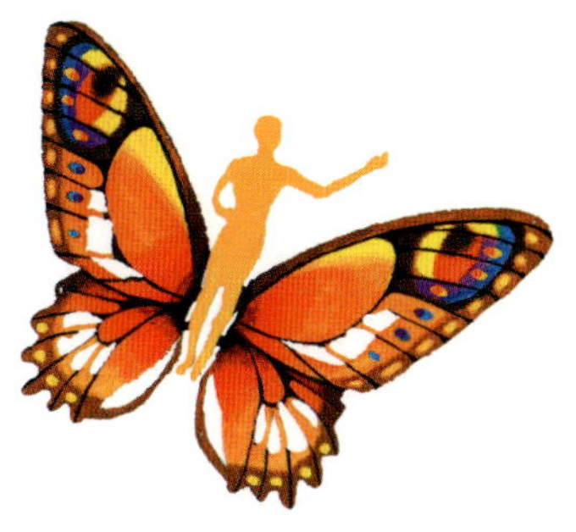

NATURAL RESERVE

ZADOK BEN-DAVID

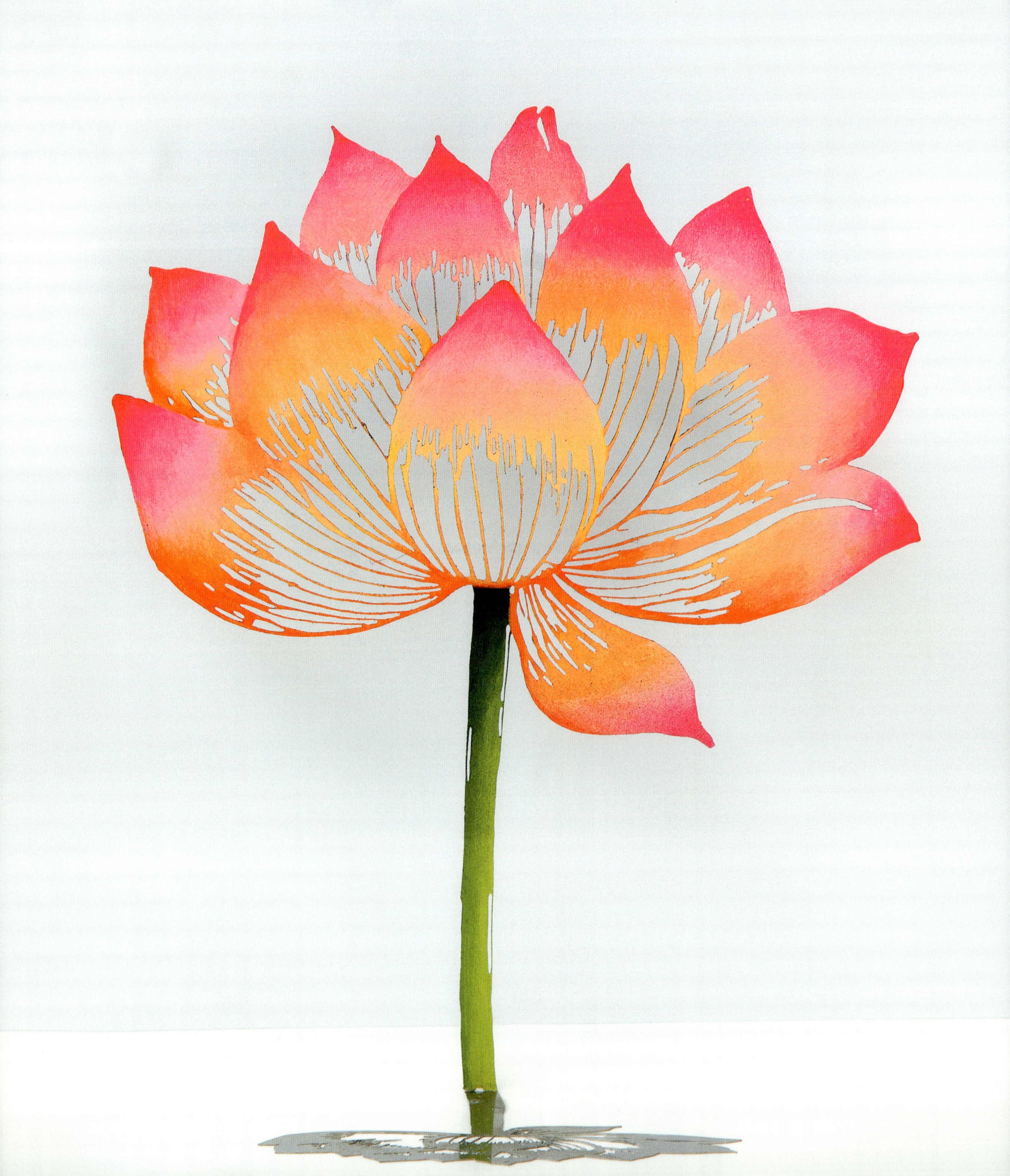

ZADOK BEN-DAVID

NATURAL RESERVE

Kew Publishing
Royal Botanic Gardens Kew

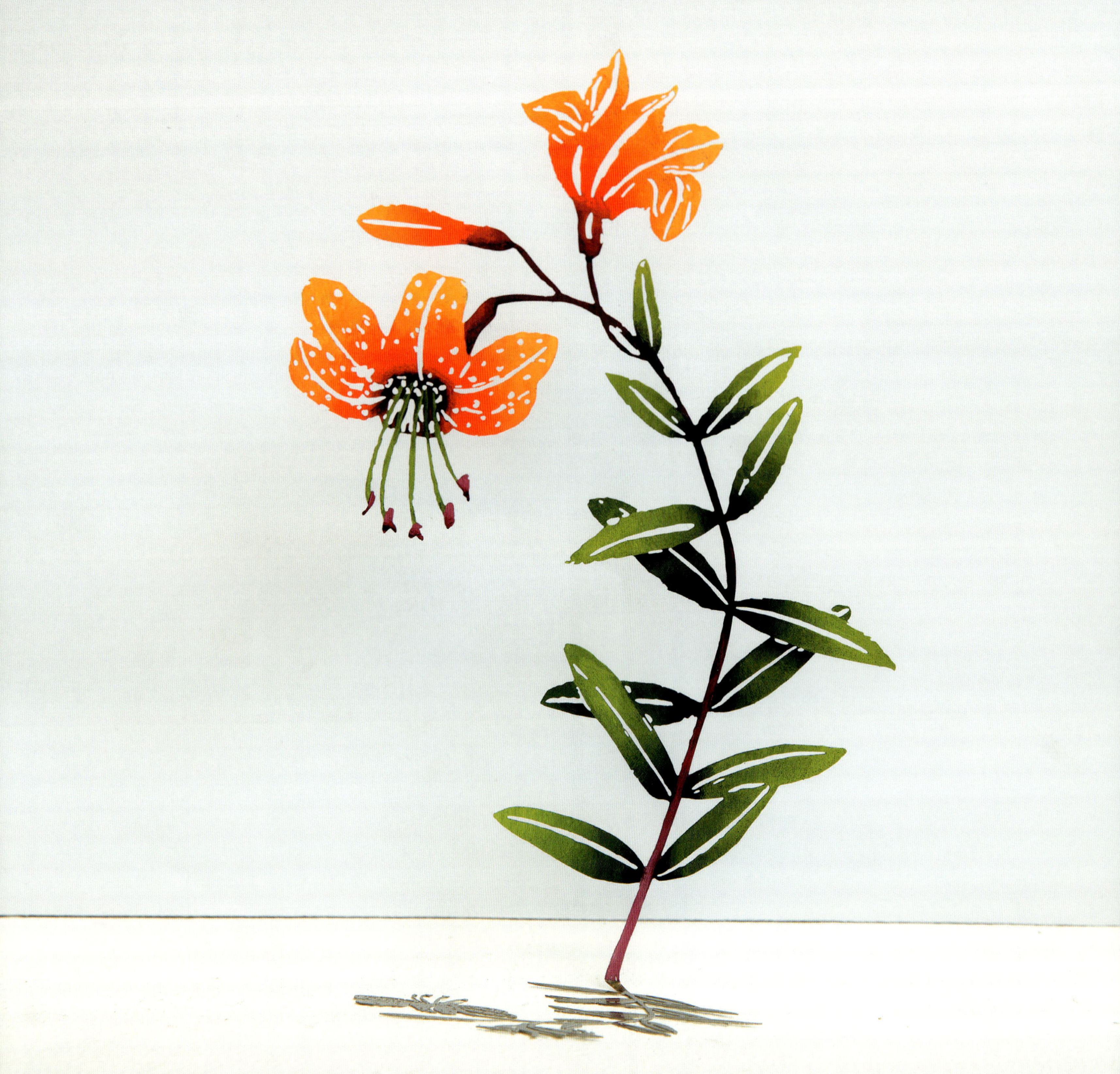

7 **Foreword**

9 **Artist's statement**

11 **An introduction to Zadok Ben-David**

13 **Interpreting Zadok Ben-David's *Blackfield***
Yael Guilat

23 ***Blackfield***

59 ***Blackflowers***

69 ***Black Box***

73 ***Conversation Peace***

81 ***Evolution and Theory***

89 ***Natural Reserve***

99 **Outdoor Sculptures**

110 **Zadok Ben-David: Life and exhibitions**

114 **Bibliography**

116 **Further reading**

118 **Acknowledgements**

119 **Image credits**

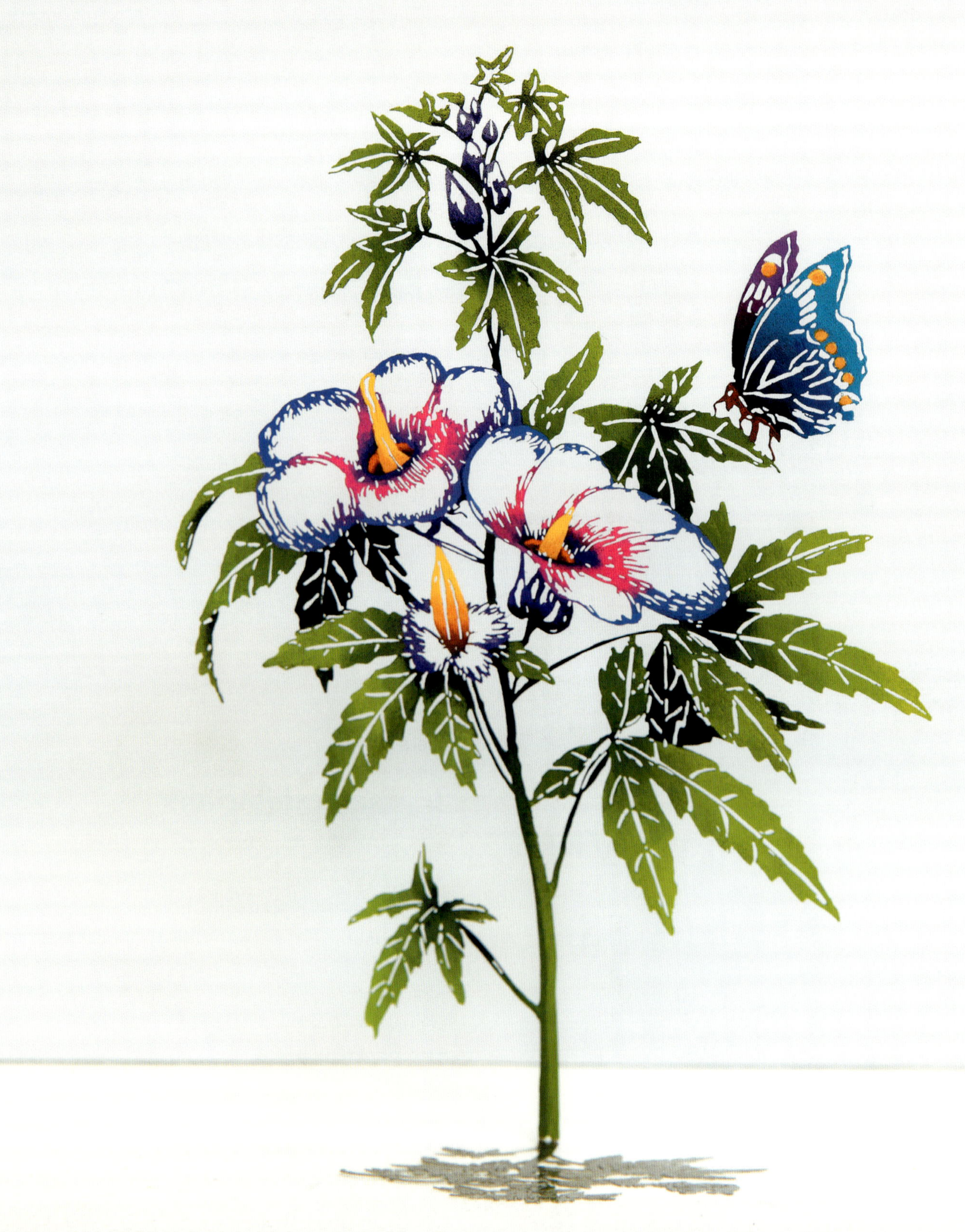

Foreword

This book marks an exhibition at Kew Gardens, showing the work of internationally renowned artist and sculptor Zadok Ben-David, who provides a unique, creative perspective on the relationship between humanity and the natural world.

His thoughtful artworks are shown through a variety of installations that he has brought together, exploring themes of tragedy and hope, and the fragility of nature.

The headline installation, *Blackfield*, contains over 17,000 steel-etched flowers, representing 900 different plant species, painted and assembled entirely by hand. It plays upon sensations of perception and perspective. It has been exhibited to critical and public acclaim in over 20 countries worldwide. Yet the installation at Kew, home to the single largest collection of living plants in the world, places it in a new context – the work confronts its sources; the plants themselves, the richness of biodiversity, scientific rigour and botanical illustration – all central to Kew's work.

The pages of this beautiful book capture not only the show at Kew but provide background, detail and insight into the singular variety of the work of the artist. This includes new wall-mounted work derived from 19th century botanical illustrations from Kew's archives. The stills from the video *Conversation Peace* incorporate depictions of trees, butterflies, insects, flowers and human shapes. *Winter Lights*, a large Corten steel sculpture outside the Shirley Sherwood Gallery of Botanical Art at Kew, takes the form of a tree comprising interlinked human silhouettes, which rusts when exposed to the elements, thus allowing the sculpture to constantly evolve and mirror the changing seasons in nature.

In presenting this new exhibition within the context of Kew as a world-leader in conservation and sustainable development research, Zadok Ben-David comments that it reinforces the theme that humans are an intrinsic part of nature rather than separate from it.

These vivid perspectives of our natural world are particularly timely in light of the climate emergency we are facing, and also in the wake of a global pandemic that has highlighted the precarious balance of life on Earth.

Richard Deverell
Director (CEO)
Royal Botanic Gardens, Kew

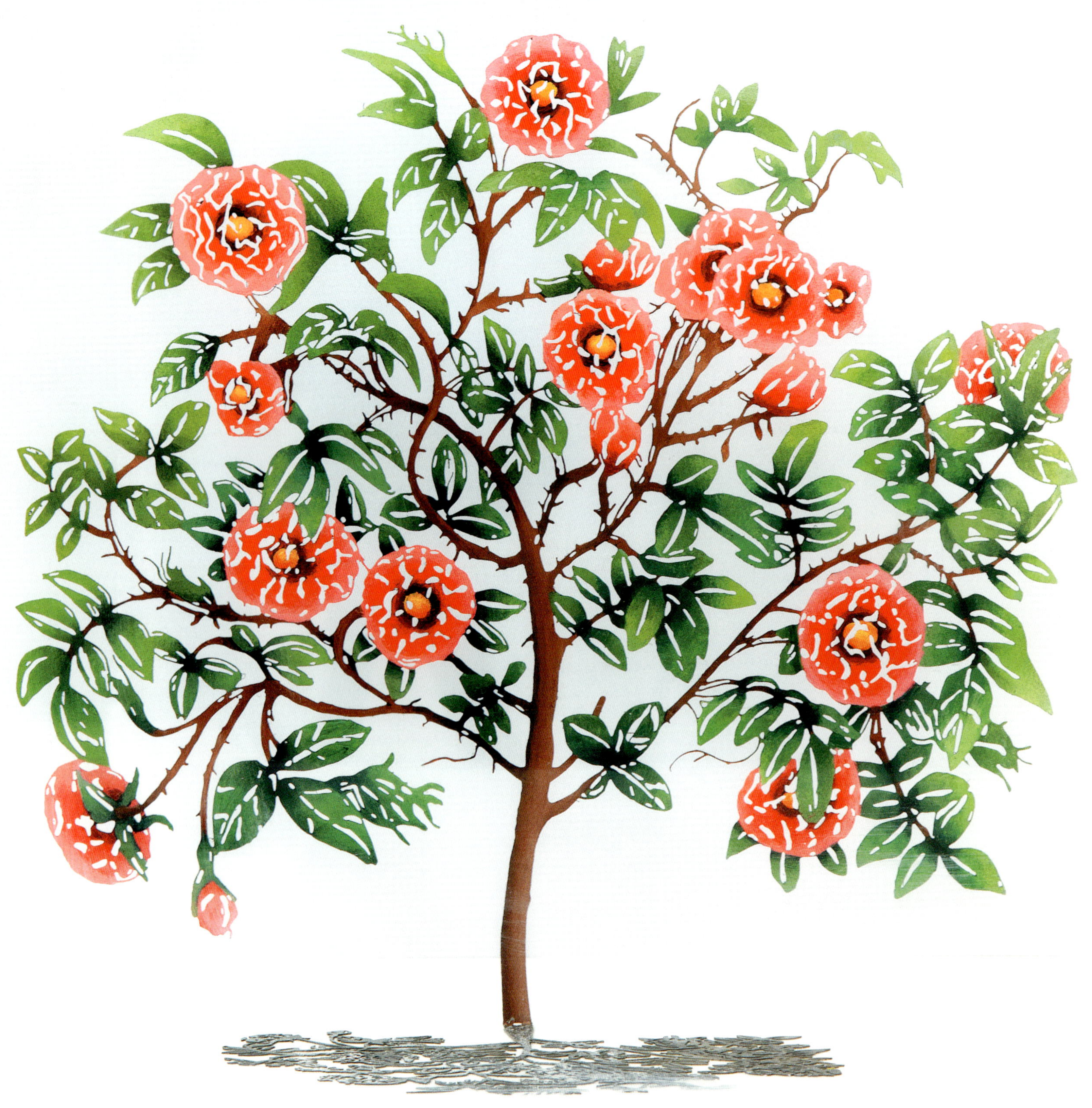

Artist's statement

The exhibition *Natural Reserve* at Kew Gardens has provided the first opportunity to see under one roof, the floor installation *Blackfield*, the video installation *Conversation Peace* and wall installations *Evolution and Theory* and *Natural Reserve*. It also includes new works inspired by old drawings from the 15th to 18th century, made in China, Japan and Europe.

The selected images from nature, including flowers, trees and insects appear in my works as metaphors for psychological and mental human attitudes. We as human beings tend to forget that we are an equal part of nature and guests on our planet. Unfortunately, we are exploiting and constantly experimenting in order to control it to suit our immediate needs and as a result there are backlashes. We are now facing a world climate crisis; global warming. Furthermore, we are currently suffering from a world epidemic caused by a tiny virus, paralysing and endangering our future on the planet.

The central installation is *Blackfield*, a moody installation, containing over 17,000 miniatures of flowers, duplicated and hand painted from 900 different species. *Blackfield* first appears to spectators as sad and sombre, like a black land after a devastating fire or a battlefield, the other side changes the mood revealing joy and optimism.

Evolution and Theory is a nostalgic installation, concentrating on a period of the 19th century when experiments in modern science took place, leading to the future, mixing Darwin's theory of evolution and exploring the human past.

Conversation Peace contains images used from my works over the past ten years, including various natural species. It tells a vicious, circular story of a futile war and self-destruction, threatening to destroy our planet.

I would like to thank Paul Denton and the gallery curator Maria Devaney, for giving me this special opportunity to bring together various aspects of my works, showing them in this spectacular and unique garden, so I can share them with many nature lovers. To Gina Fullerlove, Lydia White and Jo Pillai who helped to realise this book.

Finally, my gratitude to my devoted studio team, who helped me to prepare this show during this difficult epidemic period.

Zadok Ben-David
September 2021

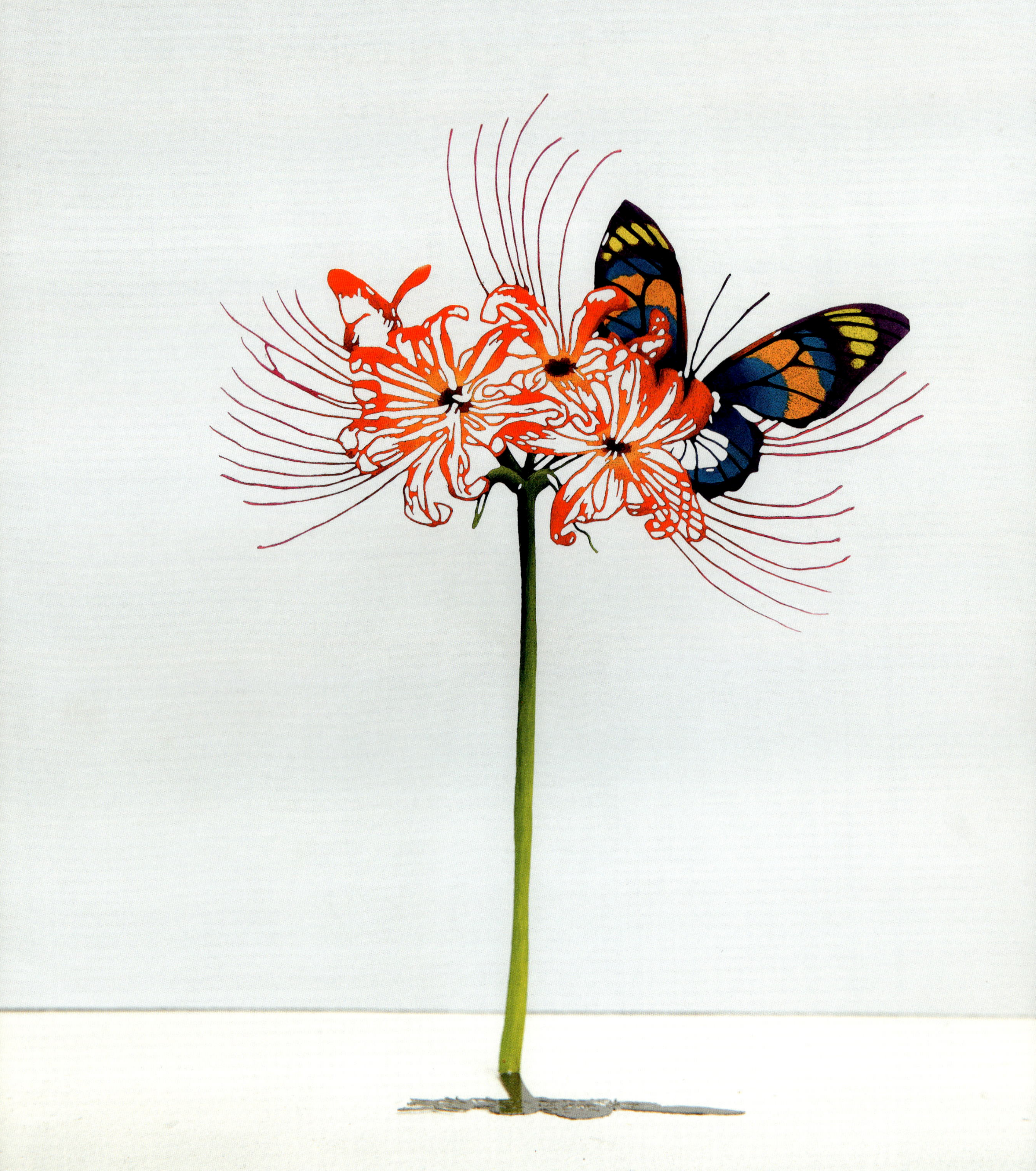

An introduction to Zadok Ben-David

Born in Bayhan, Yemen in 1949, Zadok Ben-David immigrated to Israel the same year and graduated in Advanced Sculpture from St Martin's School of Art in London, where he taught from 1977 to 1982. He lives and works in London.

As an award-winning artist, widely acclaimed for his sculptures, installations and public artworks, Ben-David explores themes linked to human nature and evolution. His work is often referred to as poetic and magical, always oscillating between delicate miniature-work and monumental installations. Metalworking has become Ben-David's preferred language in contrast with the subtle optical illusions that he creates.

Ben-David represented his country Israel at the Venice Biennale in 1988 and has participated in prestigious biennales worldwide including Krasnoyarsk Museum Biennale, Russia (2019), Busan Biennale, South Korea (2010), Biennale Cuvee, Austria (2009), *Wonder* Singapore Biennale, Singapore (2008) and Sculptuur Biennale, Netherlands (2007). The artist's work has been exhibited in illustrious national museums including the Musée de la Chasse et de la Nature, France (2018), Kenpoku Art Festival, Japan (2016), Israel Museum, Jerusalem and Art Gallery of Uzbekistan, Tashkent (2015), National Museum of the Republic of Kazakhstan, Astana (2014), Singapore Botanic Gardens, Singapore (2012), Mysteski Arsenal, Ukraine (2012), Tel Aviv Museum of Art, Israel (2010), Guangdong Art Museum, China (2007), Neanderthal Museum, Germany (2000) and Museum Beelden aan Zee, Netherlands (1998). Ben-David has also exhibited extensively in art galleries across Europe, Australia, America, Central Asia and the Middle East.

Zadok Ben-David is the recipient of numerous awards including the Grande Biennial Prémio at the XIV Biennale Internacional de Arte de Vila Nova de Cerveira, Portugal (2007) and the Tel Aviv Museum of Art Prize for Sculpture in 2005. In 2008, he was commissioned by the Beijing Olympics to install a sculpture at the Olympic Park.

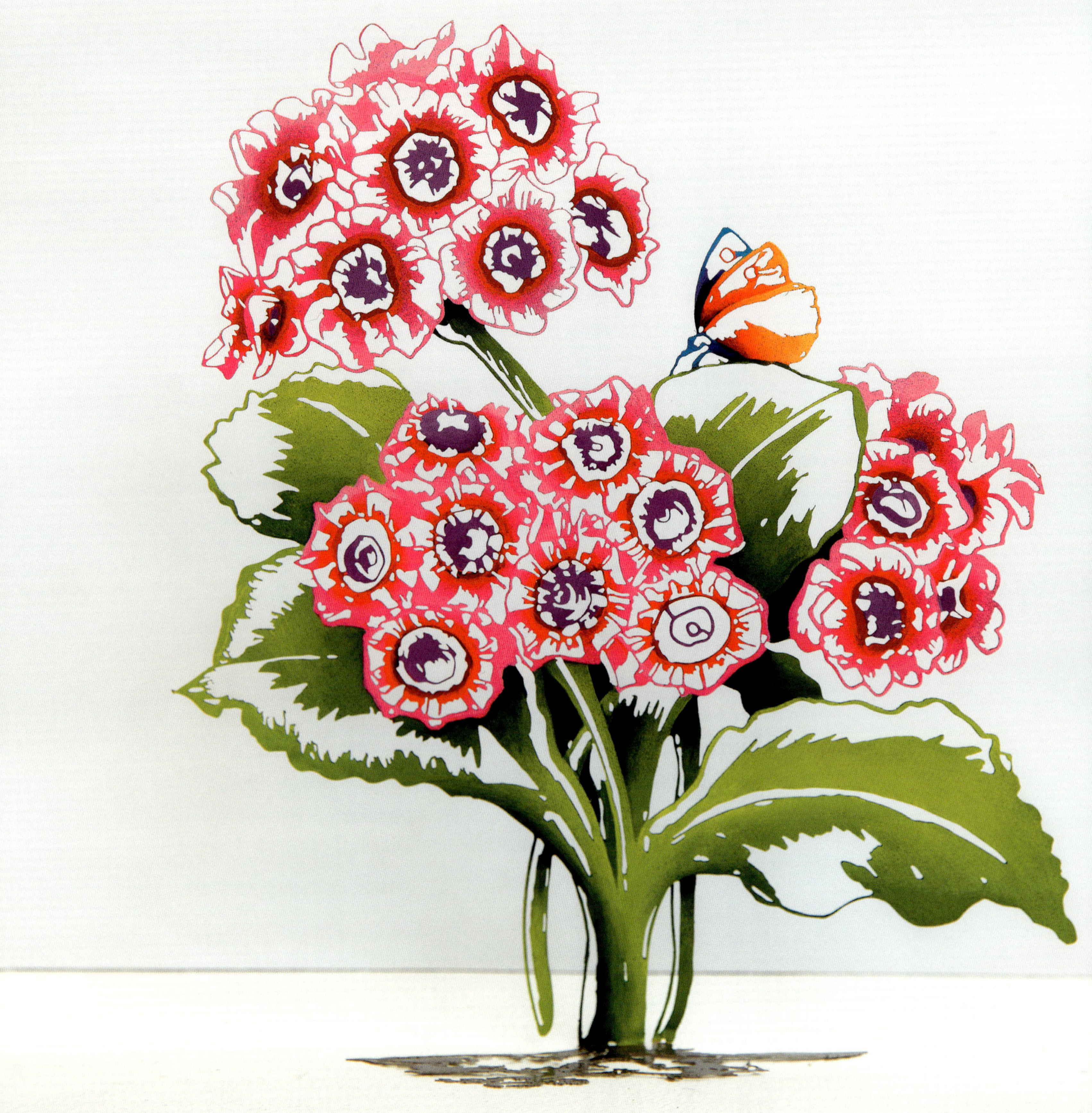

YAEL GUILAT

Interpreting Zadok Ben-David's *Blackfield*

AT THE ROYAL BOTANIC GARDENS, KEW

The presentation of Zadok Ben-David's *Blackfield* in Kew's Shirley Sherwood Gallery of Botanical Art is an invitation to contemplate the meanings evoked by its new context, which positions this work of contemporary art between two traditions: botanical painting and botanical gardens. Before it reached Kew, *Blackfield* had been set up in art galleries, exhibition halls such as the Tel Aviv Art Museum (Israel) in 2009, art events such as the Singapore Biennale in 2008, and an enormous basketball facility as part of an art festival in Japan in 2016. In its installation at Kew, 17,000 tiny flat silhouettes, based on botanical flower illustrations from encyclopaedias and botanical textbooks, are displayed within a rectangular contour that matches the contours of the gallery. All the previous installations, despite their differences and similarities, fell into the broad context of exhibiting contemporary art. This time, in contrast, a conceptual challenge to its interpretation is added. The work confronts its sources – a field, a garden, and botanical illustration – and, no less, positions the artist on the two paths that converge and diverge in his work, those of sensuous experience and the scientific model of knowledge.

By installing the silhouettes, Ben-David constructs a wonder box or magic lantern of sorts that creates the illusion of an observed landscape.

An installation, the theoretician Boris Groys claims, is a contemporary medium based on context; it derives its meaning not from contemplation of the individual work but from the relationship of the details and the whole. In the latter, questions of scale, material, and positioning that are so relevant to the medium of sculpture do not stand on their own; they are joined by questions about the site's history and, more so, the conditions of observation and the place and role of viewers as active participants. Groys also sees the installation as a democratic, participatory medium and, in the spirit of remarks by the curator and researcher Claire Bishop, I would add that it is a medium that contains a past, a present, and a future as an intensive and subjective experience.

Unlike site-specific installations that are contingent on place and cannot be moved, *Blackfield* is a 'migrant' installation that undergoes 'implantations' and 'transplantations' that attest to its nature as a cultural work far from nature. Like landscape – a cultural product and, as the cultural researcher W. J. T. Mitchell asserts, a medium in the full sense of the word – *Blackfield* is an artificial metaphor that announces its belonging to the twilight zone between imagination and fiction, a place that allows us, as viewers, to plunge into the kingdom of dream and the experience of magic, where everything is still possible. This experience, with its property of aesthetic distancing, invests us with emotional intimacy and insights that re-illuminate and cast in new light its host contexts and the conceptual and sensuous world it references.

Silhouettes as a poetic modality in the oeuvre of Zadok Ben-David

Blackfield is a floor-installation of hand-painted stainless steel silhouettes that stand atop filtered sand – a performance of sorts, I dare say, that the viewer 'activates' by walking around. Silhouettes are recurrent elements in Ben-David's work. They are flat; the connection between and within them and their installation in the exhibition space creates what Rosalind Krauss calls an 'expanded field' of sculpture and turns the spatial experience into an optical illusion. The silhouettes operate on the principle of cumulative experience and function as a drawing in space, their slender materiality not attenuating the power of their appearance as an optical projection. In this kind of sculpture, the third dimension includes the void within and around the work. Sometimes the very shape of the silhouettes evokes a photographic negative or a scientific transparency of dimensions that create amazement both in miniature virtual reduction and in sizeable enlargement. The tree-silhouettes are metonyms of observed nature, an entity not present but projected onto the observed present. From this standpoint, by installing the silhouettes, Ben-David constructs a wonder box or magic lantern of sorts that creates the illusion of an observed landscape. Like a landscape, the silhouetted human image is revealed as an optical and cultural construction. The human silhouettes are more brittle than the tree images. They are open, perhaps in a process of growth, as undergone by trees, or a dangerous process of erosion. In Ben-David's video installation *Conversation Peace*, also exhibited at the Shirley Sherwood Gallery, the characters

As a migrant installation, *Blackfield* has been displayed in various states of accumulation and scale.

are silhouettes but concurrently containers of sorts that hold life and death. Paradoxically, their flatness extends to endless depths. There is something disturbing in these silhouettes, something deceptive about the gap between what we observe and what we know; something stands between the constitutive and the constant. Physical light establishes the presence and fruitfulness of the silhouettes; it causes plants, flowers, and butterflies to sprout within them all at once; it becomes a flame that consumes everything it has created. The fullness of the cycle in which these inversions occur assures continuity. One may construe the silhouettes as a personal and contemporary interpretation of the cherubs atop the Biblical tabernacle, who watch over the Deity and the sanctity of creation. They are the guardians of the Garden of Eden, as the sources say: 'After [God] banished the man, He placed east of the Garden of Eden cherubs and a flaming sword flashing back and forth to guard the way to the Tree of Life' (Genesis 3:24). The light of wisdom, or sanctity, is seemingly trapped in its figurative metaphors and returns like a pensive reflection on nature and humankind, human nature, and the cyclicality of life and death or of destruction and construction.

The sculpting of silhouettes evidently creates a corpus of 'look-at' sculptures which stand apart from the 'touch' sculptures that typified Ben-David's endeavours in the 1980s and the early 1990s. Their materials and colour are crude and primary, whereas the silhouettes at their outset were colourless. When they became colourful and resplendent in their beauty, as in *The Other Side of Midnight* (2013), their chromatic abundance became an alluring trap behind which roaches scampered. Yes, every butterfly symbolises a metaphor, but the entire work discusses metaphor, doing so in horror and amazement in view of creation and processes of metamorphosis that exhibit binding existentiality. It is the field of vision, one may say, that grounds this work and our multisensory experience as its viewers, as happens in many other Ben-David opuses. In this respect the experience, while spatial, resembles the aesthetic one that occurs when viewers face a painting that metaphorises matter. In Ben-David's work, deviation from the medium is an aesthetic quality that bases itself on the shifting of elements of one medium to another. Thus the abstract fundamentals that nourish his work, and on which its conceptual and narrative stratum rests, come into sight.

Blackfield

As a migrant installation, *Blackfield* has been displayed in various states of accumulation and scale. When the process of creating the work began in the early 2000s, and during ten years of labour, the artist produced more than 30,000 tiny flat silhouettes that replicated illustrations of 900 plant species and their flowers, harvested from botanical illustrations of flowers in nature that appeared in old printed encyclopaedias and botanical textbooks. Before the digital information revolution, those were the ultimate vehicles for mass diffusion of science-based knowledge.

The result is a metallic and miniature field of invented species that has geometric and orderly contours.

In the first stage, Ben-David chose illustrations of flowers that were mostly smaller than their natural size. Most of them were also in black-and-white; he used a magnifying glass to modify them by connecting the loose lines, a necessary step to construct sculptural forms. Next, he used photo-etching technology to replicate the silhouettes in stainless steel. For each flower, Ben-David designed a base that resembles a water reflection of the flower shape, in unpainted silver. These bases play an aesthetic role in other pieces exhibited in mirrored boxes while remaining invisible to viewers of the installation by being covered with sand. Finally, the images of the flowers were painted in a free style, first by Ben-David himself and then by young artists he enlisted. Thus the paradoxical physical and conceptual infrastructure of the work was born.

Ultimately, in a course of reduction (of the illustrations), enlargement, and transposition that steadily distanced itself from nature, the artist created a field of flowers in which constant models are replicated with a positioning that creates proliferation and variance. The result is a metallic and miniature field of invented species that has geometric and orderly contours. Visitors experience the 'demand' of having to bend over, as though in a sensual attraction, to the pleasantness of the blossoming of spring. Their gaze, however, encounters a metallic flatness that is far from an experience that their bodies would remember. This quasi-absurd gesture and the unexpected feeling that follows it may be of central importance in making viewers active interpreters of the work, as Groys and Bishop (above) maintain. *Blackfield* does indeed require viewers to change the direction of their gaze and demands a physical gesture: kneeling, watching closely, looking from afar, and walking around. The flatness of the theatrical and gloomy black flora silhouettes and the surprising eruption of colour carry grief and joy at the same time, as two facets of human existence and as an embodiment of an inherent otherness. The viewers' emotions, experience, genetic-cultural baggage, and personal memories play a decisive role. Undoubtedly, however, the botanical awareness that inundates visitors to Kew also has a major effect. In this sense, the botanical garden is not only a host environment but an interpretive key that invites viewers to reformulate the equation of scientific knowledge and personal experience, of knowledge achieved by science and knowledge that we reach through artistic experiences.

Speaking of cultural baggage, Zadok Ben-David, an artist born in Yemen, grew up and reached adulthood in Israel, where he was exposed to the important role of wildflowers in the cultural repertoire of national identity-building. As the Israeli researcher Shahar Marnin-Distelfeld notes, the attitude towards wildflowers as a constitutive educational and ideological component was associated with the reterritorialisation of the Jews in their cultural cradle and in response to the wandering-Jew motif in European culture. This démarche reflected an ideology that, like the re-appropriation of land, transformed something 'wild' into an acquired native fundament. The establishment of the Society for the Protection of Nature in

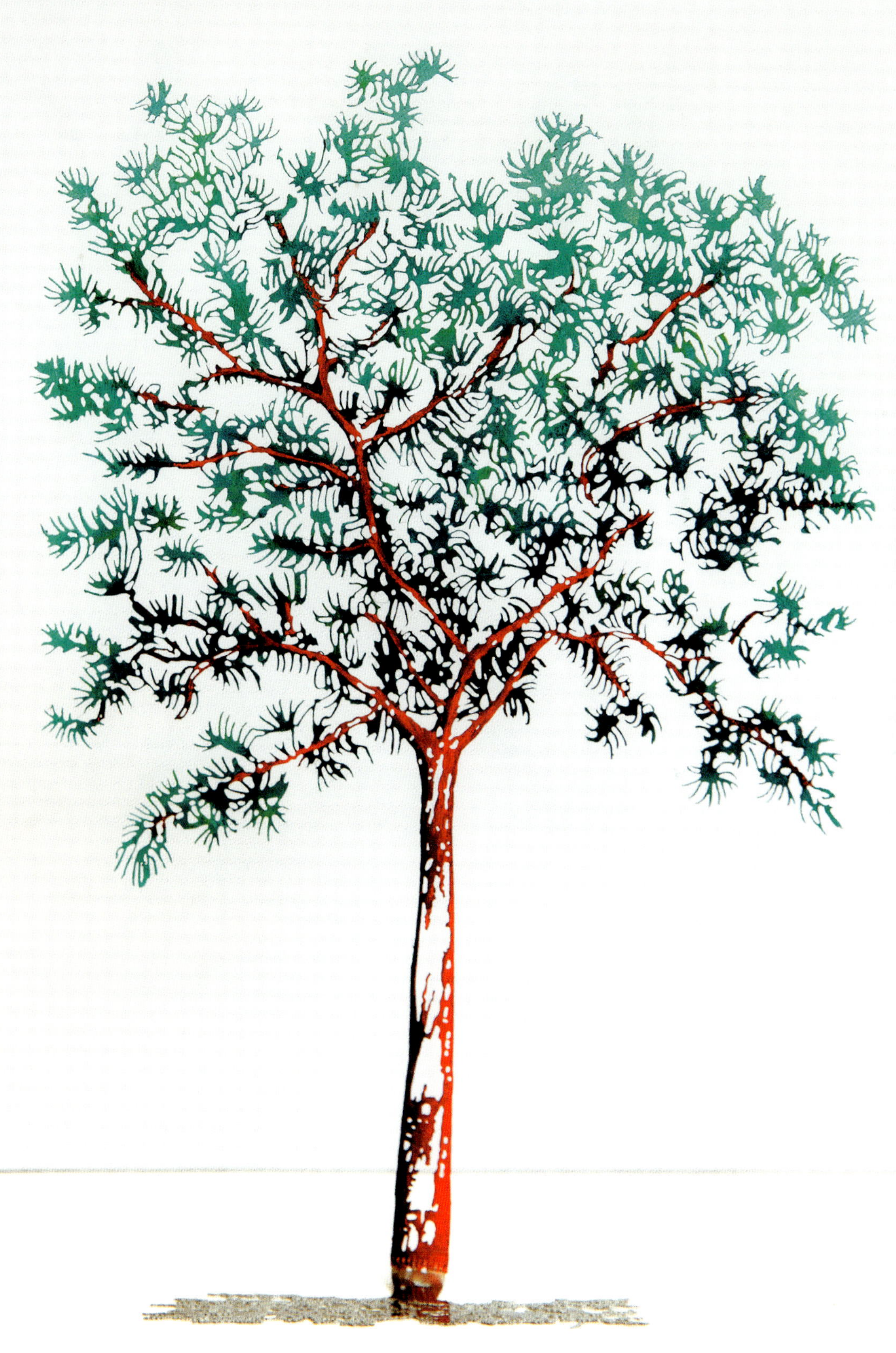

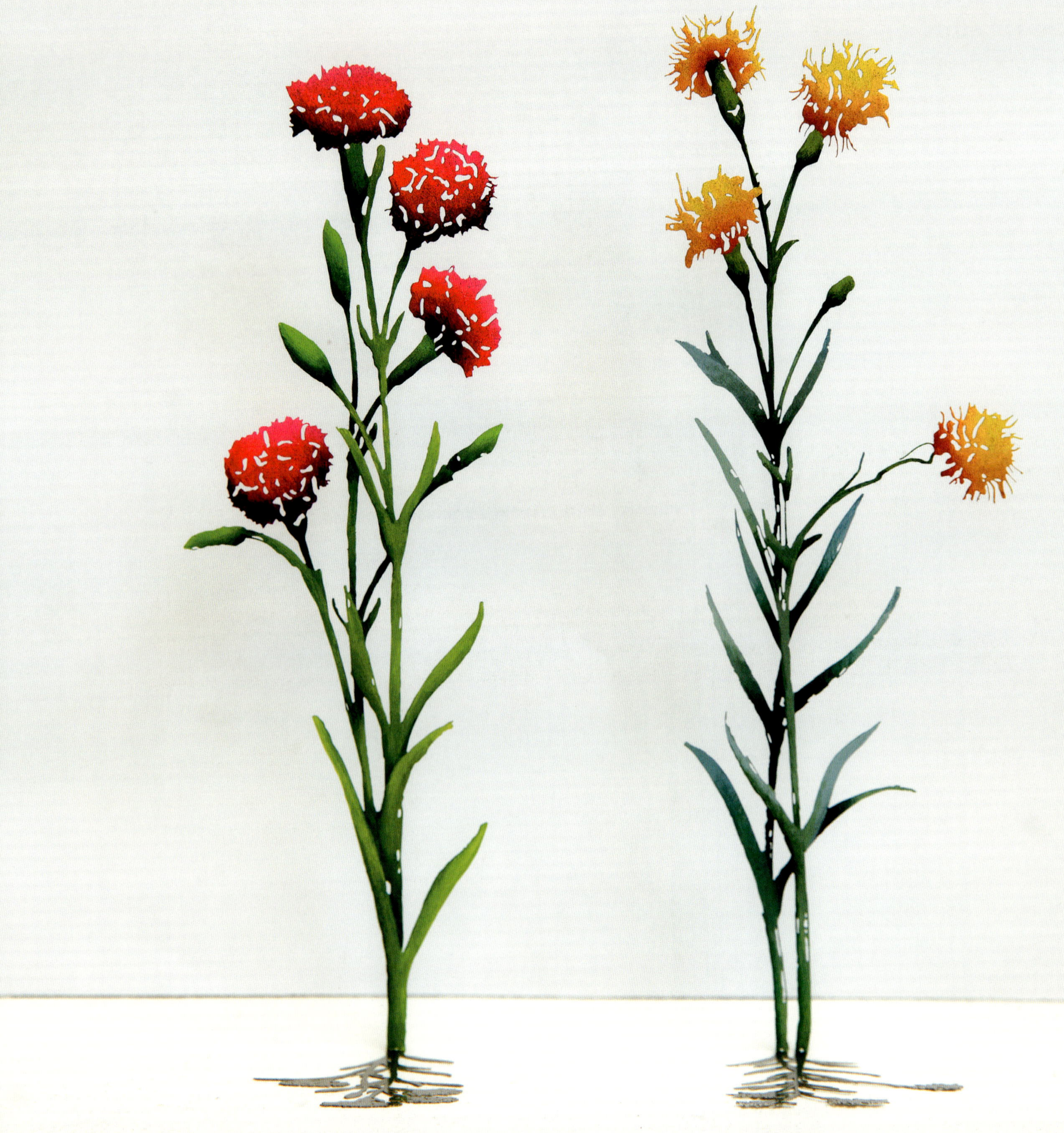

The sand in *Blackfield* serves the artist's 'field of wildflowers' as an infrastructure or, conceivably, as a flying or magic carpet of sorts.

Israel in 1953 kindled a passion for preservation and study among graduates of the Israeli public-education system. This resonated widely in Israeli contemporary art, in which exhibitions engaging in botanic illustrations –themselves part of this ideological démarche – proliferated. This cultural perspective may shed light on Ben-David's 'wandering' in fields of wildflowers as a belated reflection of that formative element of his identity. Consciously or not, in his adult England-based life and as an itinerant international artist in the global world, Ben-David confronts the childhood memory that was 'implanted' in him. The sand in *Blackfield* serves the artist's 'field of wildflowers' as an infrastructure or, conceivably, as a flying or magic carpet of sorts that also migrates from place to place – revealing yet another stratum of his work, touching upon his complex attitude towards nature and the relationship of nature, culture, and ideology.

It is not, however, botanical illustration as it evolved in Israel on which this work draws as its direct iconographic source, but rather historical scientific illustrations. Furthermore, this is not the first time Ben-David bases his work on illustrations from encyclopaedias, particularly British ones. His *Evolution and Theory*, first exhibited in 1997, was also grounded in illustrations from encyclopaedias and nineteenth-century British pamphlets. The encyclopaedia era reflected faith in progress and a positivistic attitude towards science. In an extension of the Enlightenment spirit, 'Rational Man' was crowned as the scion of creation who rules and dominates the world by virtue of his sagacity. This anthropocentric vision was projected onto nature. In the late twentieth century and more intensively today, we encounter a more sober and mindful view of the inevitable catastrophe that the continuation of this approach will bring upon the world. In this spirit, Ben-David's aluminium silhouettes, resembling scientific diagrams, measuring tools, instruments, and human silhouettes – each representing a different stage in evolution and all arrayed in a varying ahistorical order – express overt ambivalence towards science and the grand tableau that it created. Thus, observing this installation in the sunset of the previous millennium and in a more recent stationing in 2016 at the Israel Museum in Jerusalem raises the thought that the march of history may not be linear, and one may, or must, 'recalculate the route'. Ben-David does not suggest that it is possible or appropriate just to 'delete' the old way of thinking. Instead, he proposes a re-elaboration profound and critical – but not devoid of admiration, enchantment, and nostalgia – of the scientific metaphors that, on the one hand, sought truth and precision, and, on the other hand, for this very reason created an imagined picture, detached from worldly context and presenting the world as something sterile and laboratory-like. The scientific illustrations, including the botanical ones, evolved into an undifferentiated mass of metaphors devoid of background and interrelations with the broader ecology. It was the perspective of the world as a transparent backdrop for the misdeeds of the human being, the creature who conquers nature and conquers others of the same species. Over the years, Ben-David's works present

Over the years, Ben-David's works present us with a spectacle through which we may reflect on existential ethical dilemmas.

us with a spectacle through which we may reflect on existential ethical dilemmas.

The new context

With all this in the background, exhibiting *Blackfield* in the heart of the Royal Botanic Gardens, Kew and in a gallery of botanical illustrations offers an opportunity for contextual interpretation. So does the invitation from the exhibition's curator, Maria Devaney, who even asked the artist to address ancient botanical illustrations from the collection which, unlike the Victorian encyclopaedic images Ben-David had been using until then, mostly originated in the non-Western cultures of China and Japan. Ben-David accepted the challenge, which once again drew him into a dance of attraction to and repulsion from the traditional models of garden and scientific and botanical illustration, producing a current personal statement on the relationship of humanity and nature.

As previously stated, the way *Blackfield* is installed is an integral part of the work. Whether set up individually, as projections onto a wall, or dominated by their multitude, the silhouettes 'speak' the language of proportion which, of course, is a central element in the language of sculpture. Ben-David's silhouettes are perceived as miniatures relative to the size and wealth of the wings, pavilions, and gardens of the Kew site. The silhouettes, as miniature units within the model, attest to their 'landlessness' and the sand table affirms itself as a liminal playground. Certainly, they are neither a scientific model nor an illustration in the service of science. Their migration is different from that of the rare species of flora that were transported from their natural habitat to the faraway royal botanical garden in the capital of the Empire. The botanical gardens that sprouted in seventeenth-century Europe were typified by a combination of two approaches towards nature: one seeing nature as an object to contemplate in astonishment, and the other regarding it as an object for conquest by human knowledge. One who gazes at Ben-David's installation in its new exhibitional context sees clearly that the infrastructure of his work accommodates both attitudes: one originating in knowledge and grounded in encyclopaedic factuality, the other searching for the joy and pleasure of discovery.

English landscape architecture owes the secret of its success to the perception of artifice as natural – both in the English garden that developed in the eighteenth century, typified by a pictorial approach that reflected an ideal landscape and Classical vestiges, and in the representation of a 'universal garden', which originated in the colonial era and became the design policy for botanical gardens, matching buildings from non-European cultures with non-native flora. Beauty and foreignness created enchantment; size and power produced aesthetic exaltation. It was this, too, that would draw class boundaries between those who observed and enjoyed the marvels of nature and those who worked the soil by the sweat of their brow.

In its new exhibitional context, *Blackfield* serves as a platform for reciprocal reflections of past and future, of what the gardens were when established to what they are today – a public resource, in the example

The surprise effect that accompanies the moment when black and colour switch places may generate a smile of relief in some viewers and a fierce emotional jolt in others.

of the Royal Botanic Gardens, Kew, which UNESCO has declared a World Heritage site. The licence invoked in painting Ben-David's flowers and the foreignness they project suggest relativity as a value. Deep contemplation of the work evokes philosophical questions about the relationship of difference, equality, and freedom, since each flower is not only differently coloured but also presented in a free and liberated form. The surprise effect that accompanies the moment when black and colour switch places may generate a smile of relief in some viewers and a fierce emotional jolt in others. This aside, viewers seem to be asked to 'practice' changing their point of view and adopting a different and new perspective towards the same field.

Transitioning among angles of observation and testing the extent of relativity that dominates the social world were the constitutive foundations of the oeuvre of Jonathan Swift (1667–1745), one of the greatest English satirists, the author of *Gulliver's Travels*, and the offspring of the era when global explorations turned into real discoveries and created a new world order. *Gulliver's Travels* holds up a mirror – pointed and critical but also compassionate – to the way the lifestyle dictated by colonialism shapes attitudes towards ourselves and others, towards both the high and mighty and those weaker than and different from us. In *Gulliver's Travels*, what is 'natural' for one community is not necessarily a natural model for all. Along with amazement and curiosity towards the different, fear surfaces as a motor of human behaviour. It appears that Ben-David took an interest not only in seventeenth-century science fiction but also in writing that questioned human nature and humanity's relationship with nature. One may imagine those who visit Ben-David's installation at Kew as travellers in Gulliver's footsteps – 'giants' who march around a miniature forest in the main gallery and 'Lilliputians' in the gigantic groves and forests in the gardens themselves – confronting the enlarged botanical illustrations that evolved into works of art in a see-through case, and viewing the tree, a Corten-steel sculpture installed in the Gardens outside the gallery, itself composed of tiny human images.

These together are the new context of *Blackfield,* which, along with Ben-David's other works, elicit an elegiac and enchanted gaze, reflective and melancholy but still optimistic, on humankind and its journey in the world and, above all, its attitude towards nature. For Ben-David, nature, analogised as a socio-ecological environment, is a delicate web of connections, interrelations, and sustainable cyclicality. The new context of *Blackfield* places even stronger emphasis on ethical and philosophical aspects that have been present throughout Zadok Ben-David's lengthy career, which spans continents and makes contrasts converge.

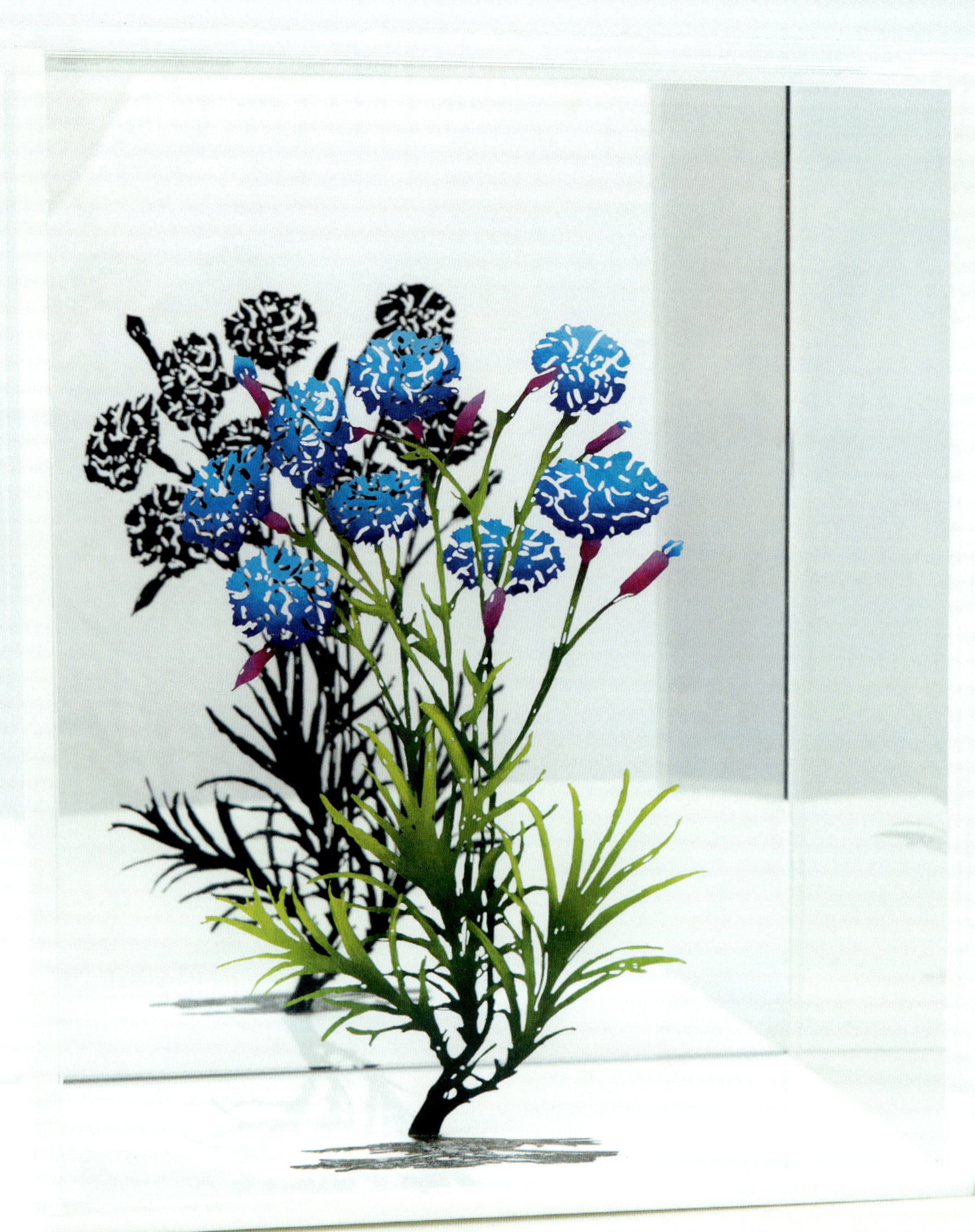

BLACKFIELD

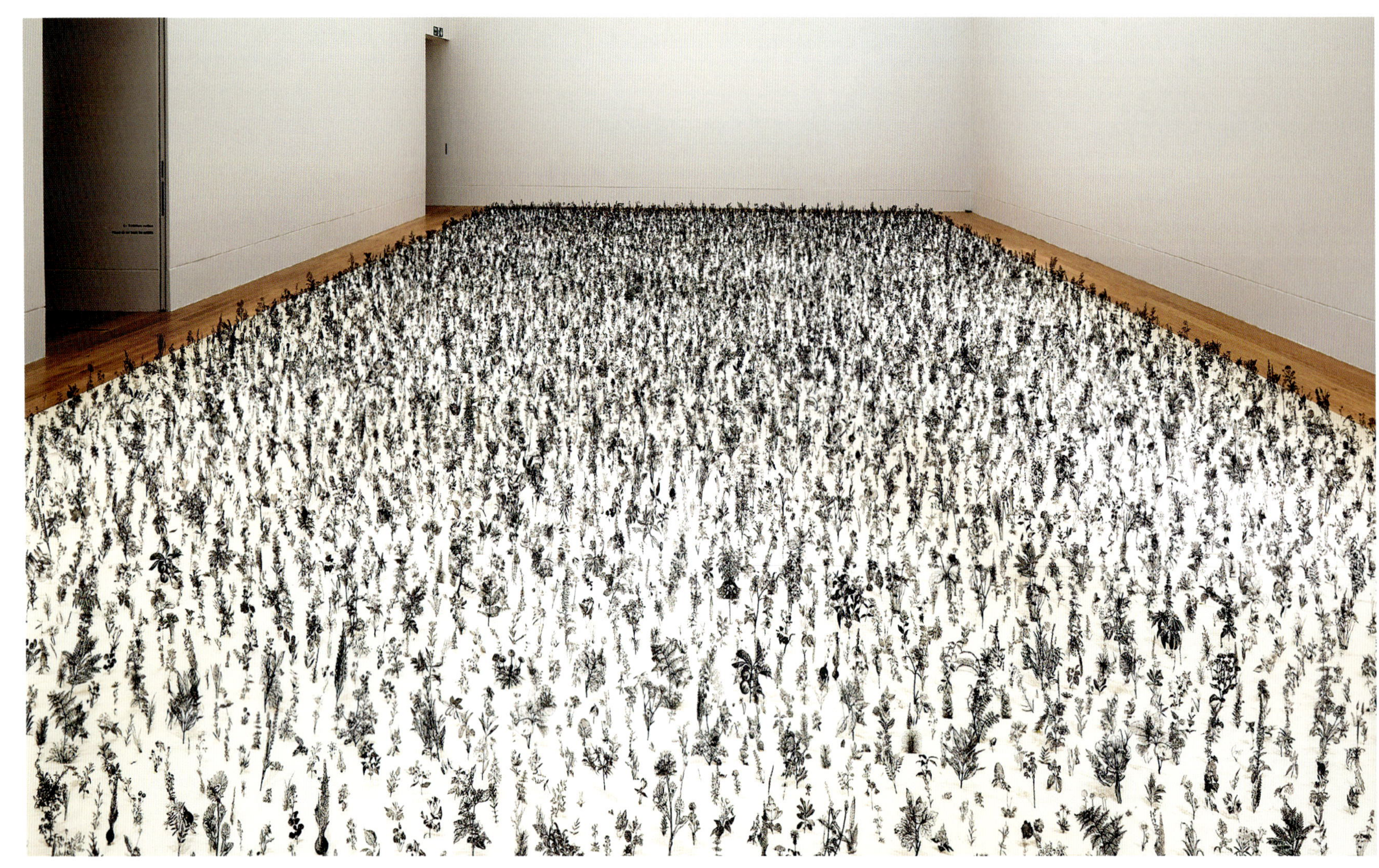

Blackfield, hand-painted
stainless steel, Royal
Botanic Gardens, Kew,
UK 2021.

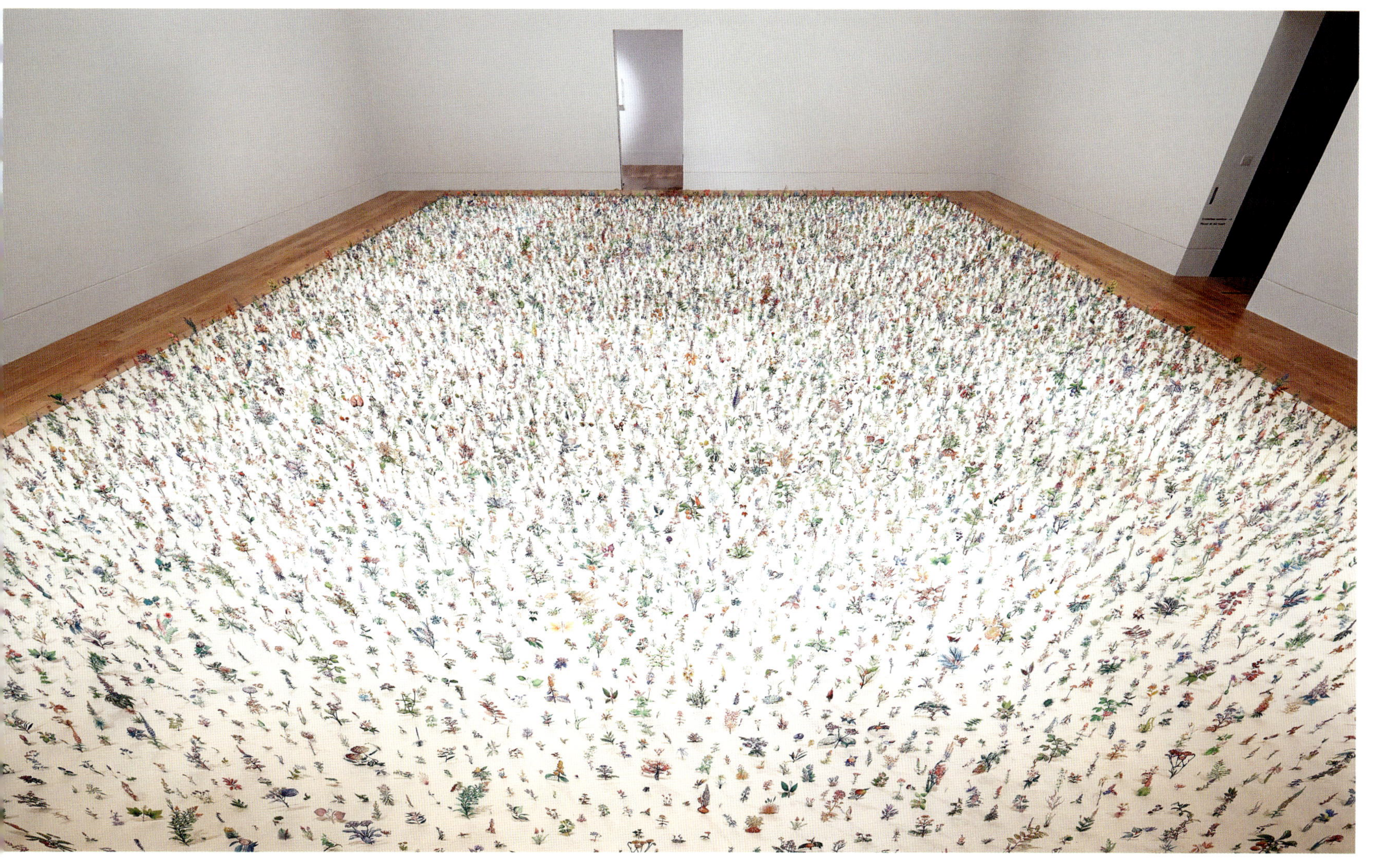

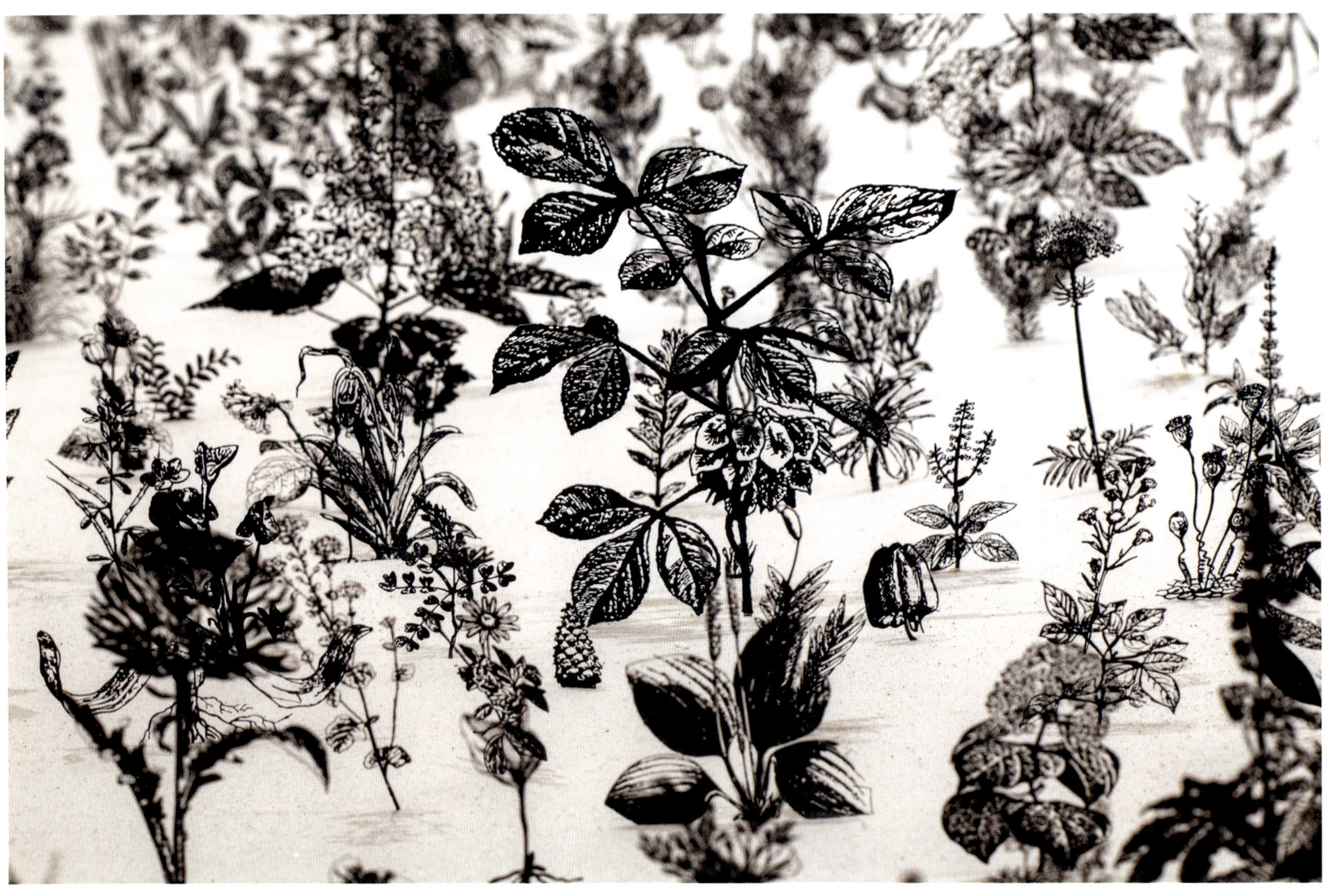

Blackfield, hand-painted
stainless steel, Royal
Botanic Gardens, Kew,
UK, 2021.

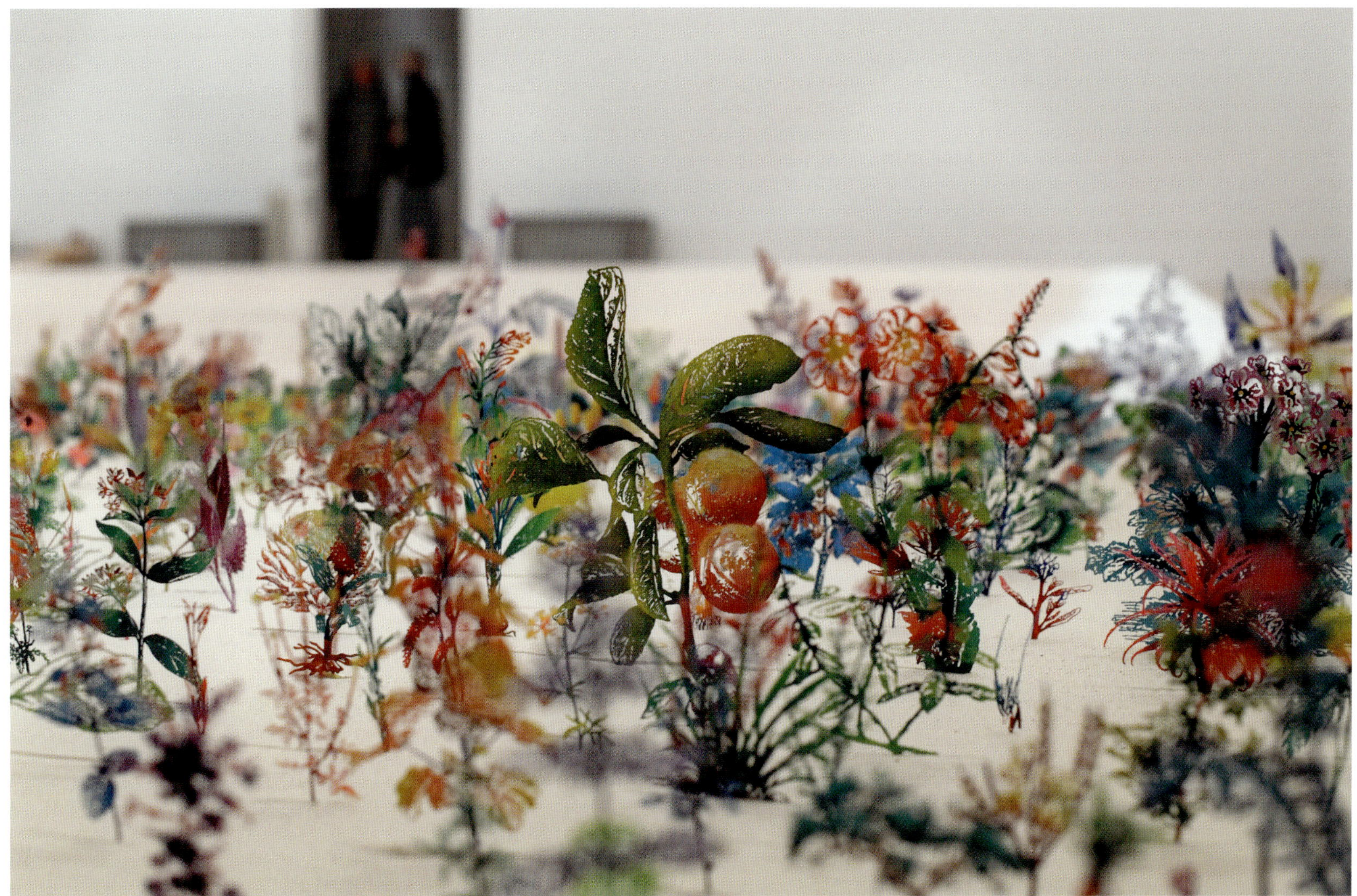

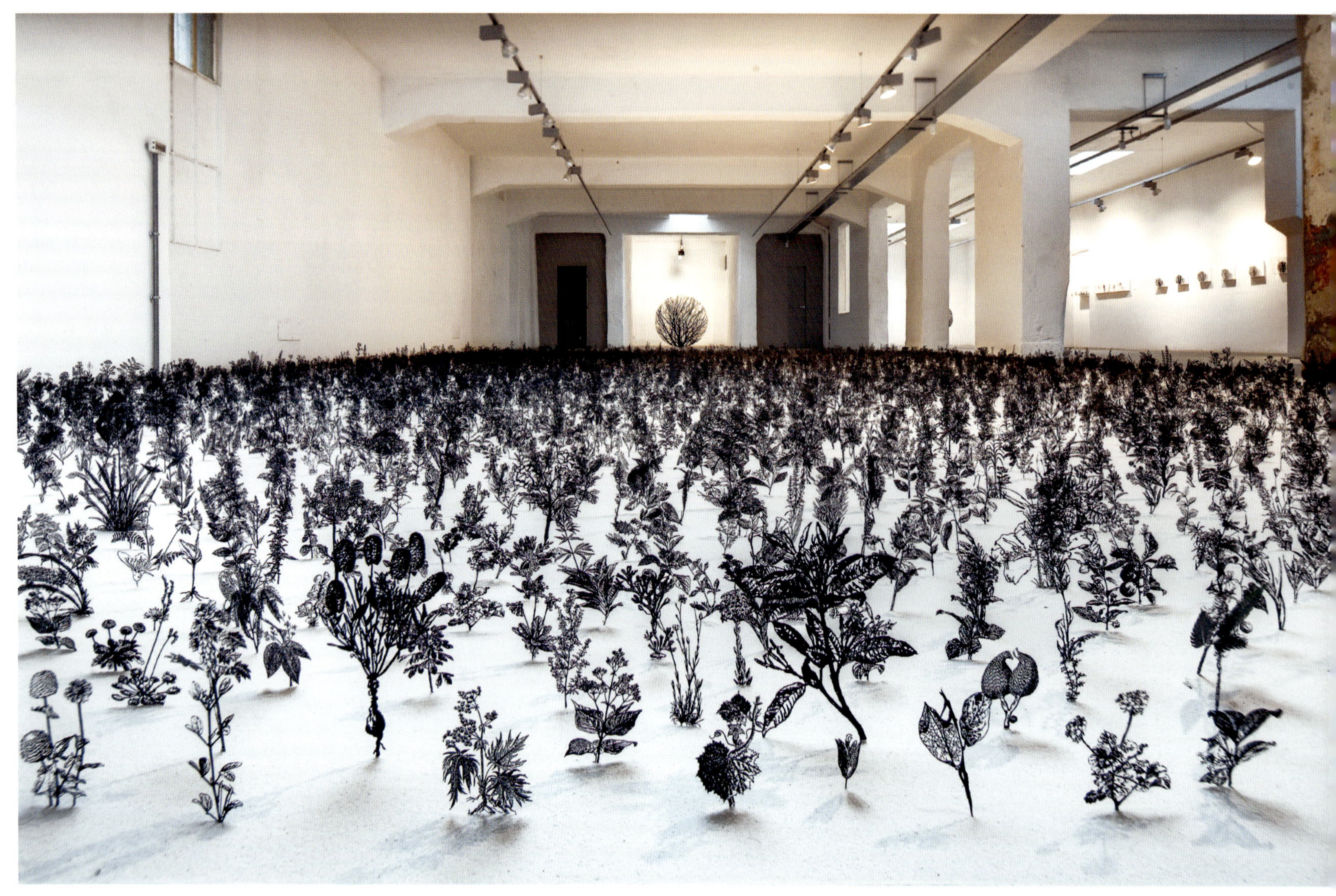

Blackfield, hand-painted
stainless steel, Verso Arte
Contemporanea, Turin,
Italy, 2010.

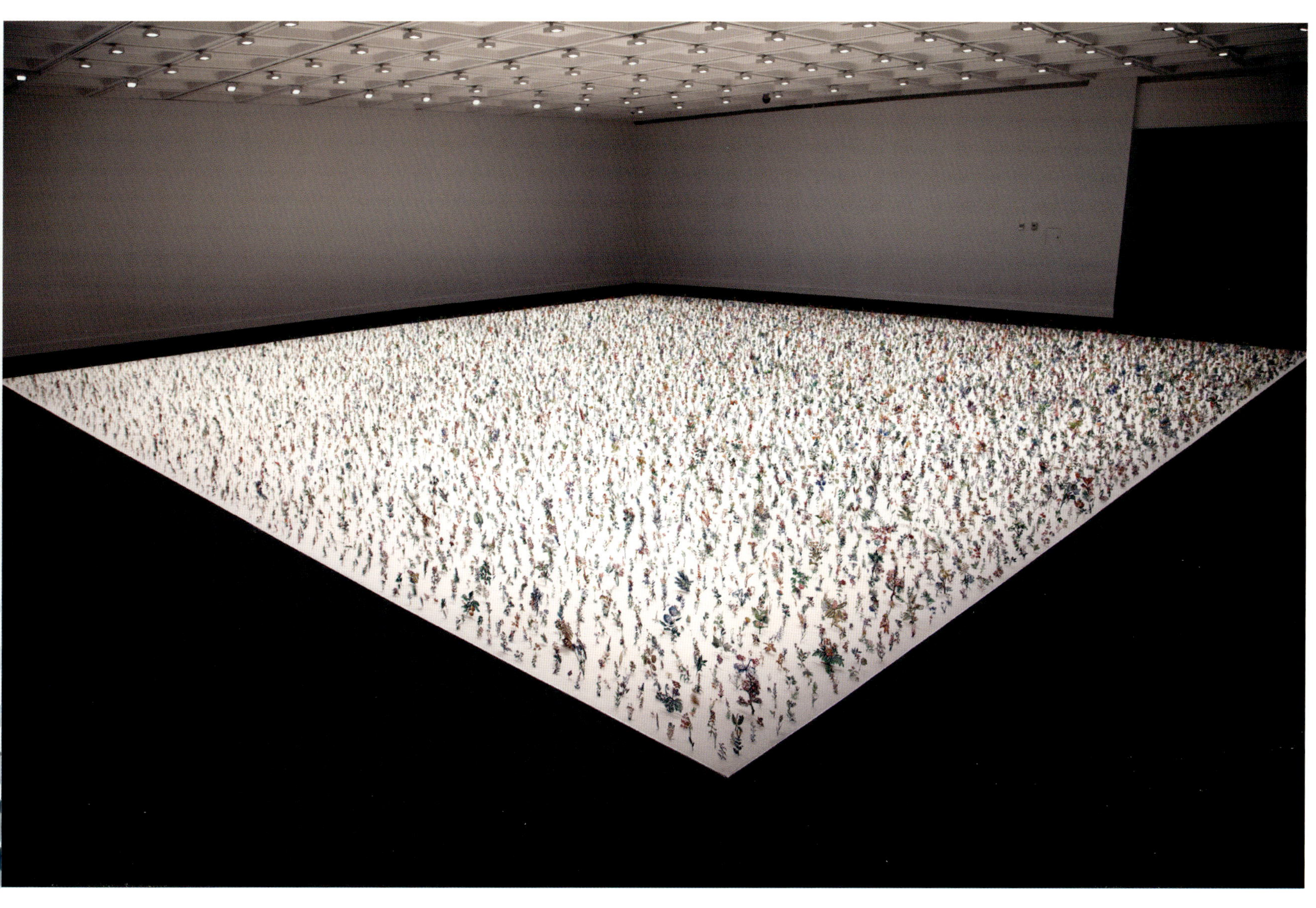

(above)
Blackfield, hand-painted
stainless steel, Perth
Festival, Lawrence
Wilson Gallery, Perth,
Australia, 2018.

(following page)
Blackfield, hand-painted
stainless steel, Musée
de la Chasse, Paris,
France, 2018.

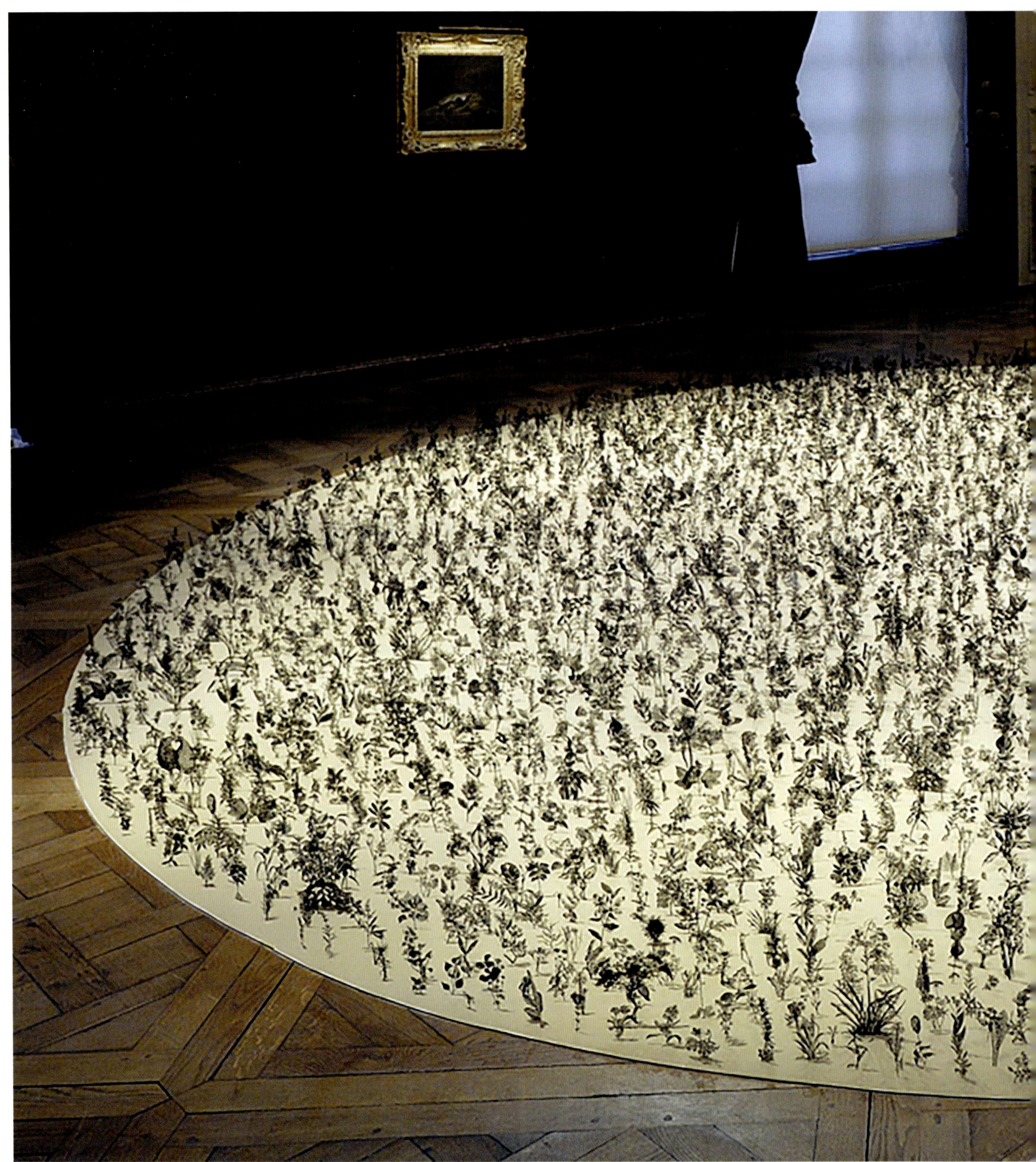

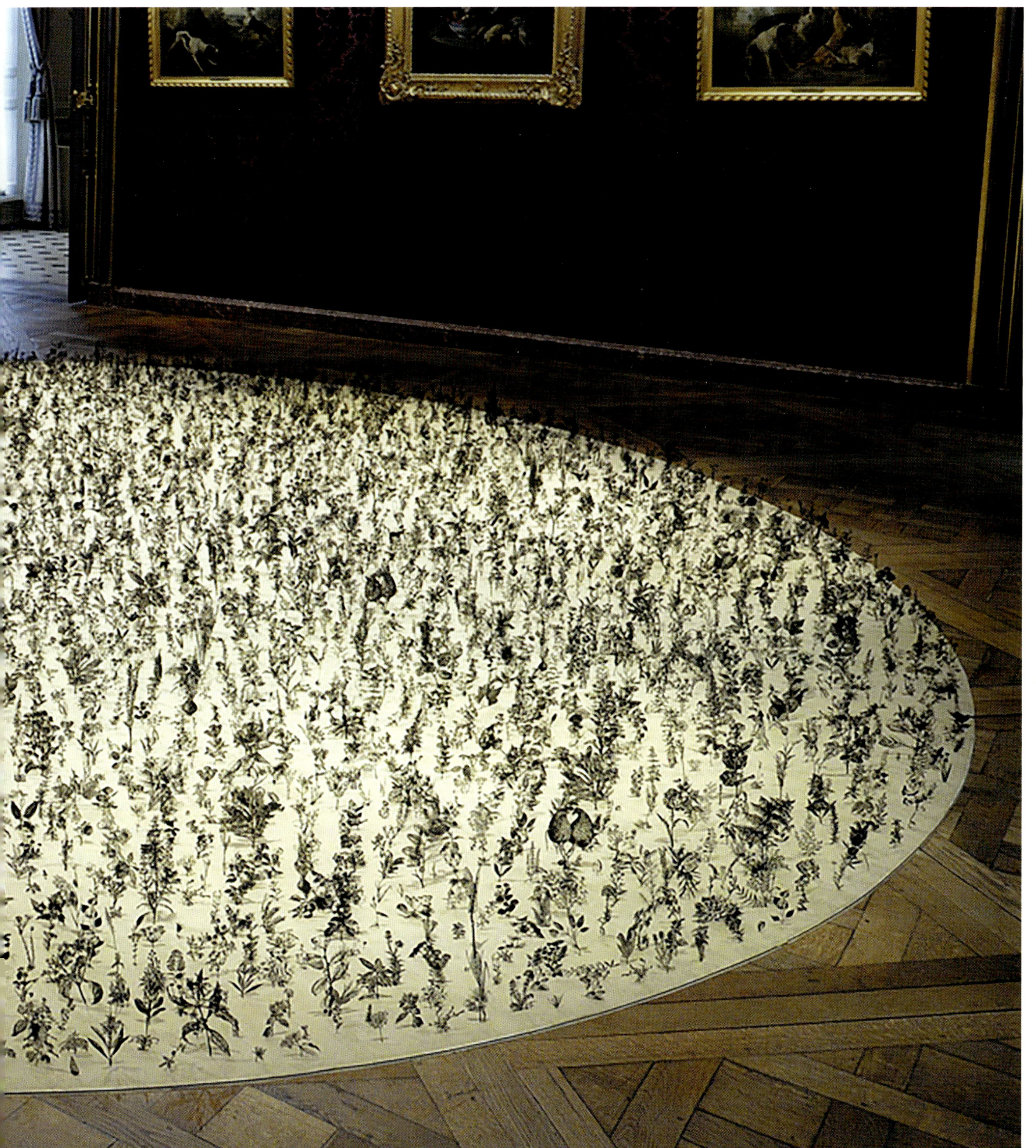

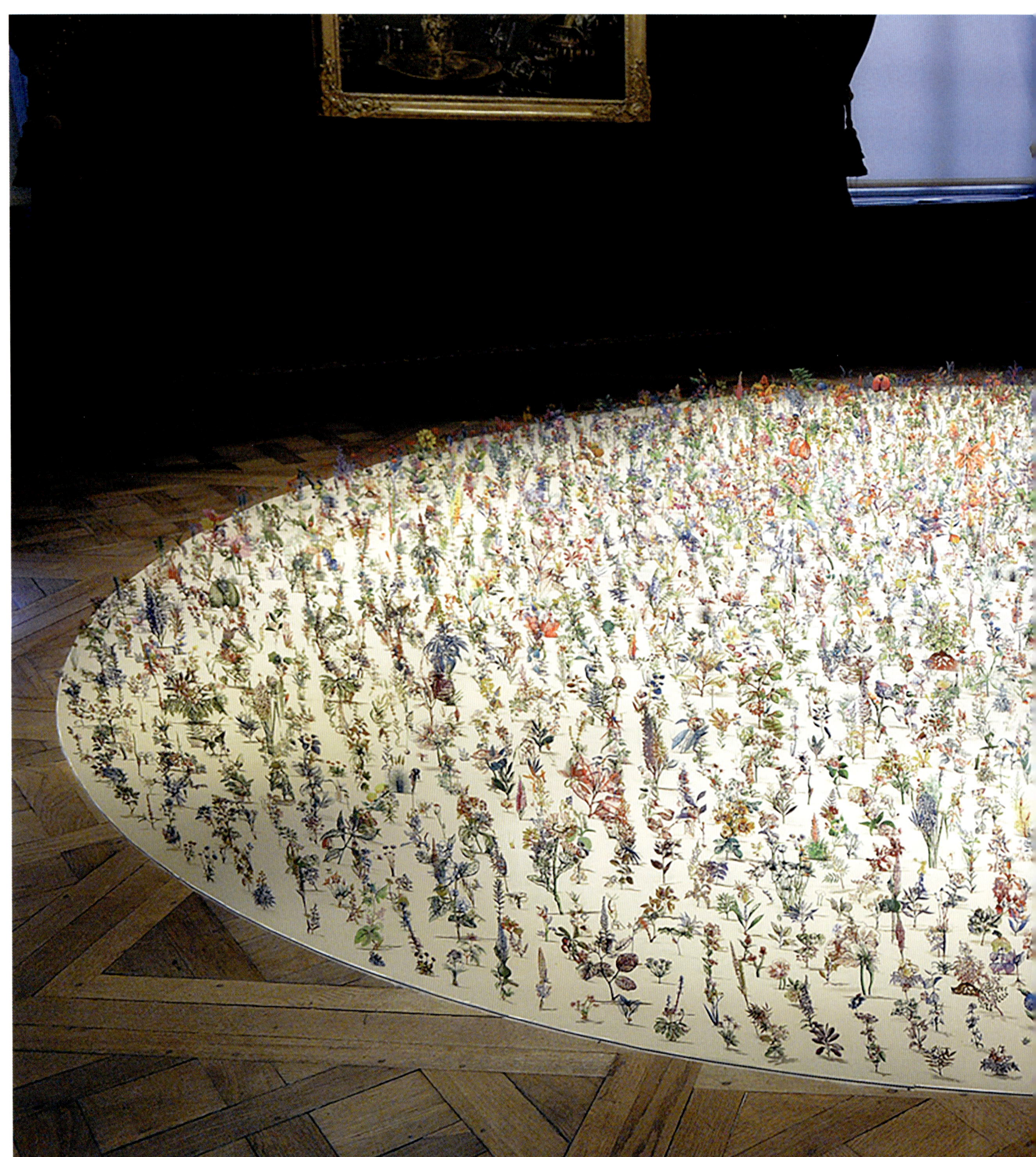

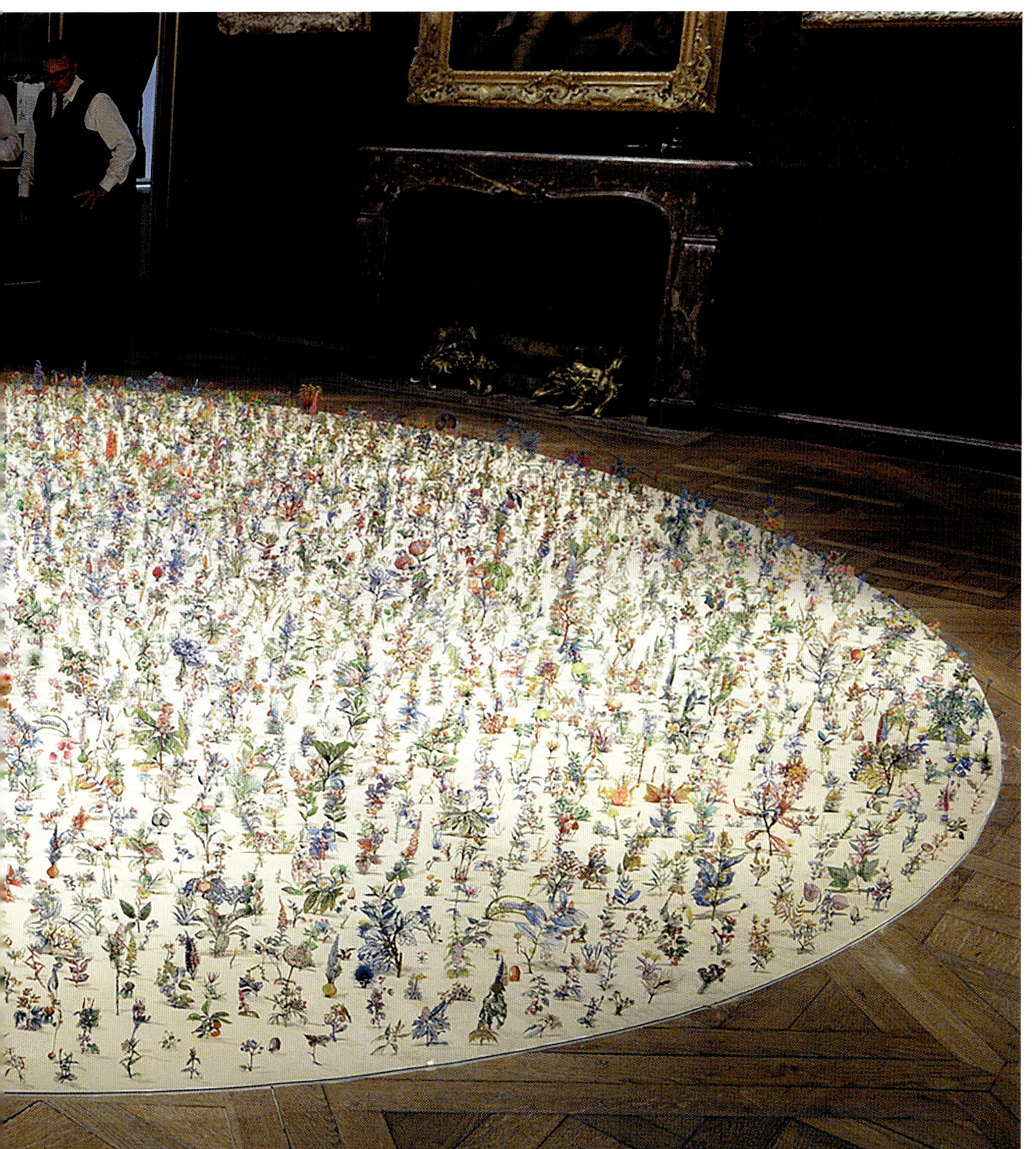

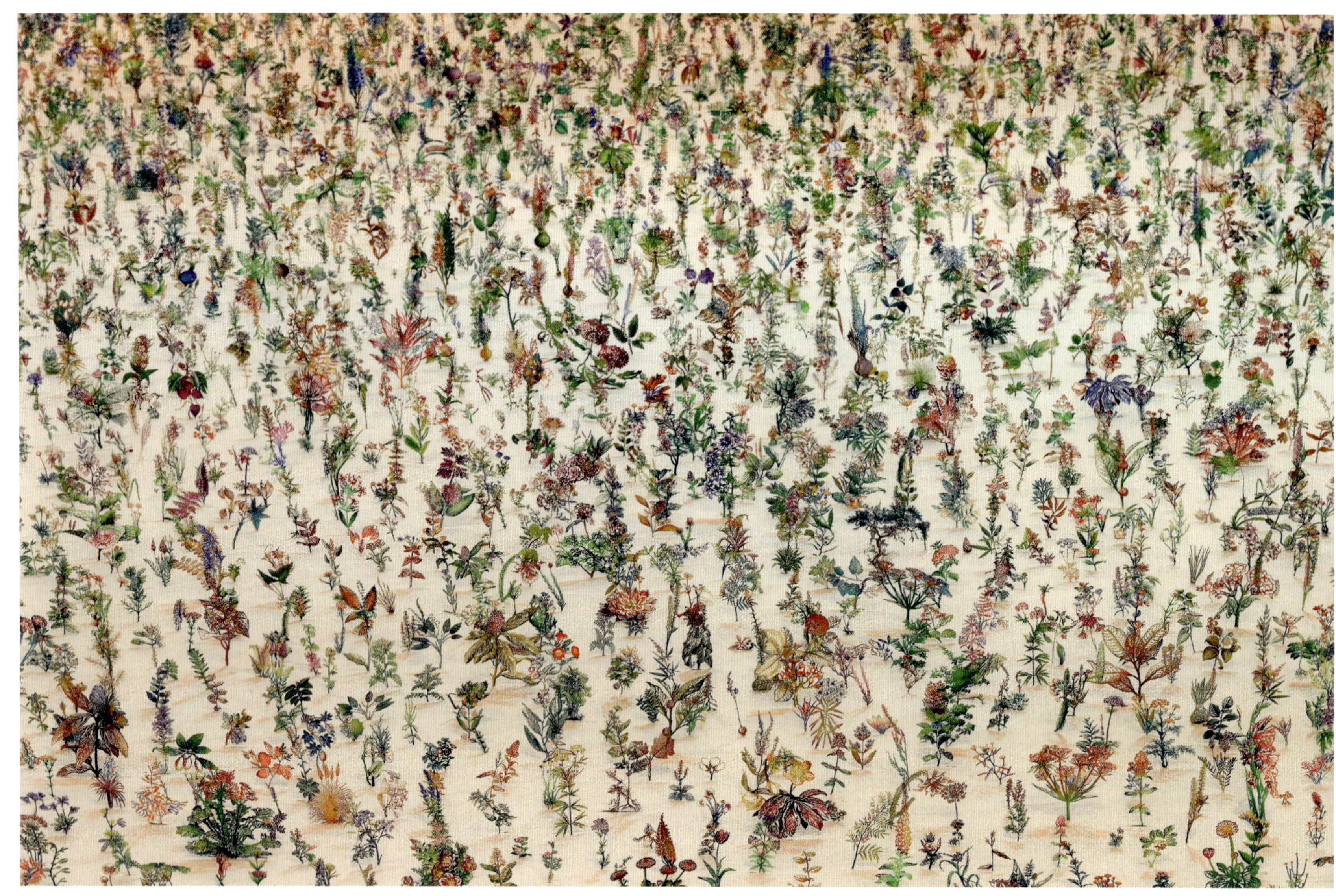

(previous spread)
Blackfield, hand-painted
stainless steel, Musée
de la Chasse, Paris,
France, 2018.

(above)
Blackfield, hand-painted
stainless steel, Tel Aviv
Museum of Art, Tel Aviv,
Israel, 2009.

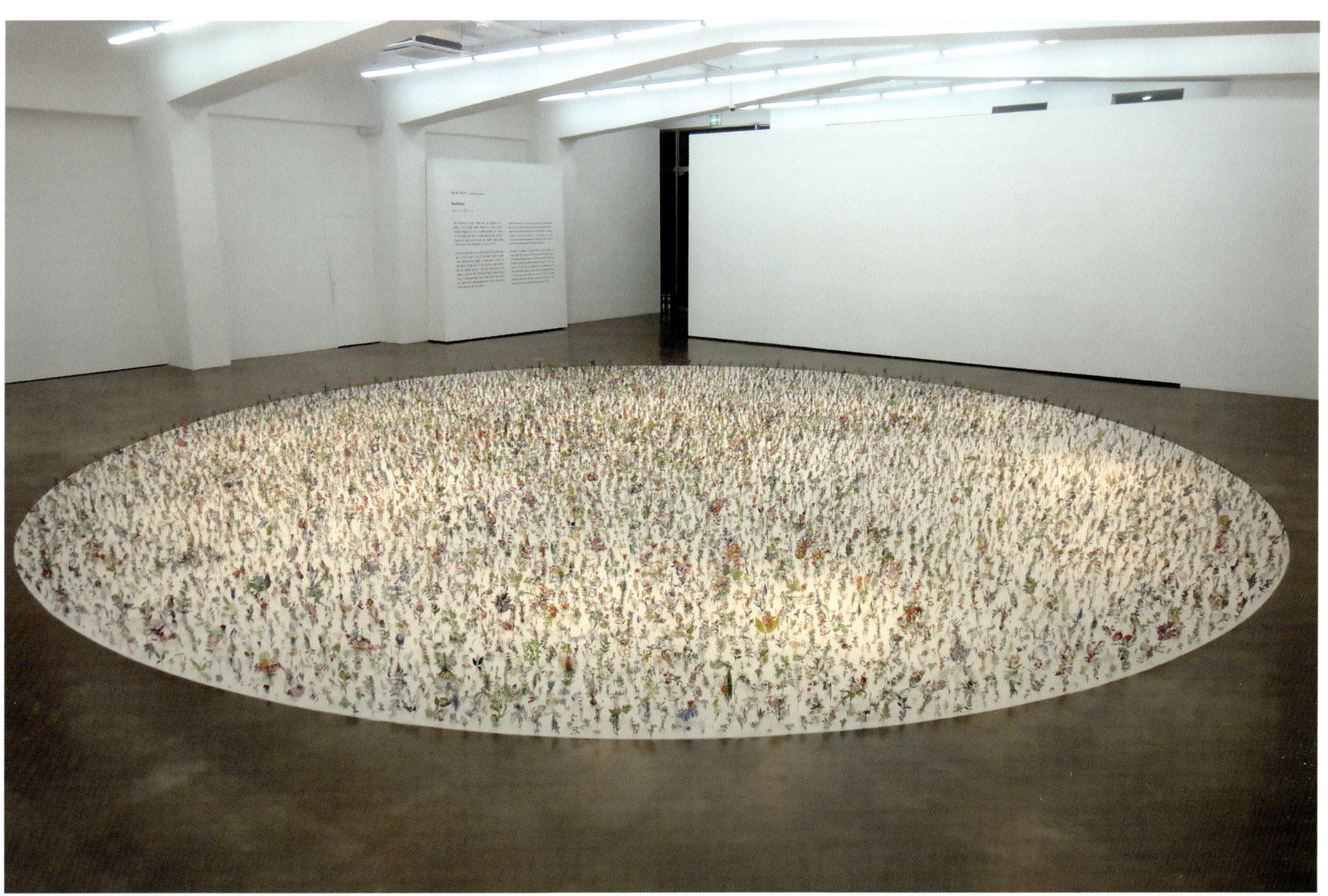

Blackfield, hand-painted
stainless steel, Artclub
1563, Seoul, Korea, 2011.

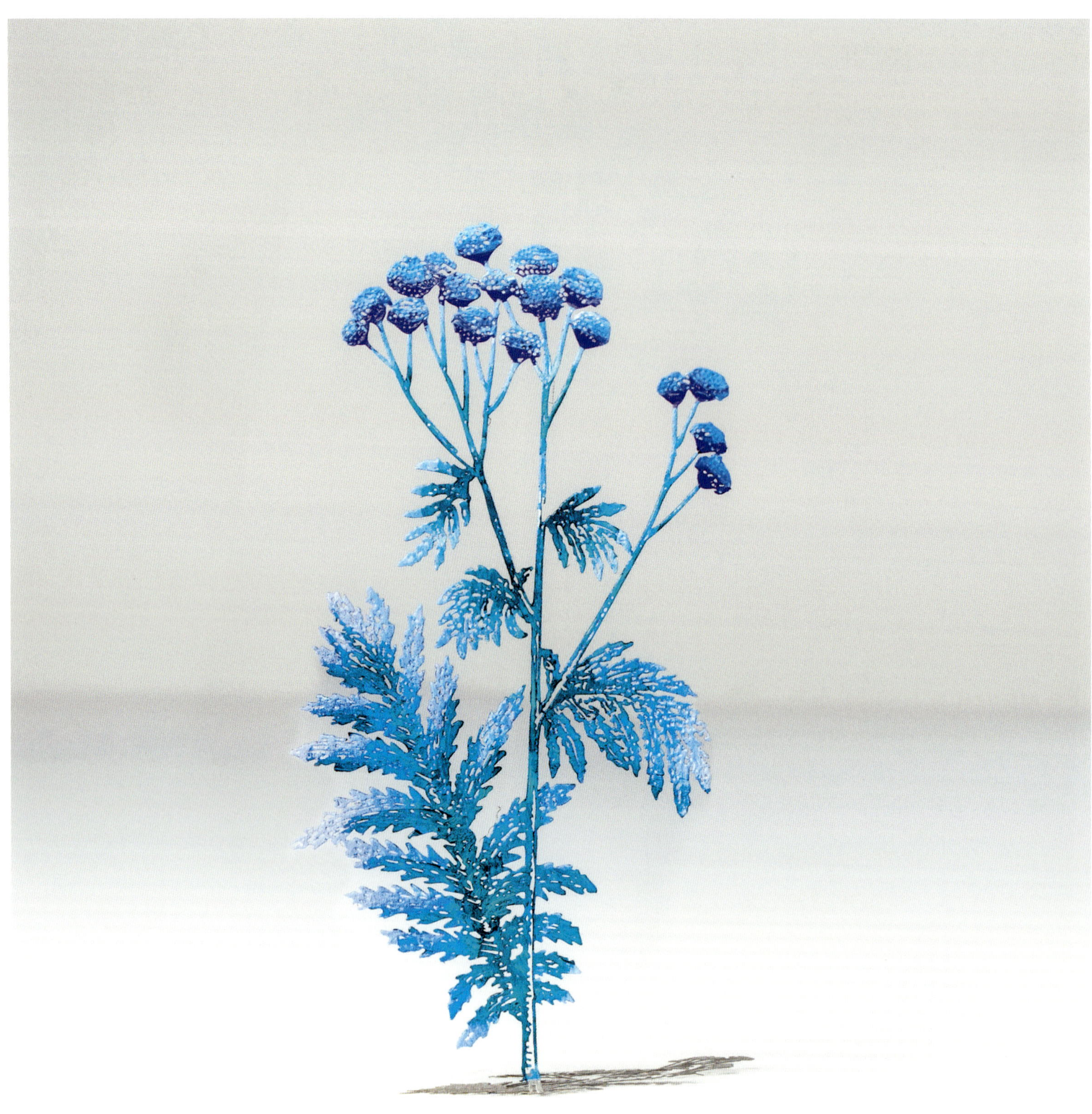

Details from *Blackfield*,
hand-painted stainless
steel, 2017.

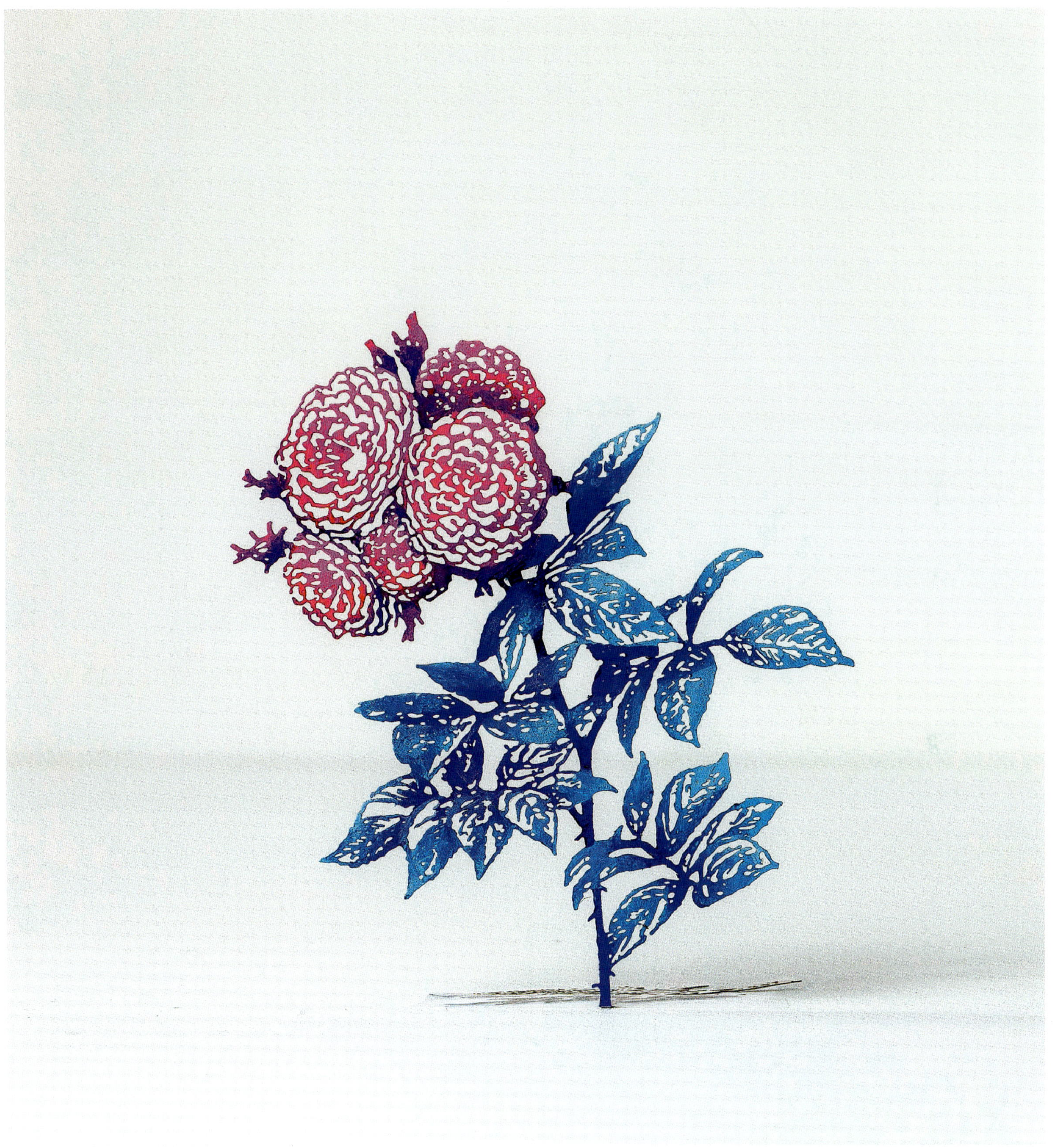

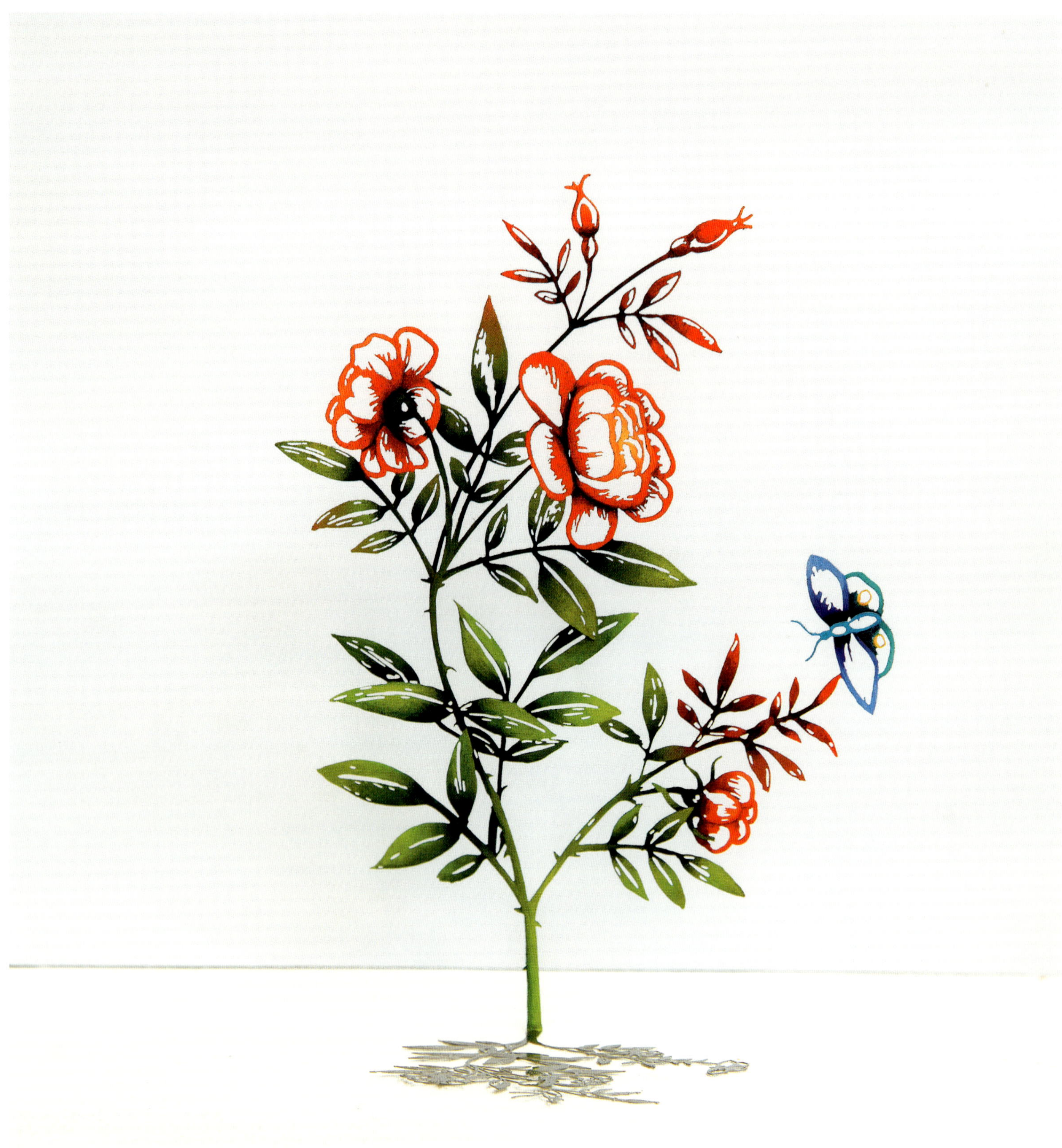

Details from *East and West*, hand-painted stainless steel, 2021

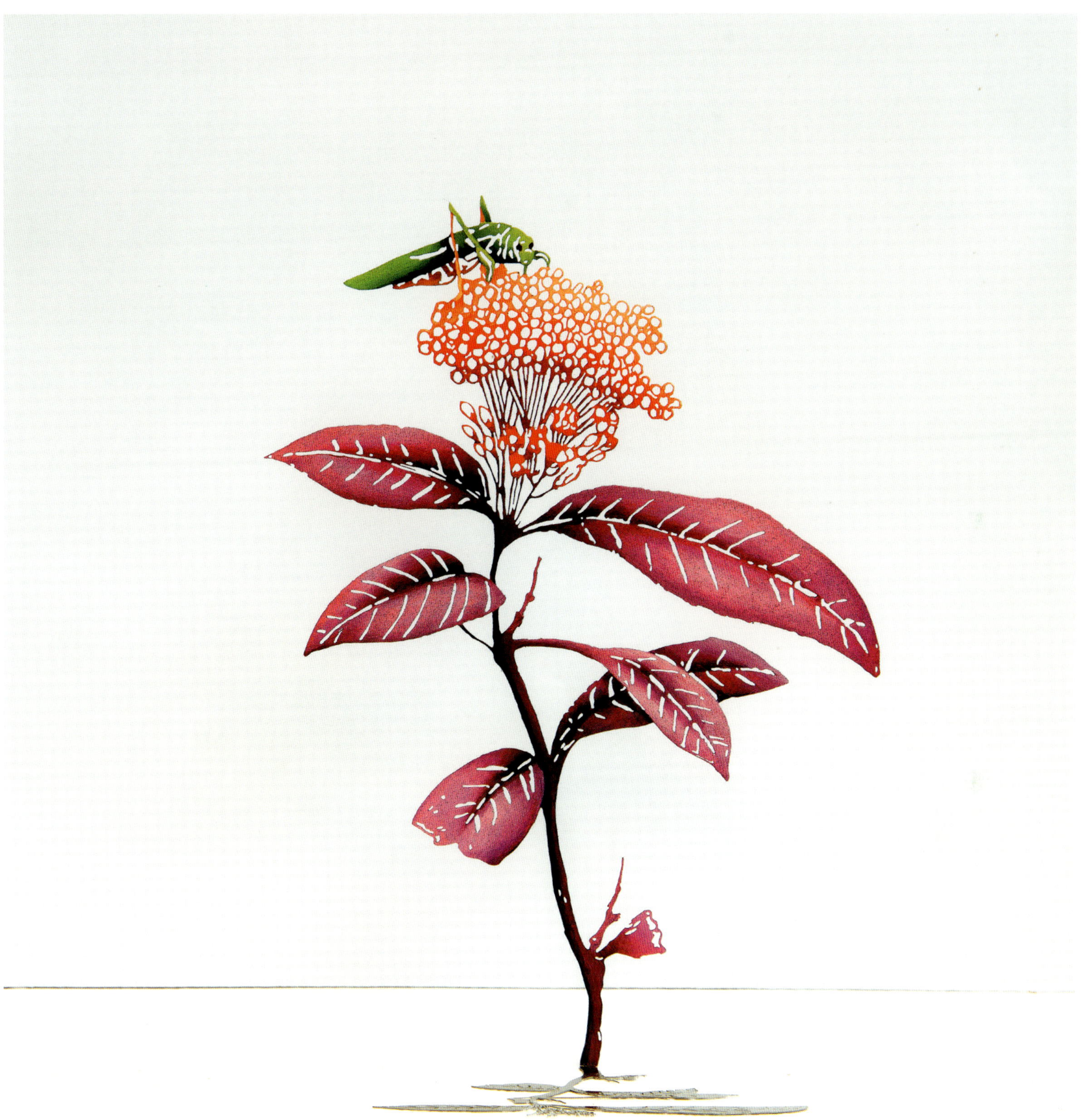

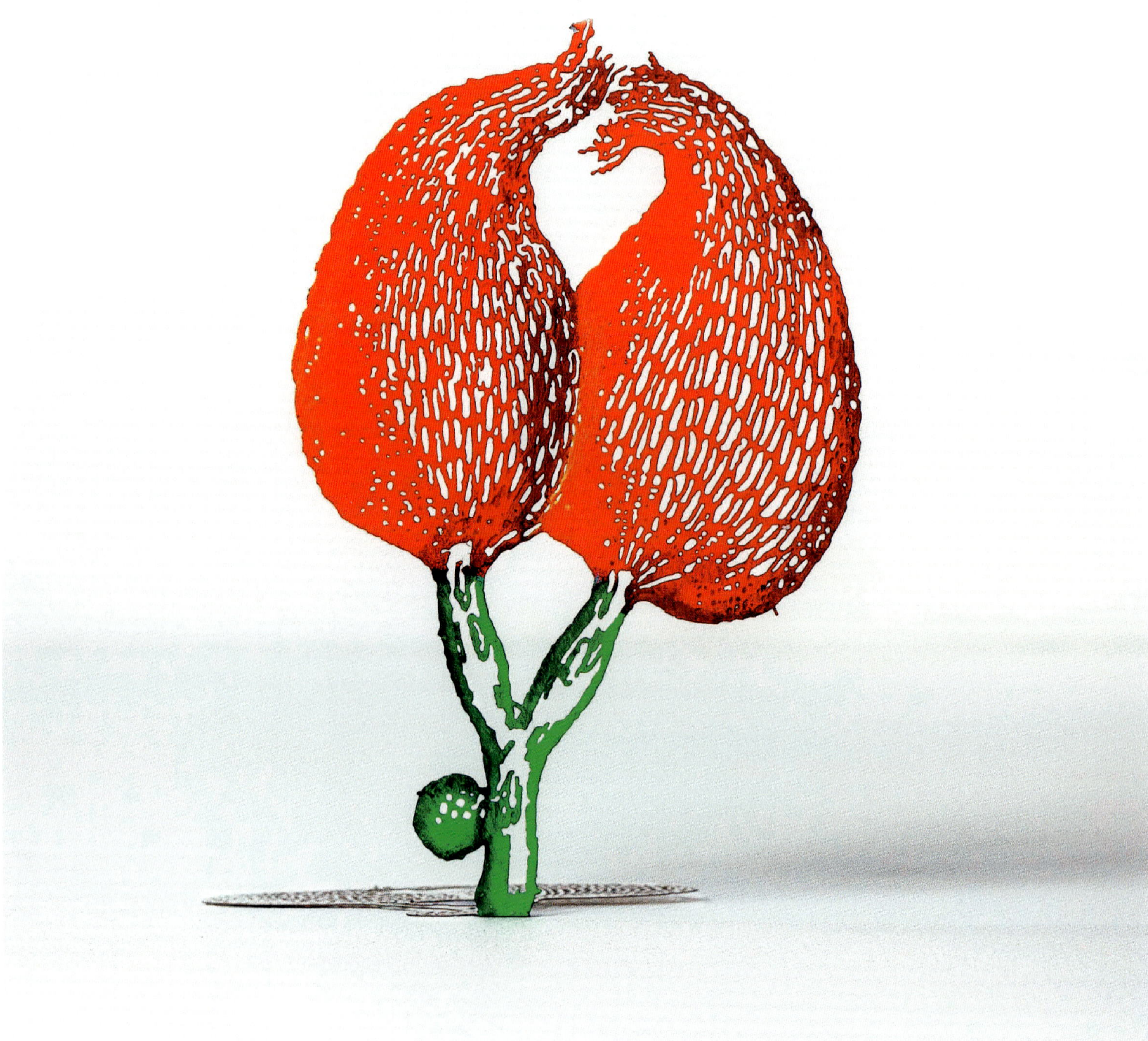

Details from *Blackfield*,
hand-painted stainless
steel, 2017.

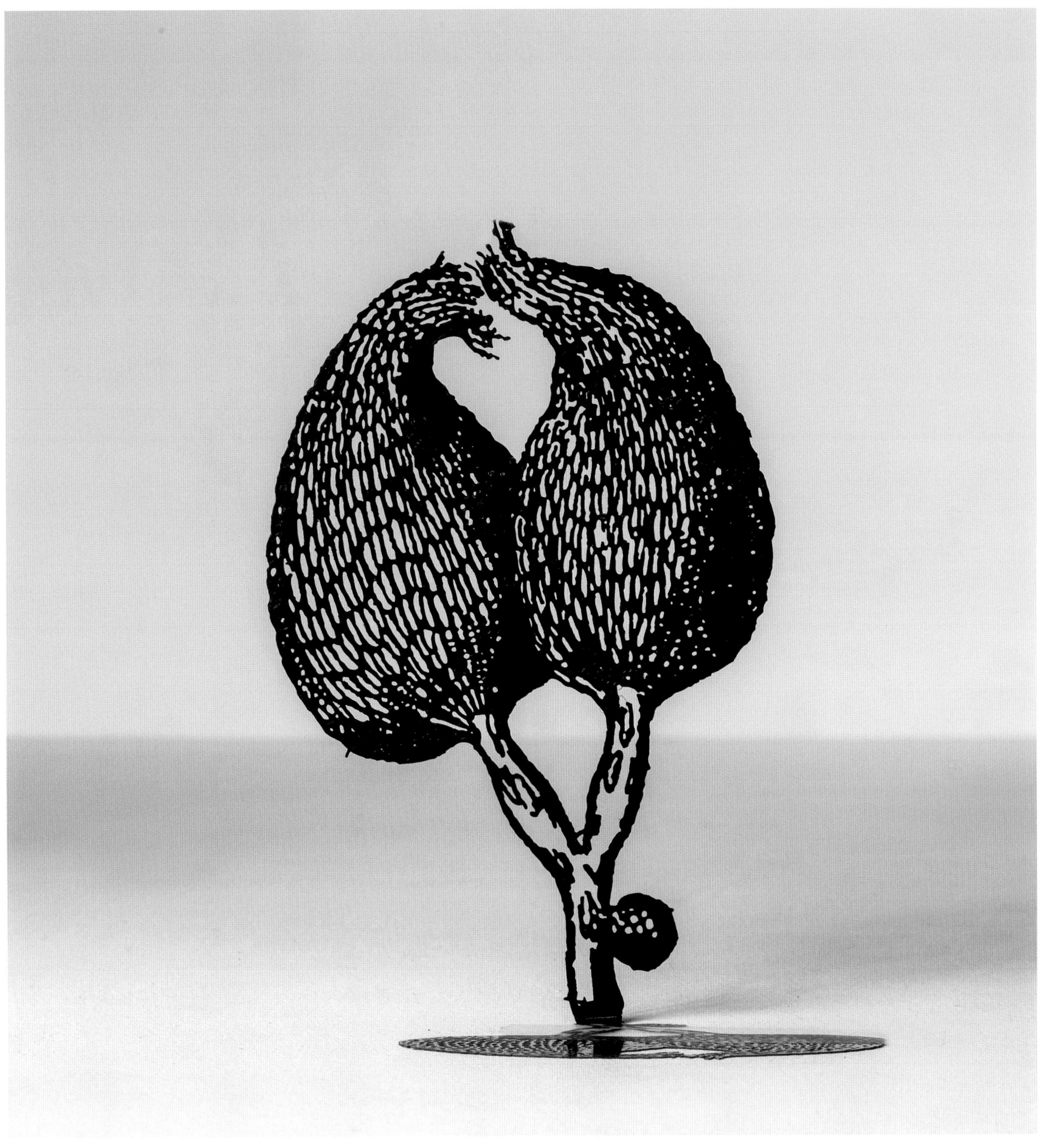

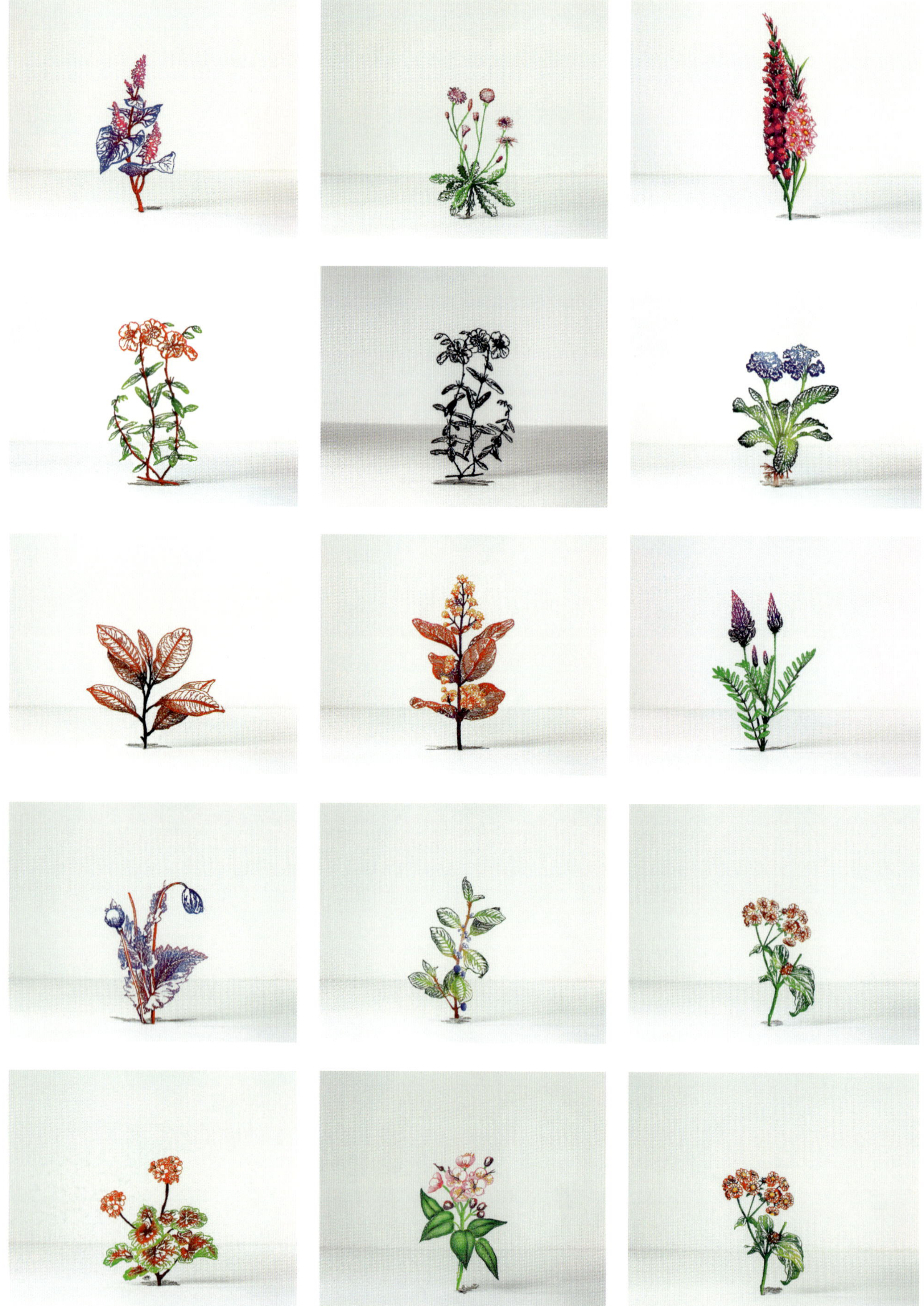

Details from *Blackfield*, hand-painted stainless steel, 2017.

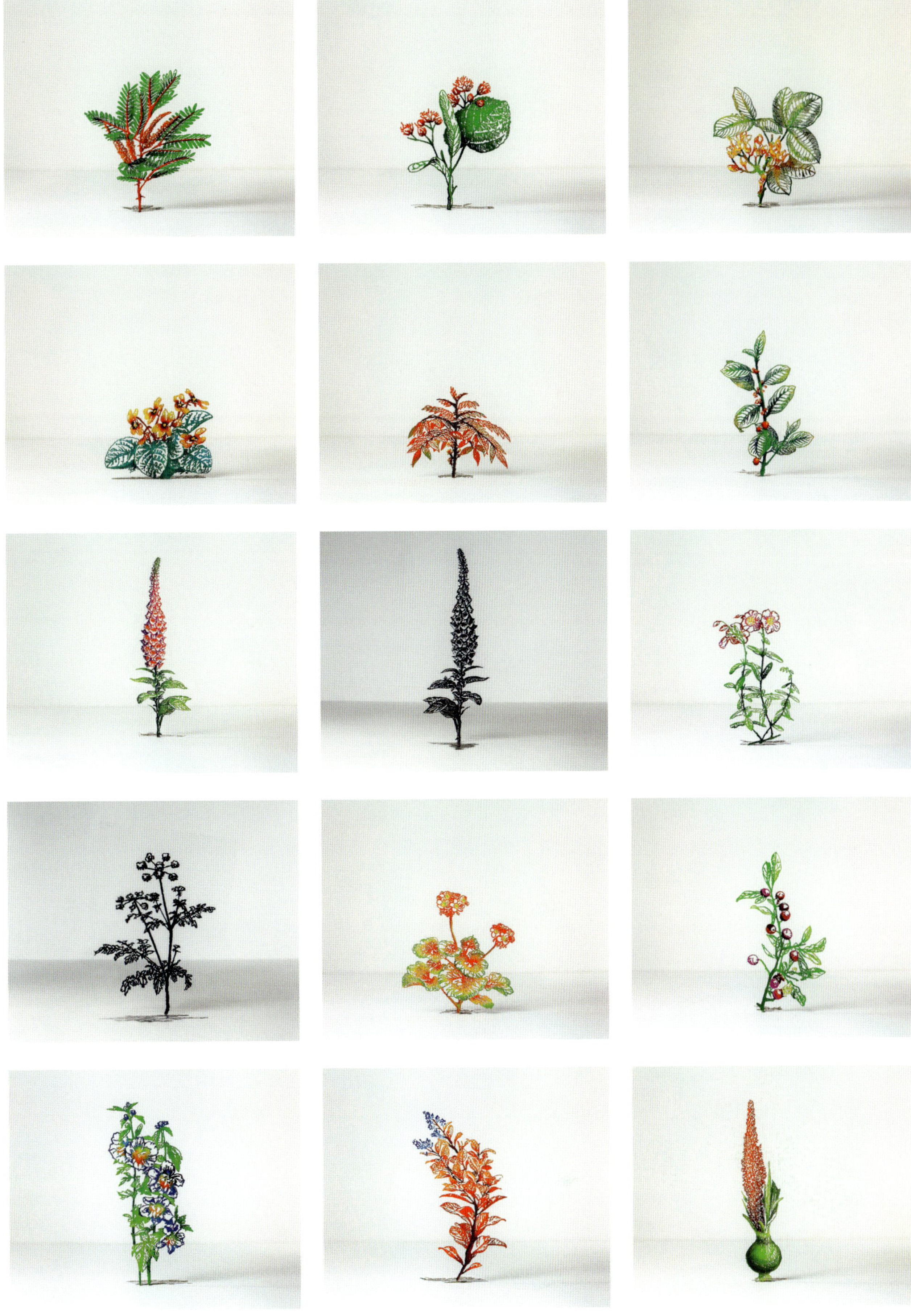

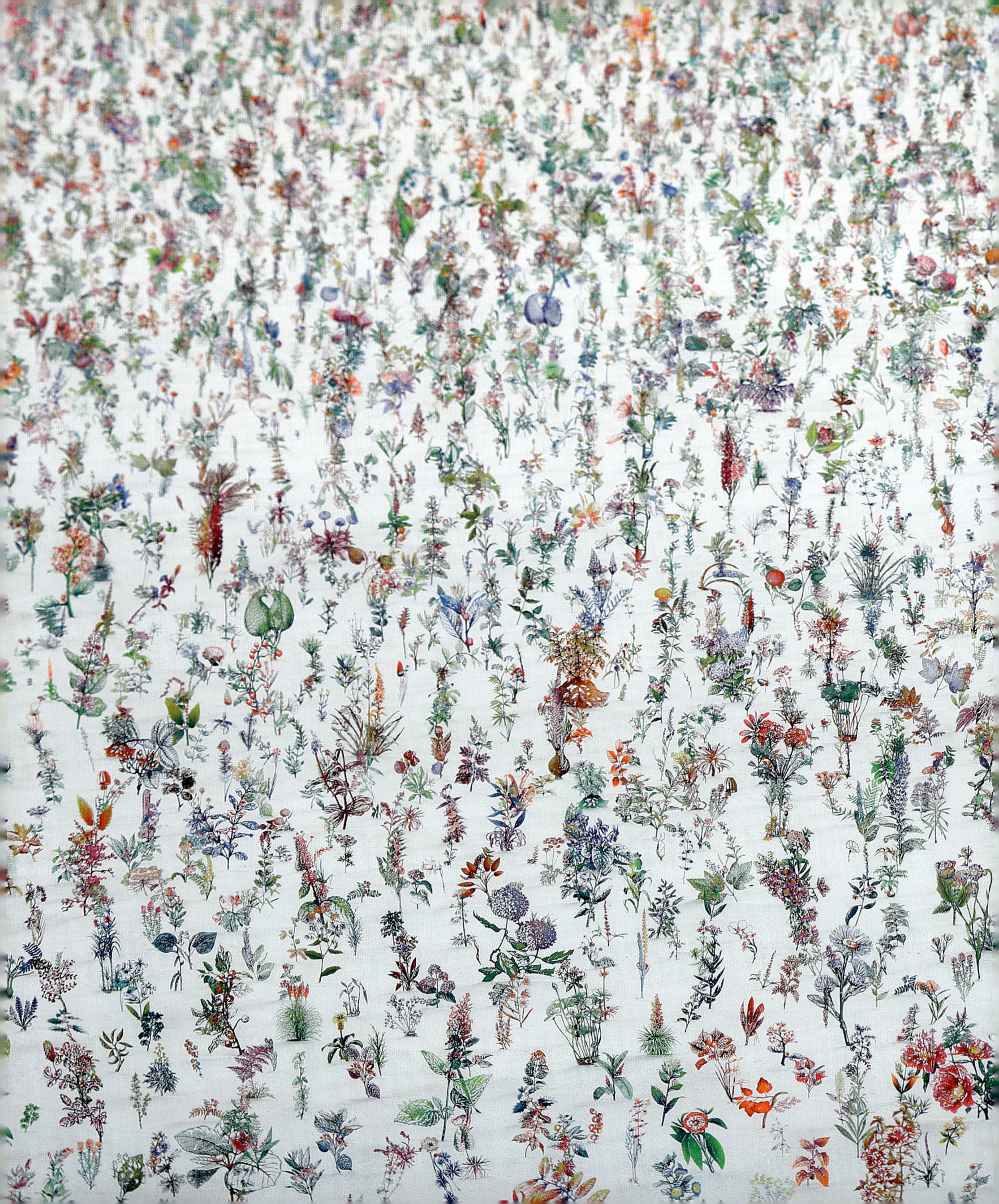

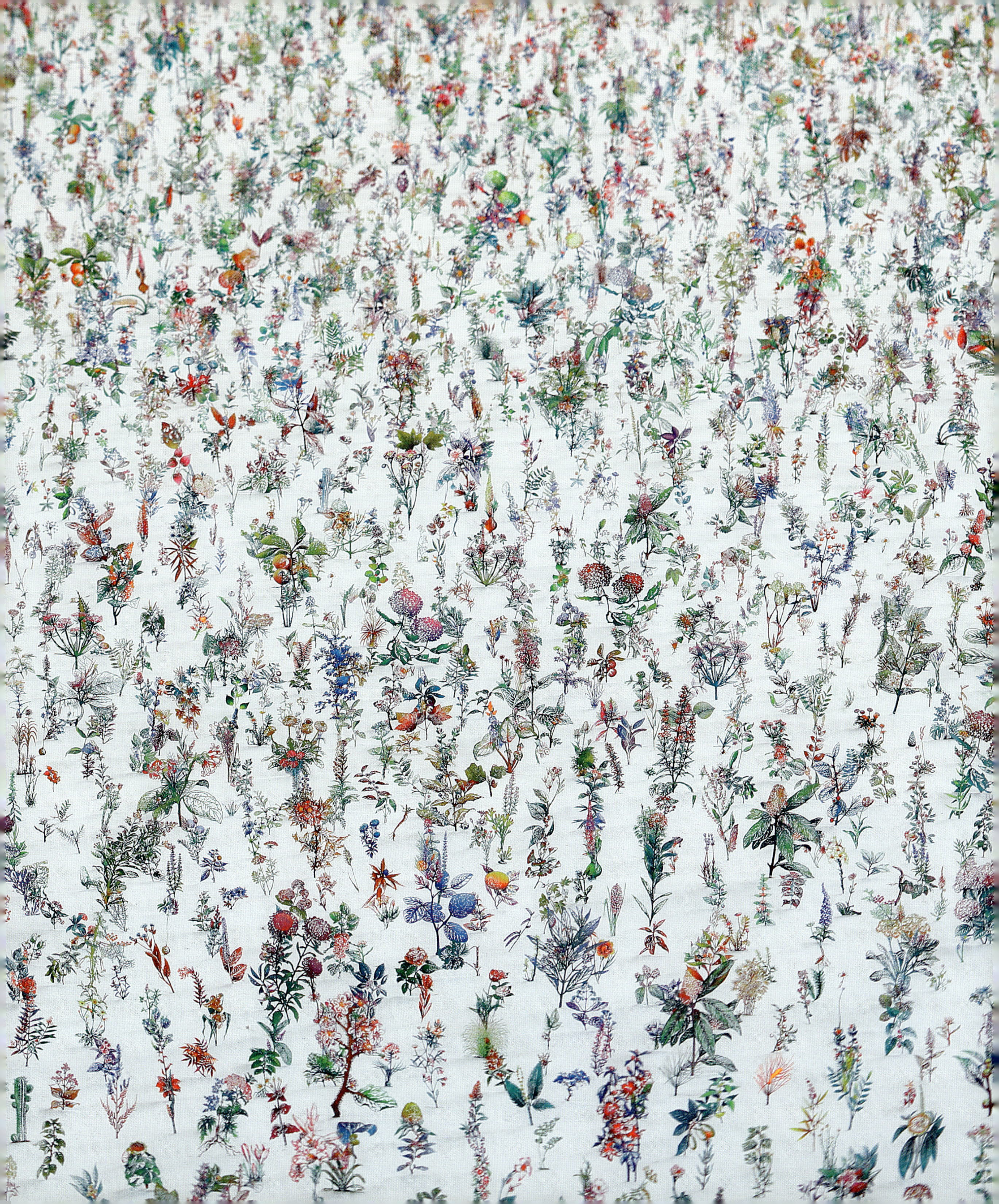

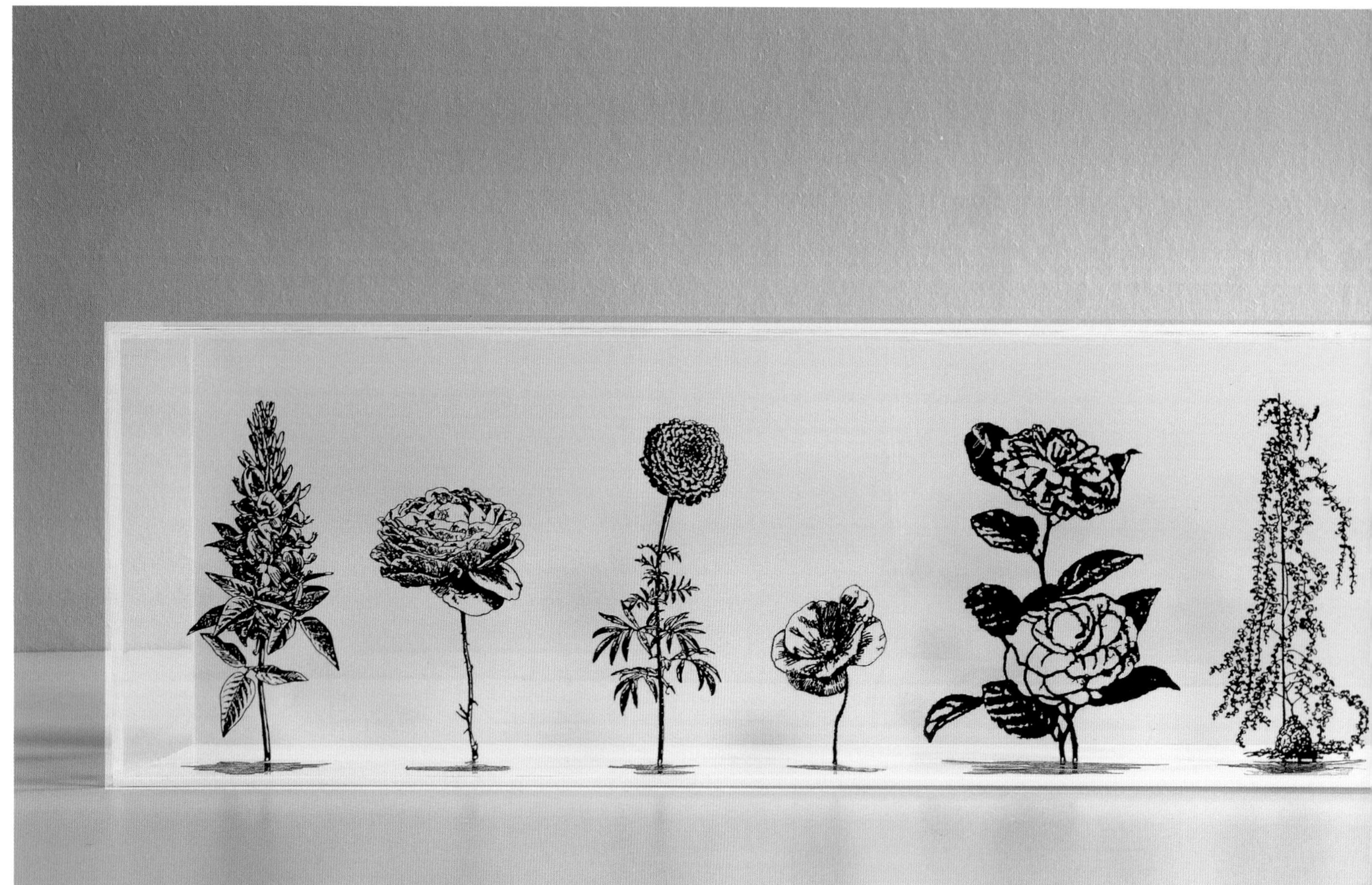

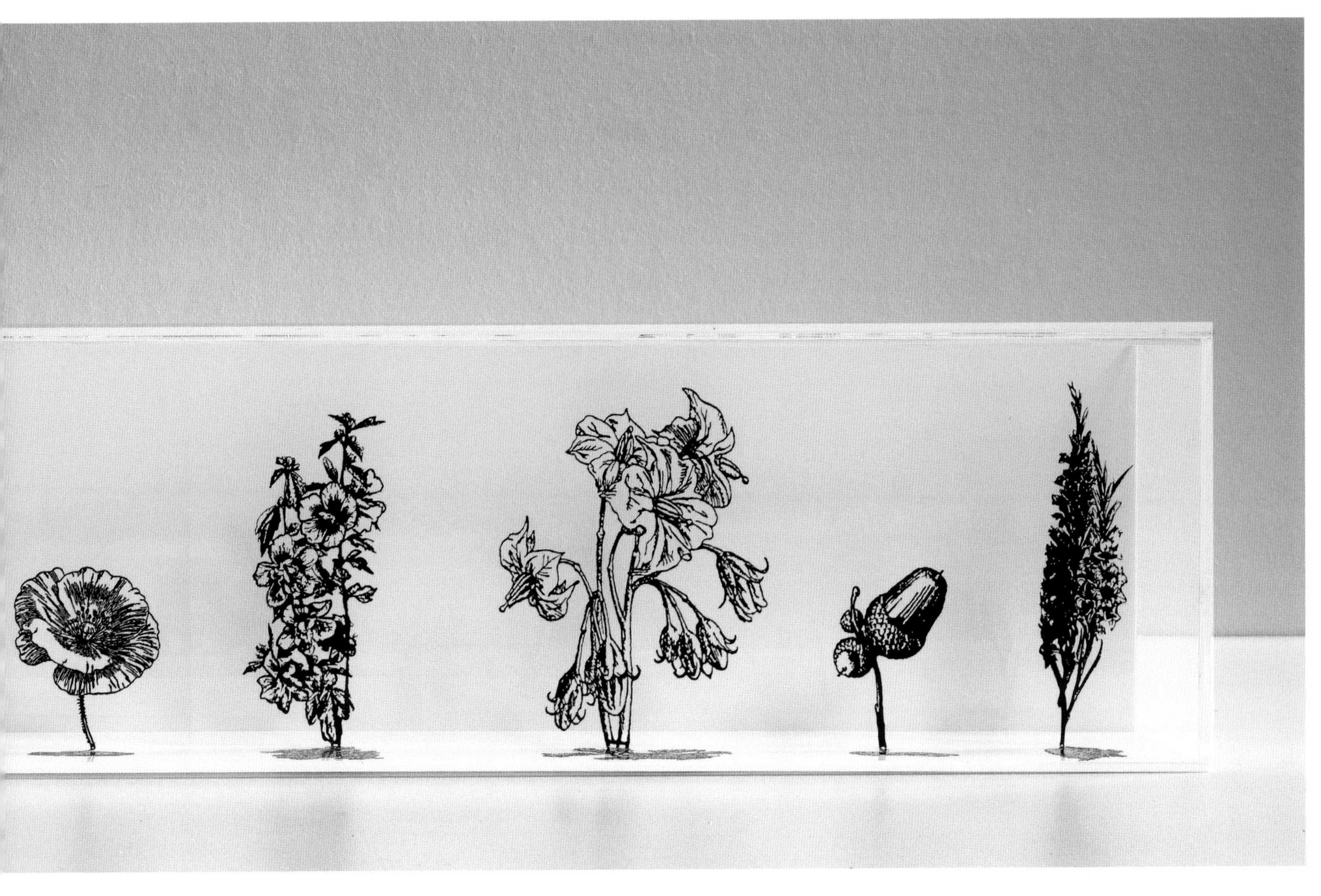

(previous spread)
Blackfield, hand-painted stainless steel, Kenpoku Art Festival, Ibaraki, Japan, 2016

(above)
Black Flowers, hand-painted stainless steel and plexiglass, H25 x W150 x D13 cm, 2021

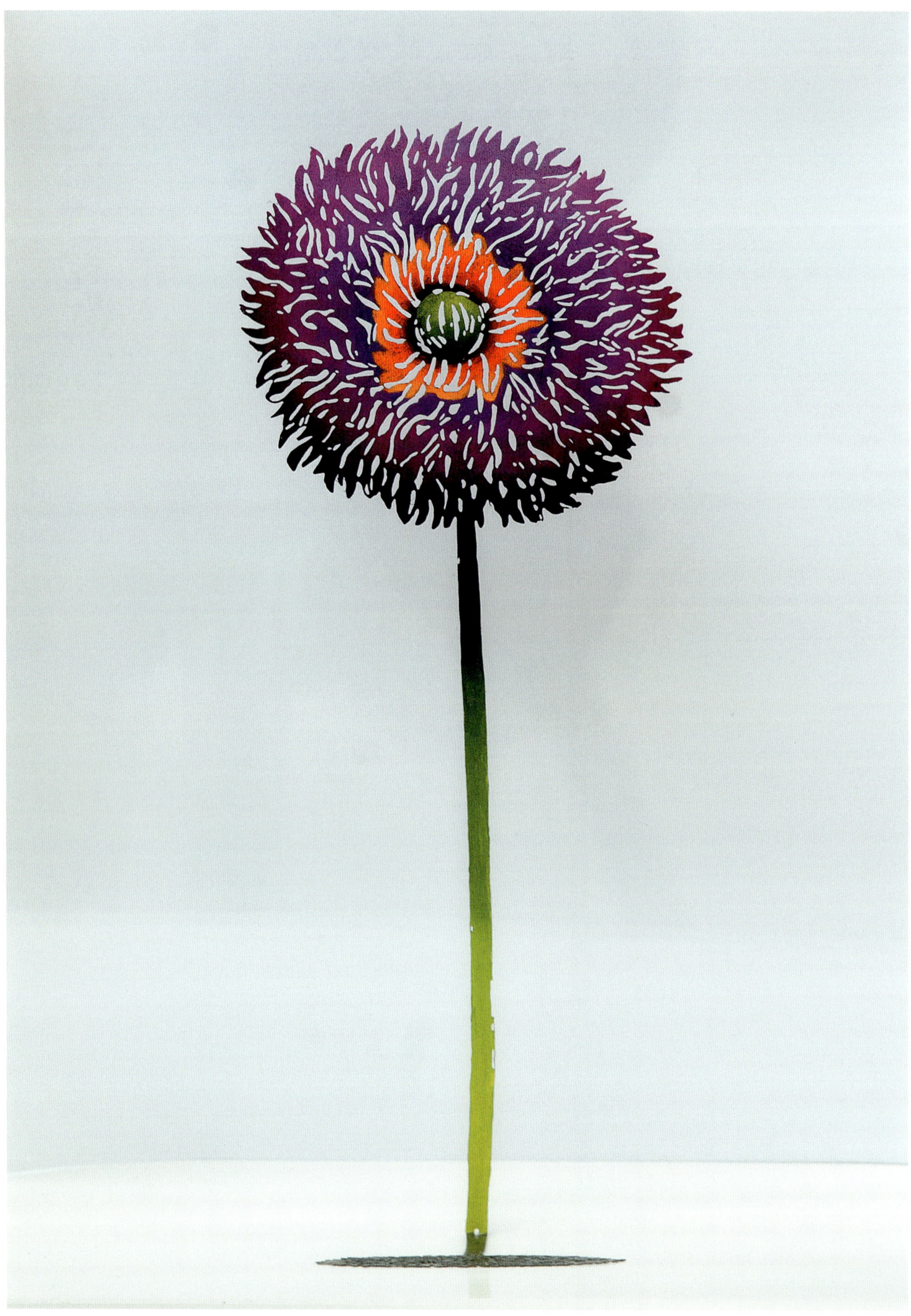

Changing Mood, hand-painted stainless steel and plexiglass, H25 x W20 x D13 cm, 2021.

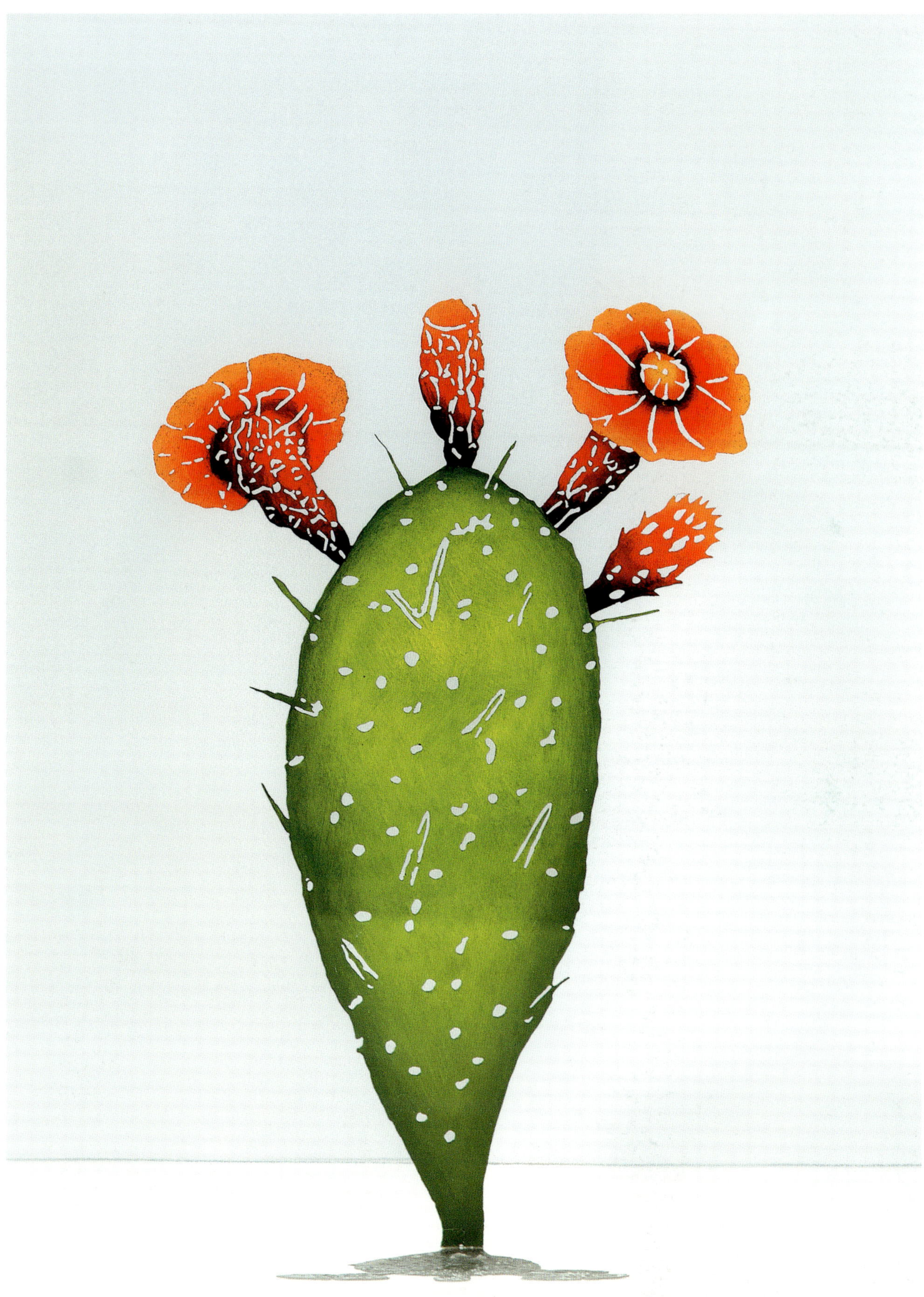

Happy Days, hand-painted stainless steel and plexiglass, H25 x W20 x D13 cm, 2021.

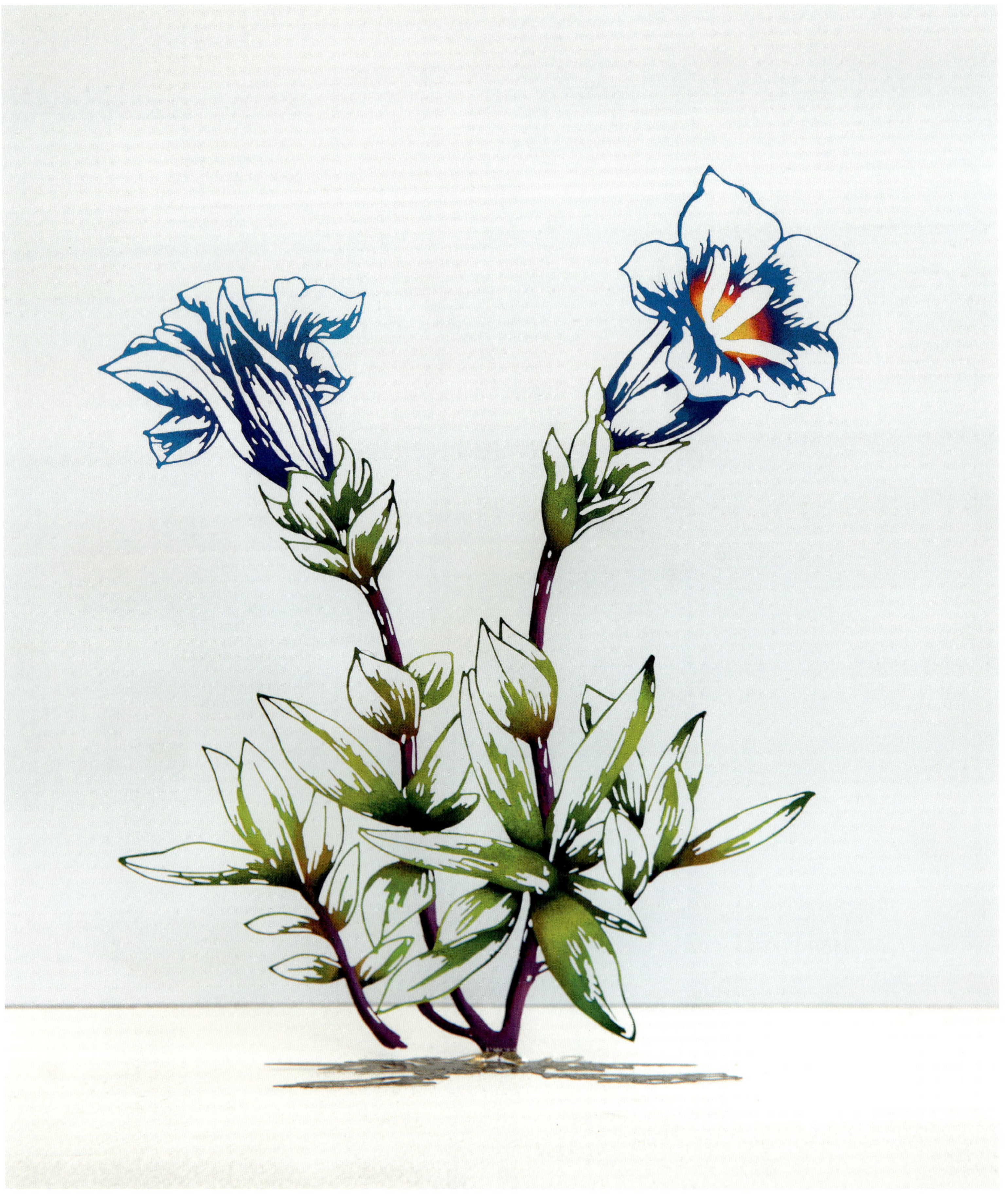

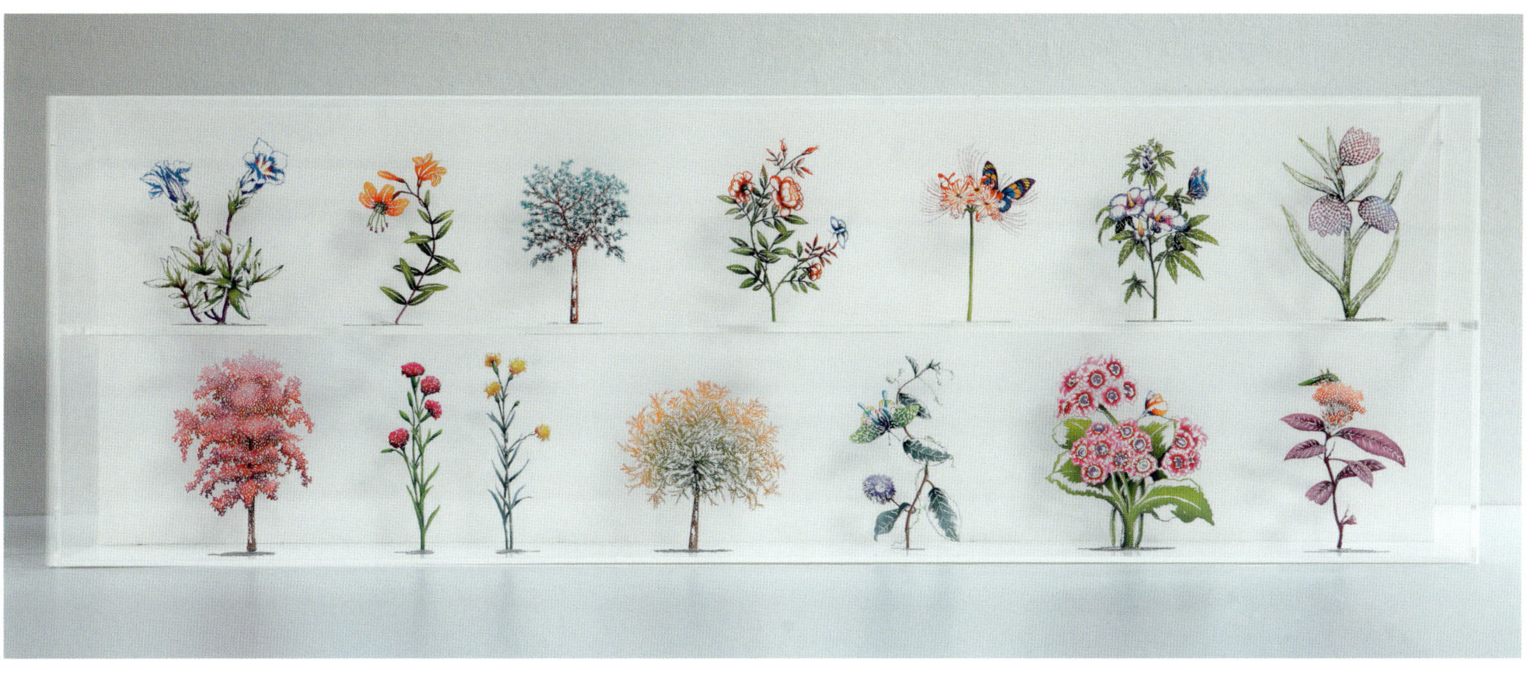

East and West, hand-painted stainless steel and plexiglass, H50 x W150 x D13 cm, 2021.

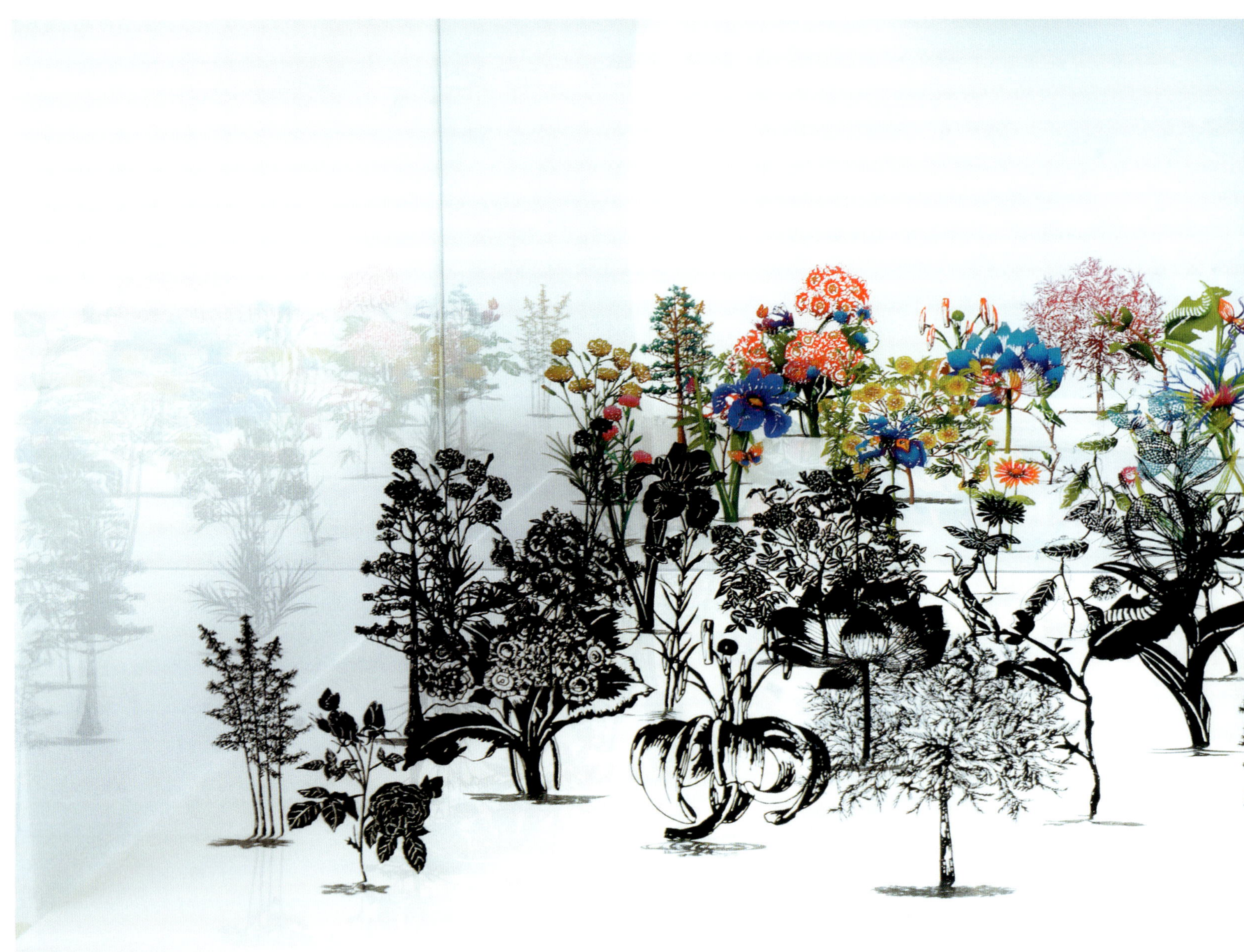

Desert Bloom, hand-
painted stainless steel
and plexiglass, H30.5 x
W75 x D53 cm, 2021.

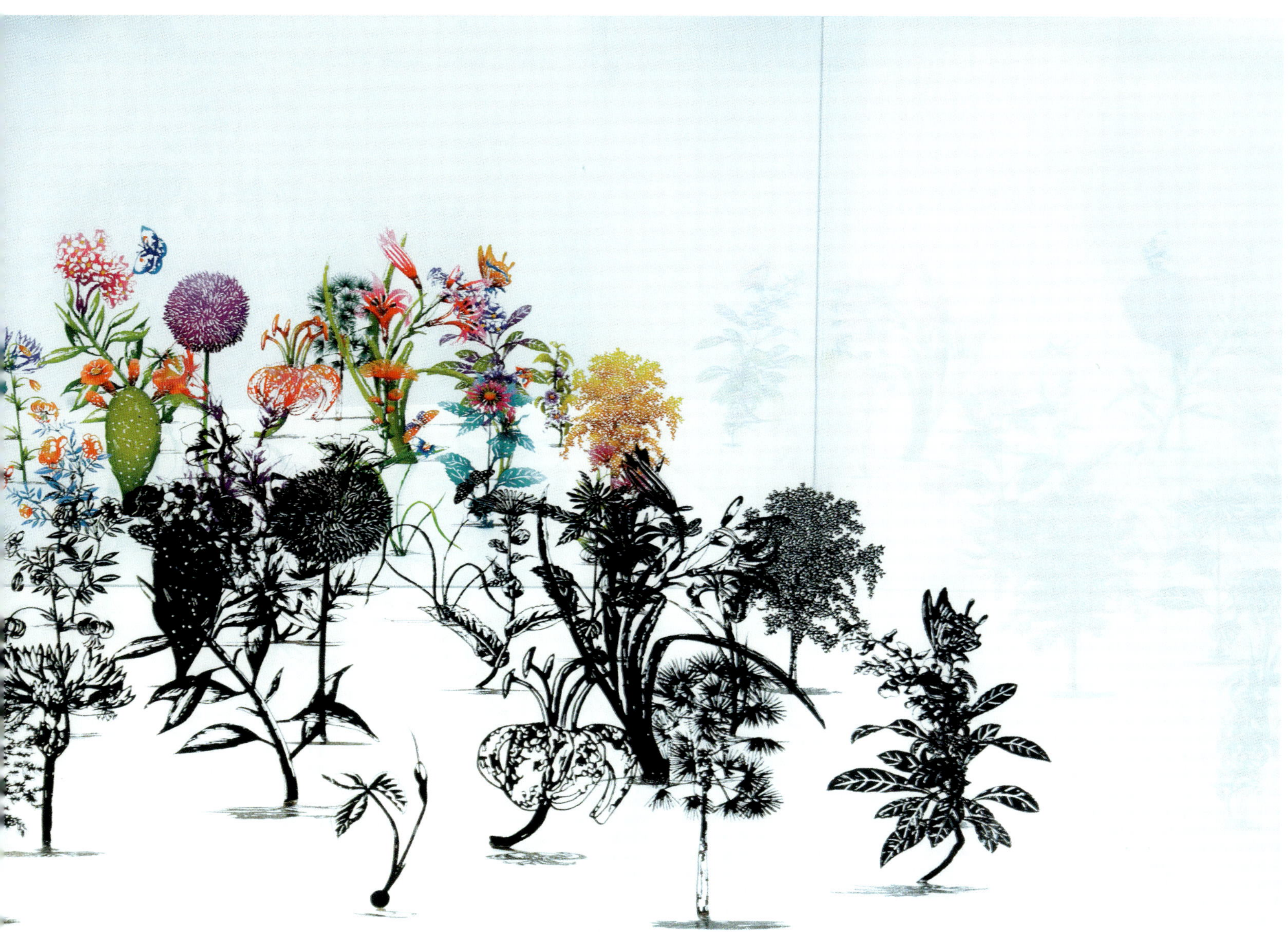

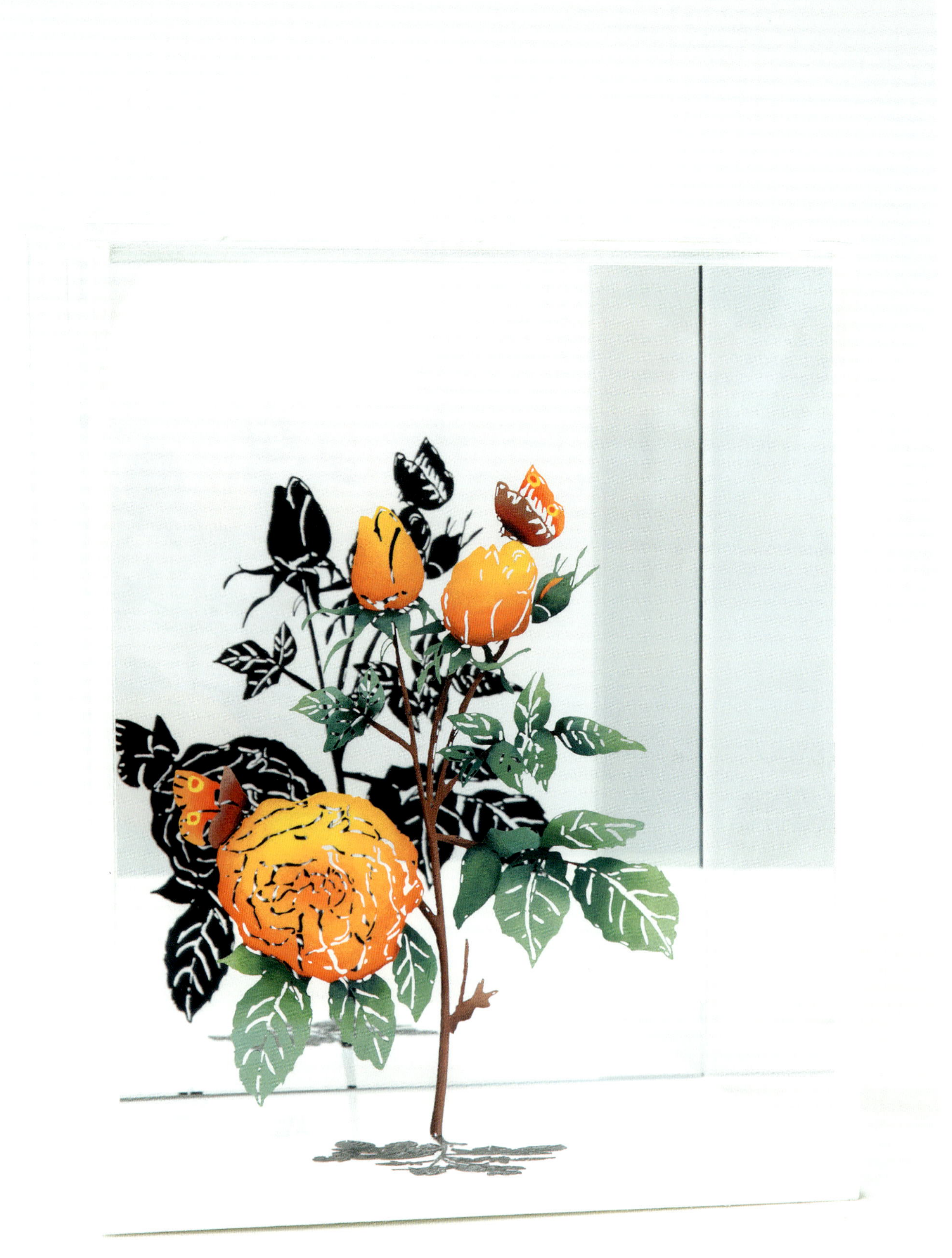

Winter's Heart, hand-painted stainless steel and plexiglass, H25 x W20 x D13 cm, 2021.

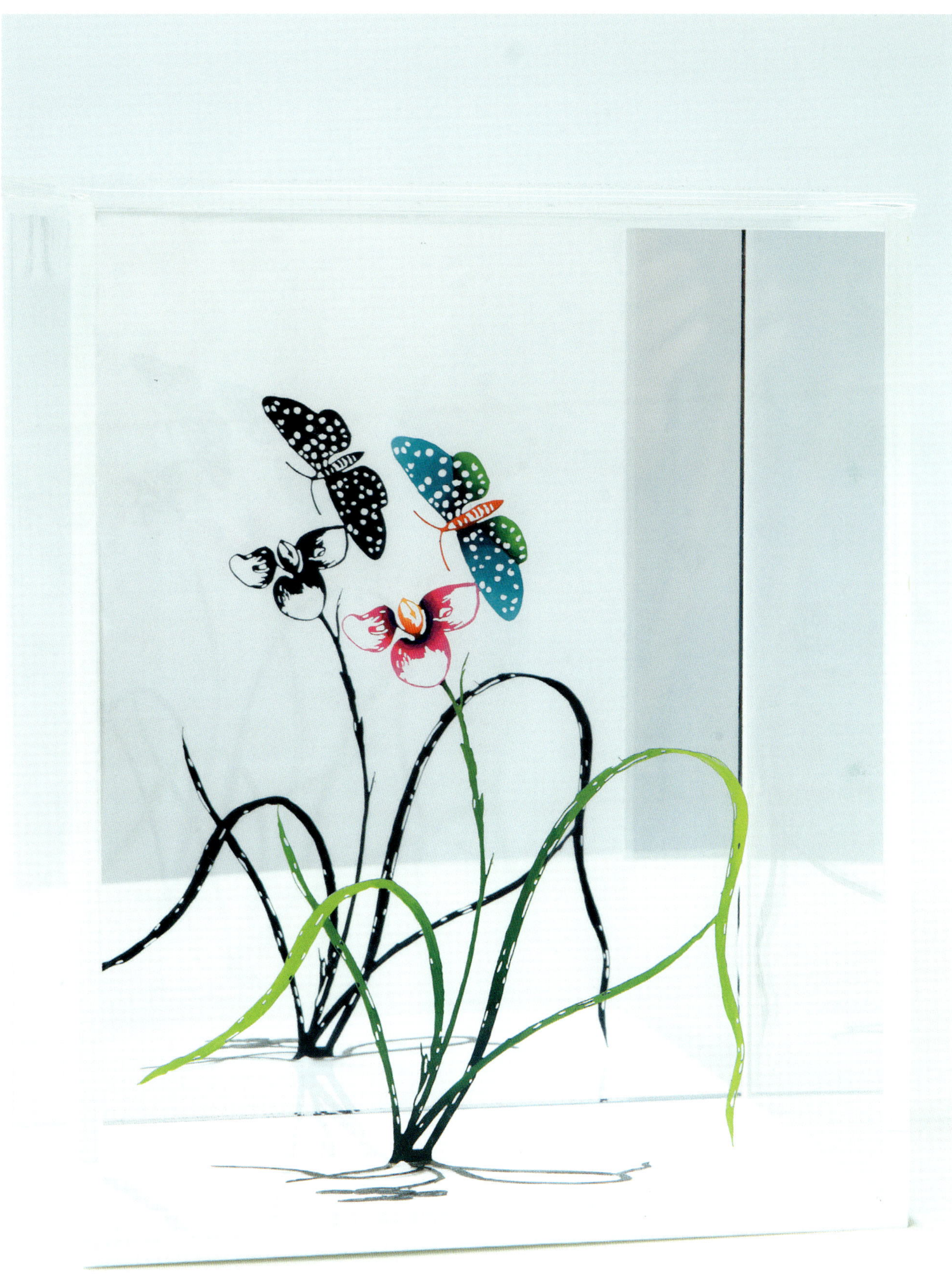

Easy Night, Easy Day,
**hand-painted stainless
steel and plexiglass, H25
x W20 x D13 cm, 2021.**

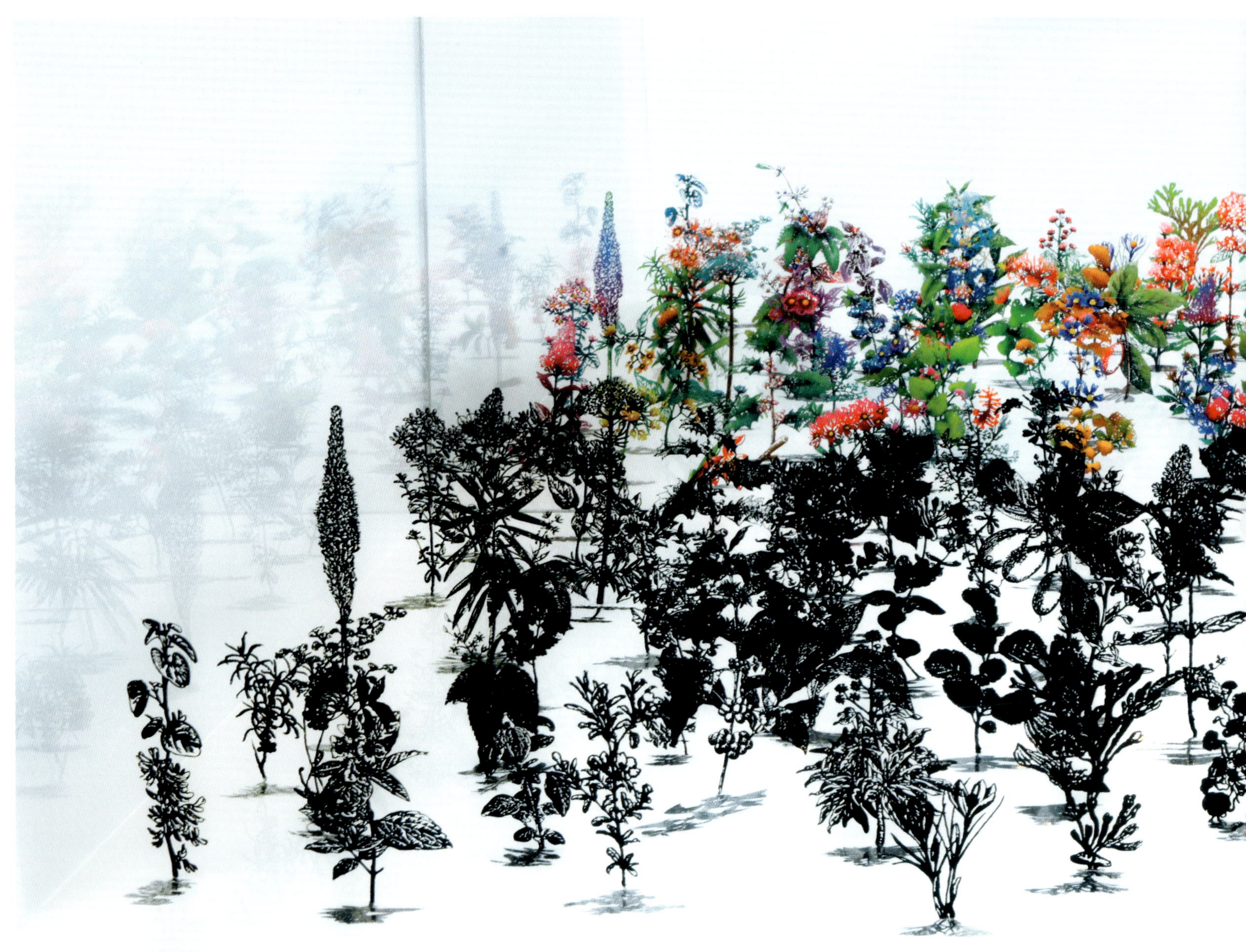

Dawn, hand-painted
stainless steel and
plexiglass, H31.5 x W76 x
D53 cm, 2021.

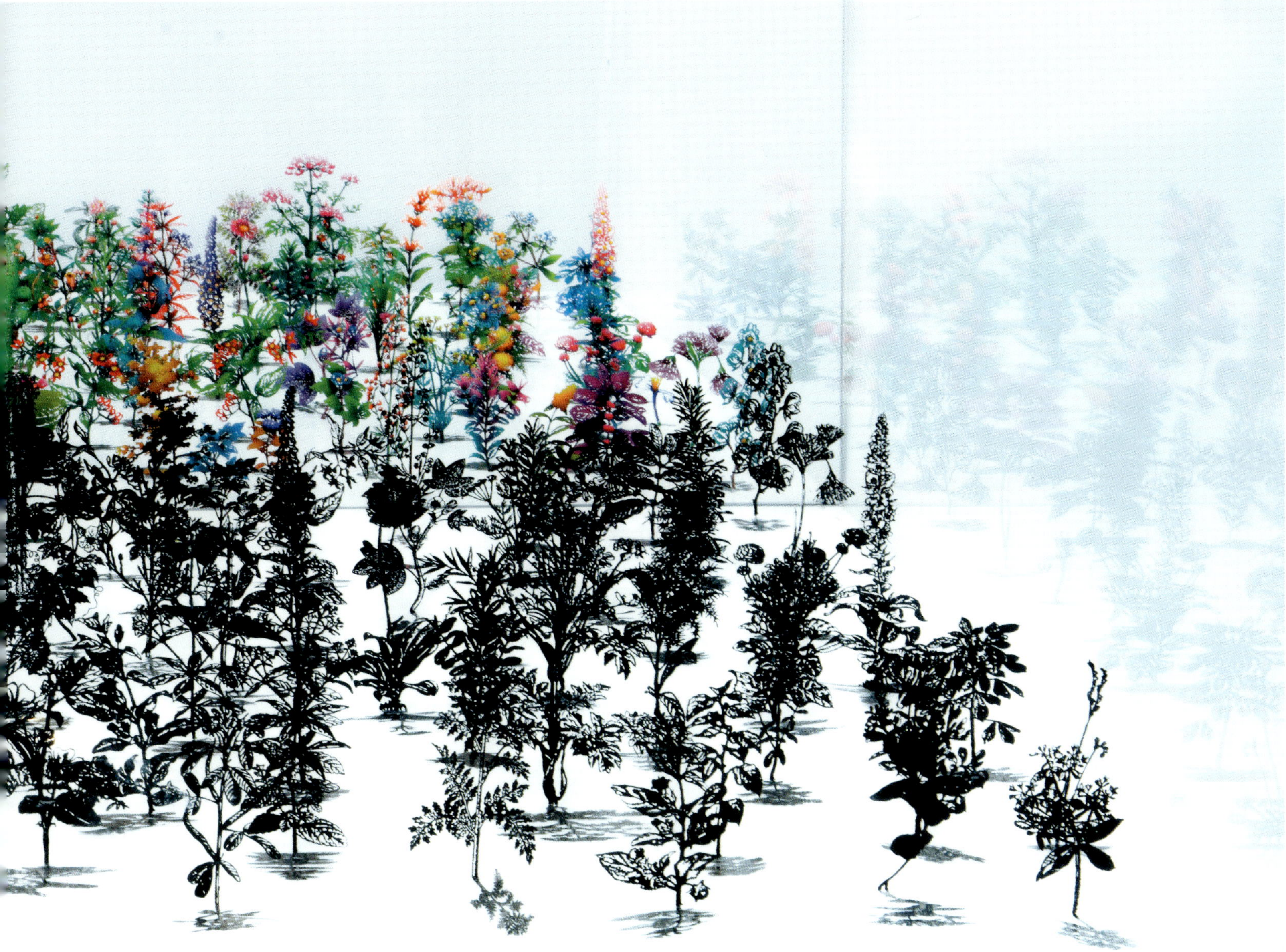

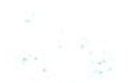

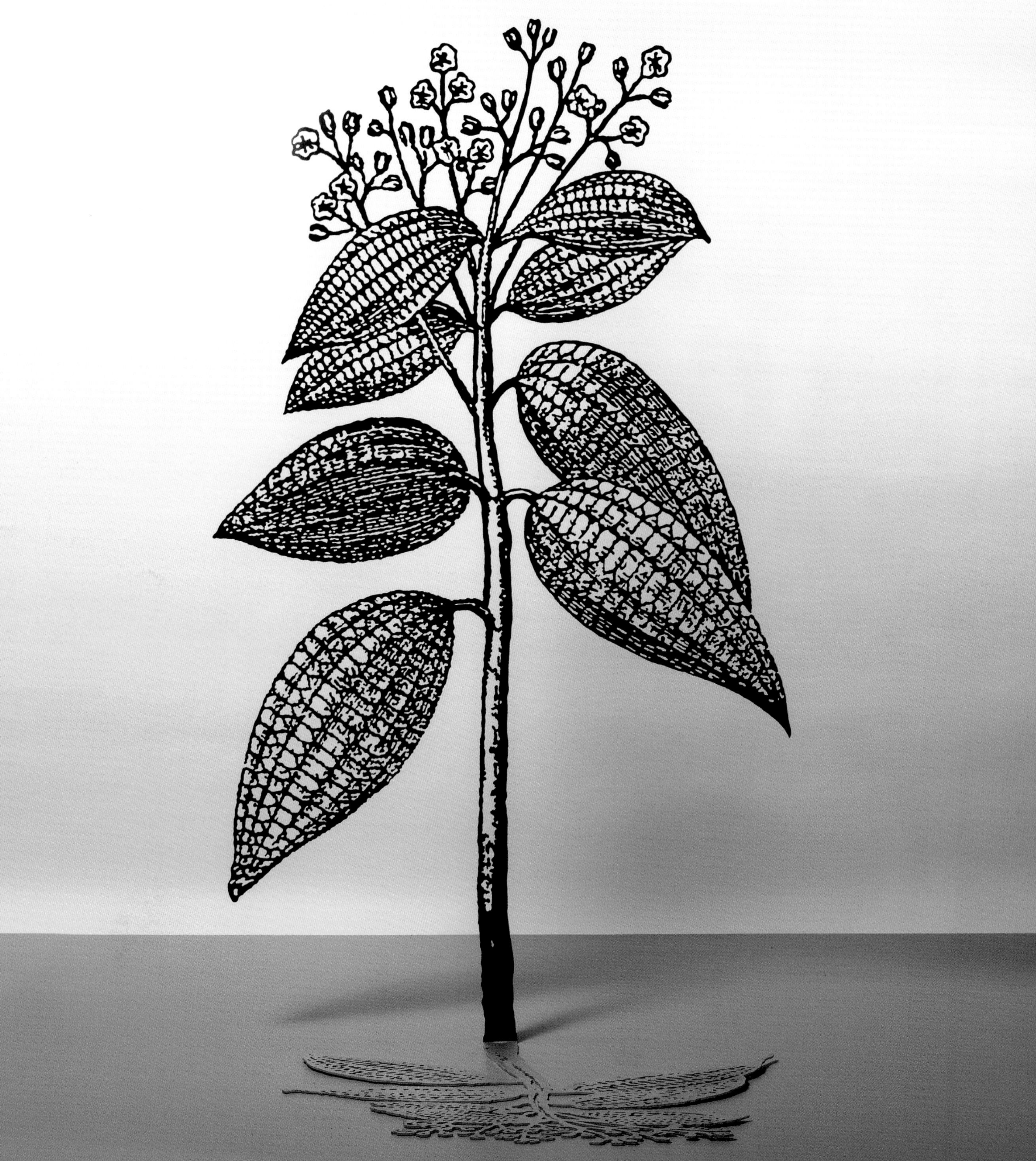

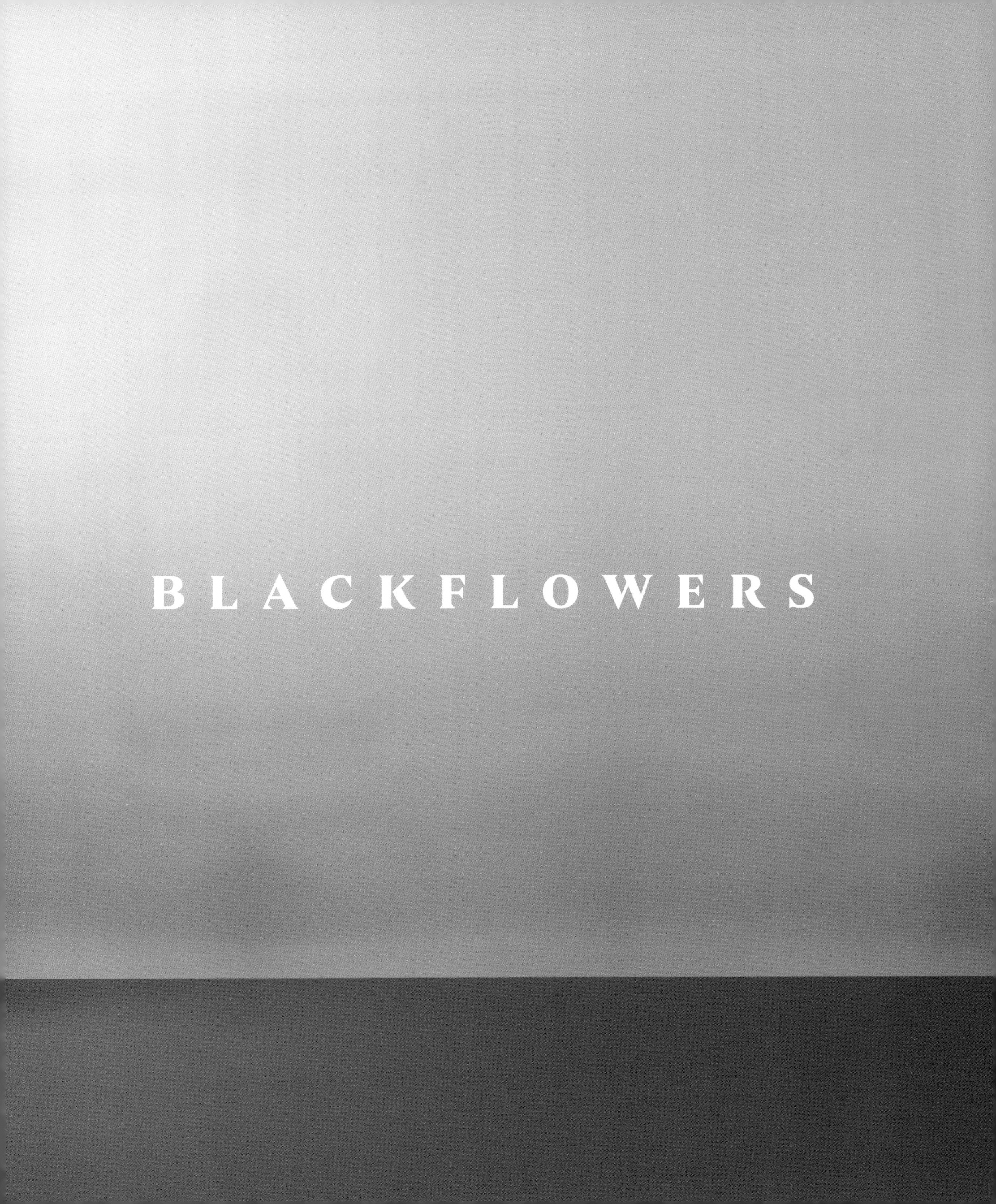

BLACKFLOWERS

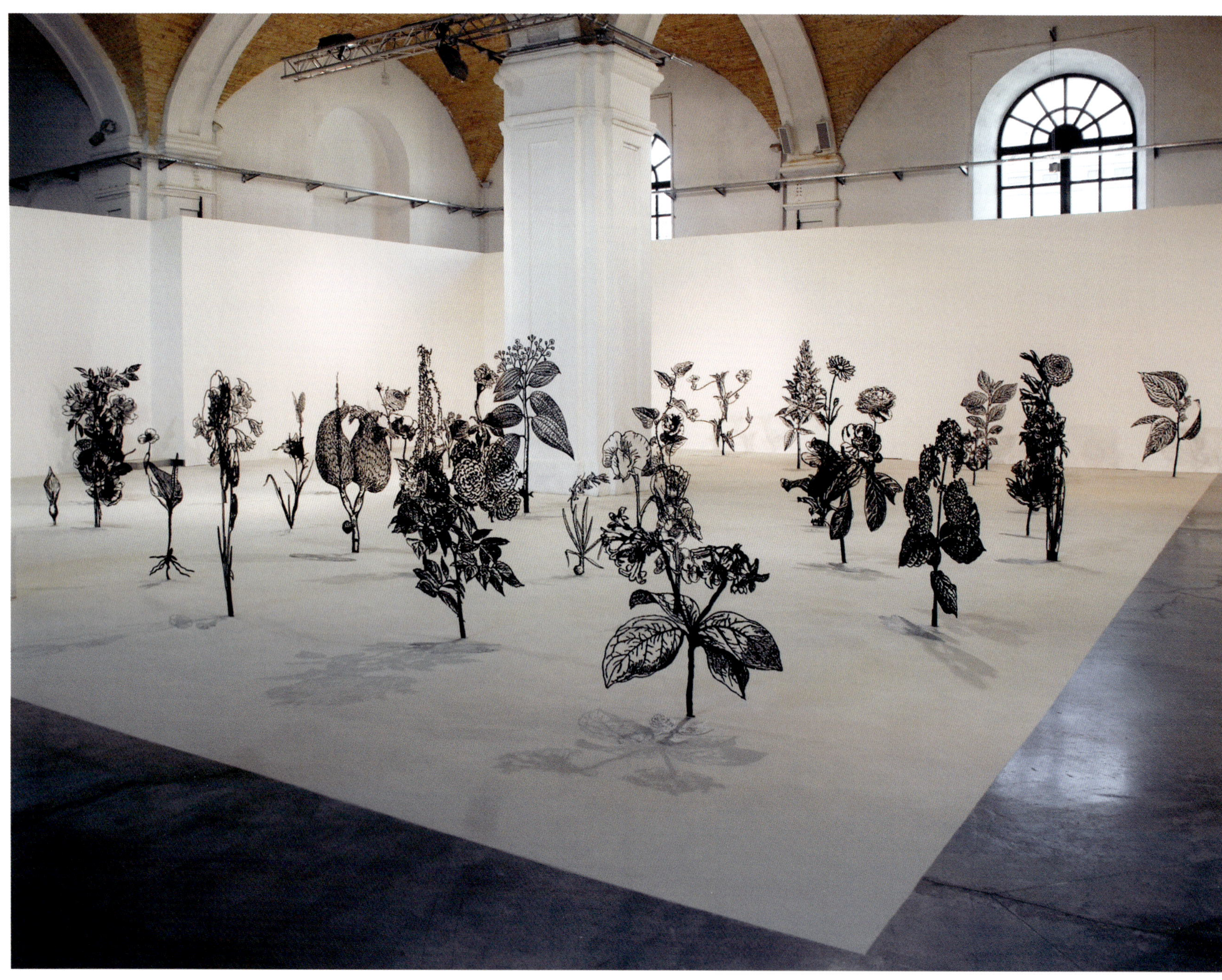

Blackflowers, hand-cut
painted aluminium,
Mysteski Arsenal, Kiev,
Ukraine 2012.

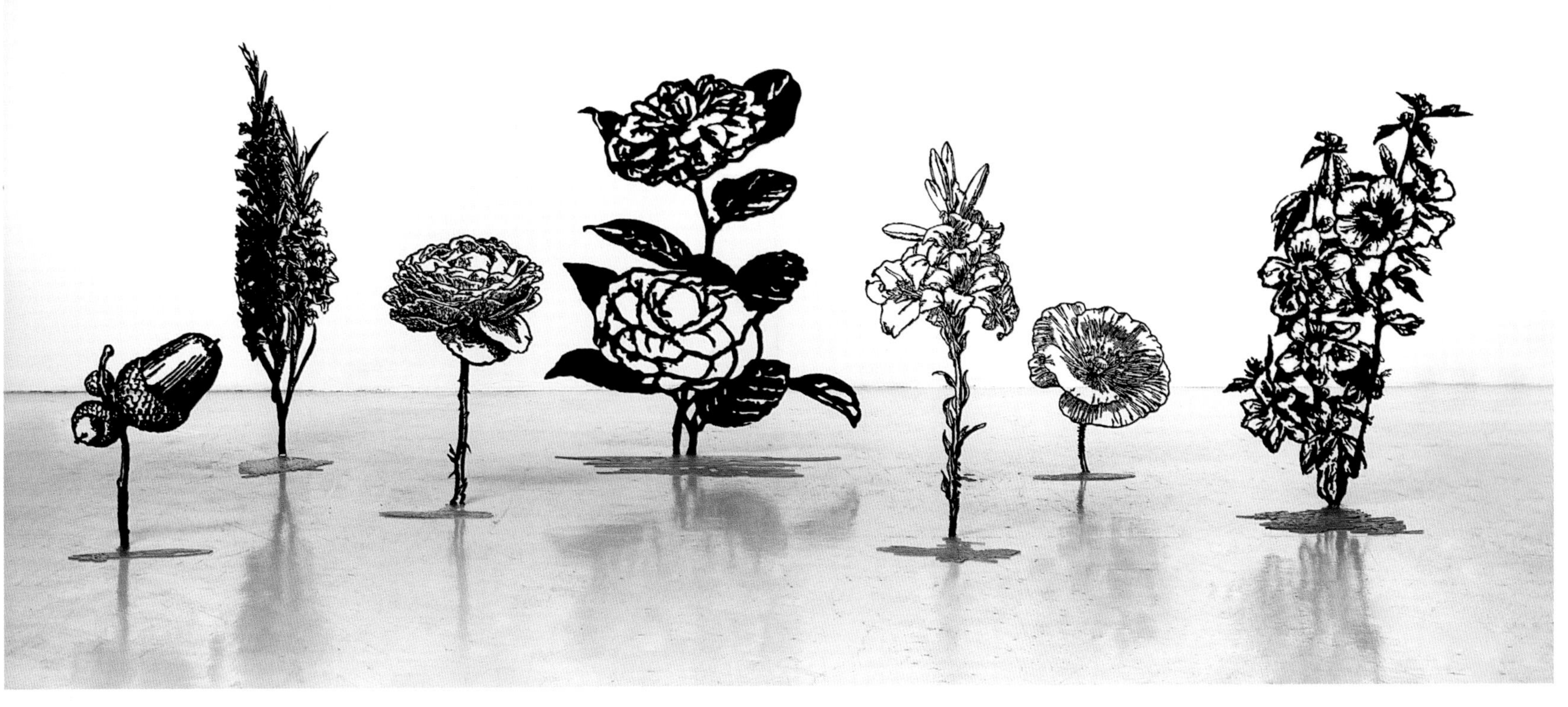

Blackflowers, hand-cut
painted aluminium,
Zadok Studio, 2010.

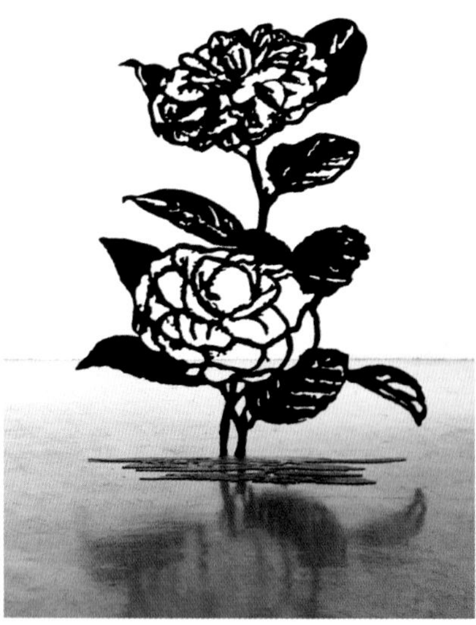 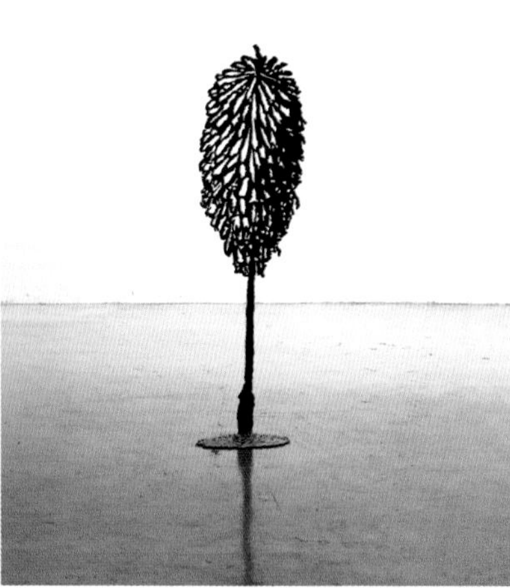 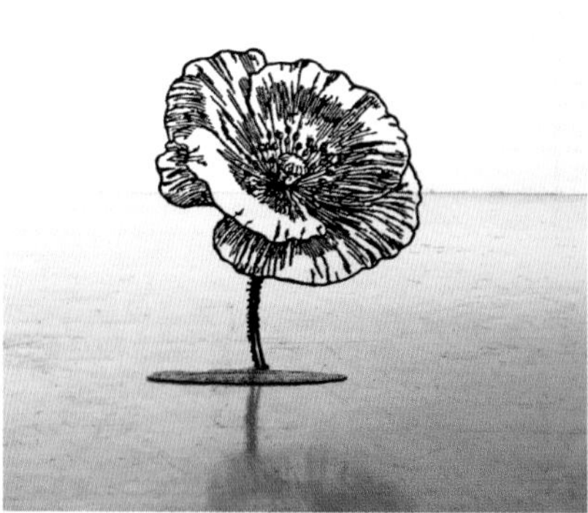

(left)
Under the Above, hand-cut painted aluminium, H171 x W139 cm, 2010.

(centre)
Back Head, hand-cut painted aluminium, H110 x W31.5 cm, 2010.

(right)
All Reveal, hand-cut painted aluminium, H72.5 x W60 cm, 2010.

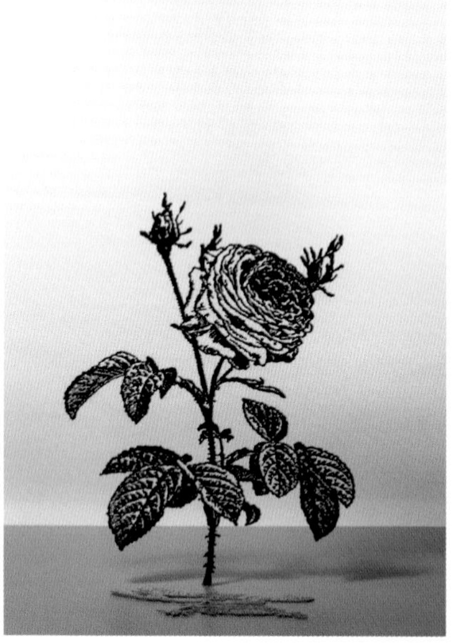 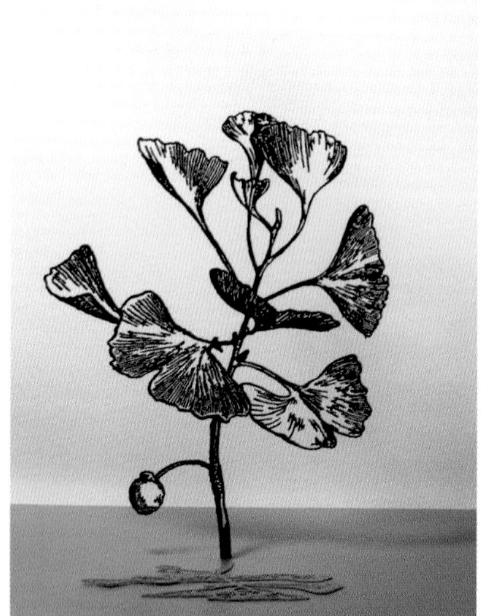 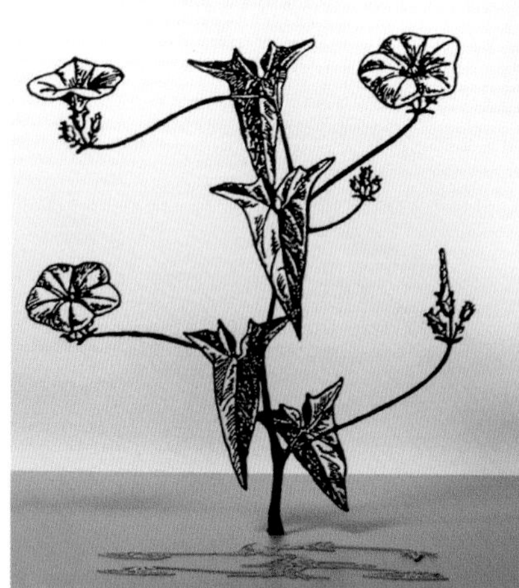

(left)
Almost Perfect, hand-cut painted aluminium, H130 x W99 cm, 2012.

(centre)
Almost Ready, hand-cut painted aluminium, H151 x W117 cm, 2012.

(right)
Balancing Act, hand-cut painted aluminium, H89 x W70 cm, 2012.

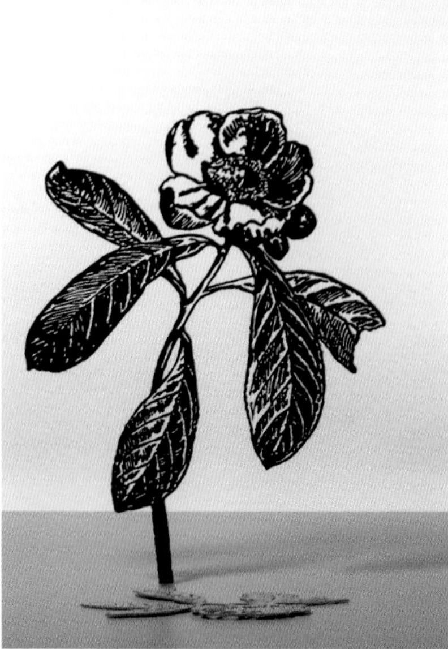 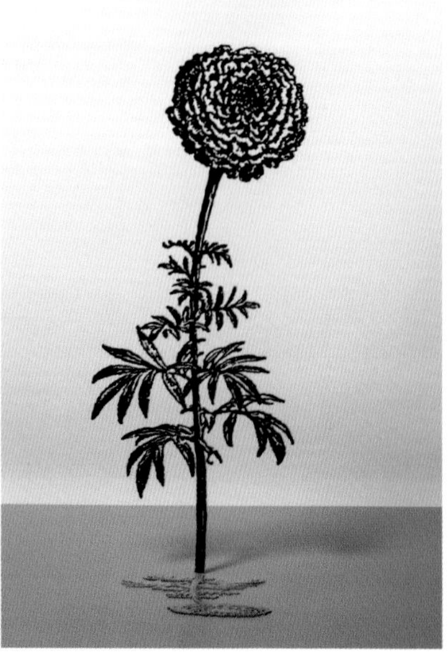 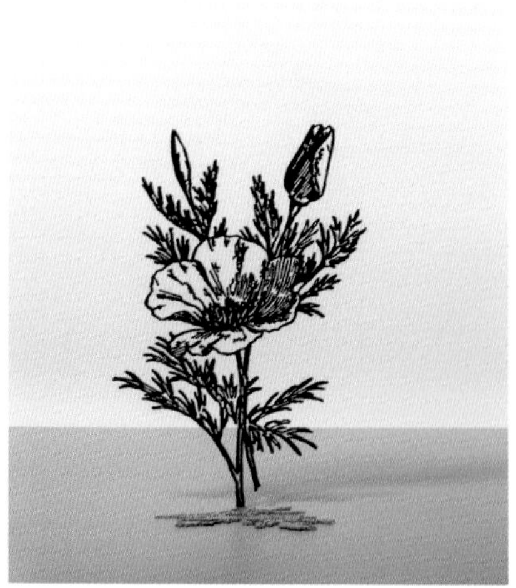

(left)
Big Bite, hand-cut painted aluminium, H108 x W83 cm, 2012.

(centre)
Big Head, hand-cut painted aluminium, H174 x W68 cm, 2010.

(right)
A Special Day, hand-cut painted aluminium, H79 x W52 cm, 2010.

(left)
Dry Leaves, hand-cut
painted aluminium, H186
x W145 cm, 2010.

(centre)
Happily Alone, hand-cut
painted aluminium, H76
x W46 cm, 2010.

(right)
Happy Life, hand-cut
painted aluminium, H114
x W96 cm, 2012.

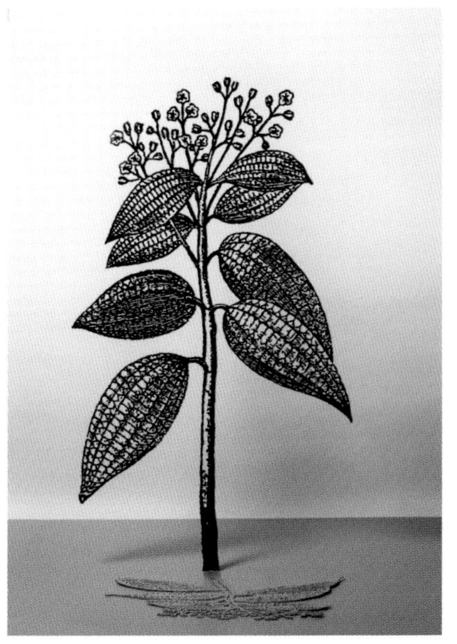
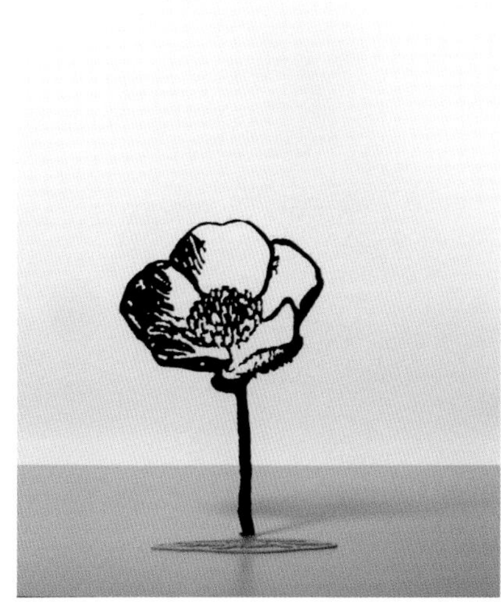
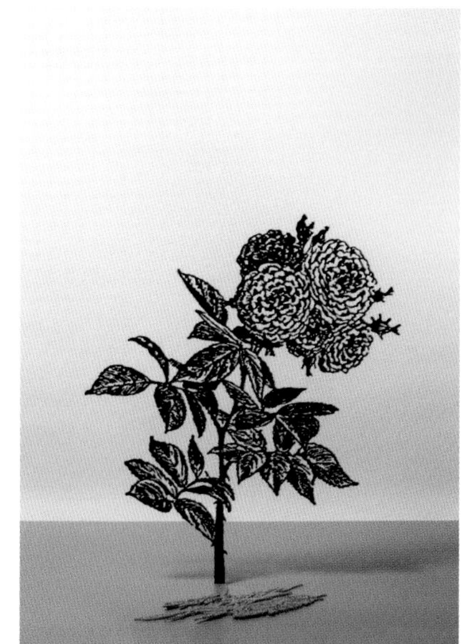

(left)
Happy Pile, hand-cut
painted aluminium, H64
x W52 cm, 2012.

(centre)
Heavy Load, hand-cut
painted aluminium, H91
x W62 cm, 2012.

(right)
Jellyfish, hand-cut
painted aluminium, H92
x W90 cm, 2012

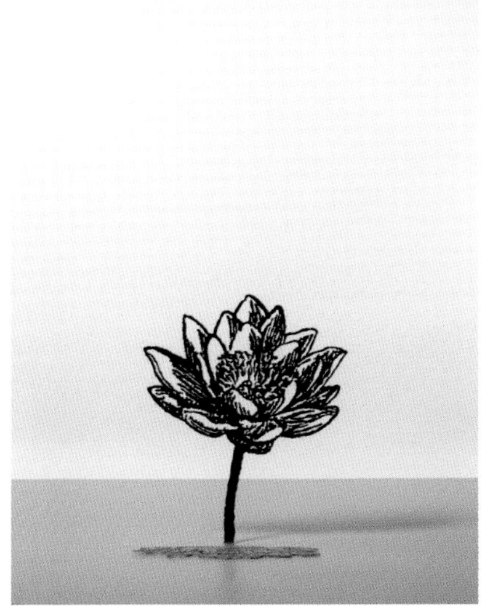
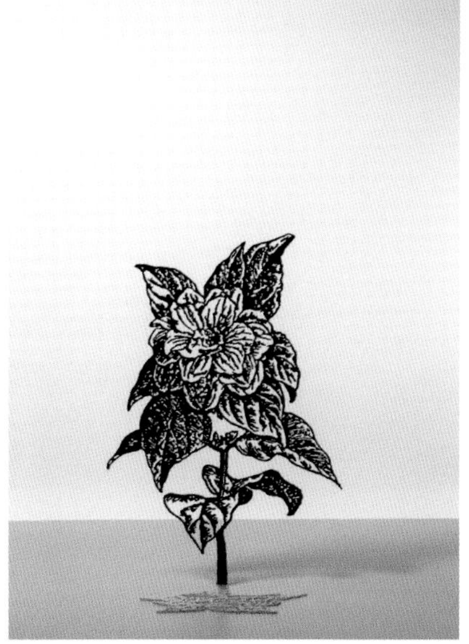
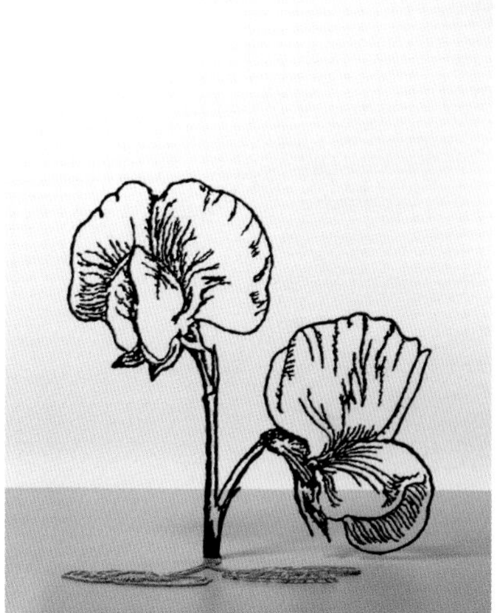

(left)
Light and Easy, hand-cut
painted aluminium, H84 x
W31 cm, 2012.

(centre)
Light Storm, hand-cut
painted aluminium, H165
x W48 cm, 2012.

(right)
Midlife, hand-cut painted
aluminium, H95 x W77
cm, 2012.

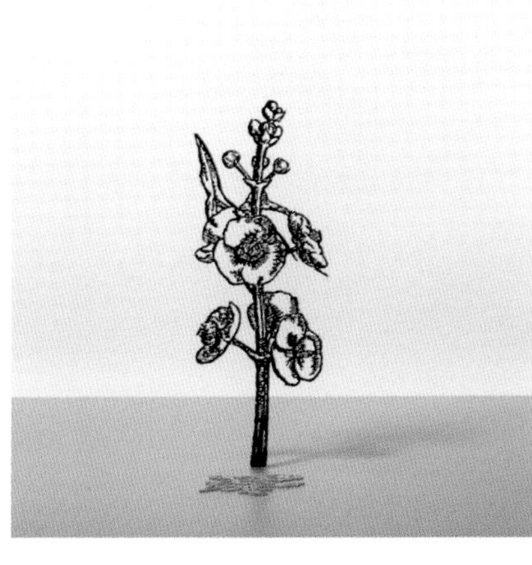
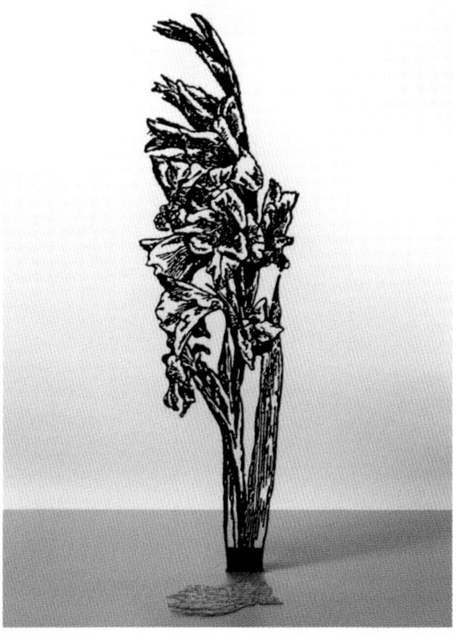
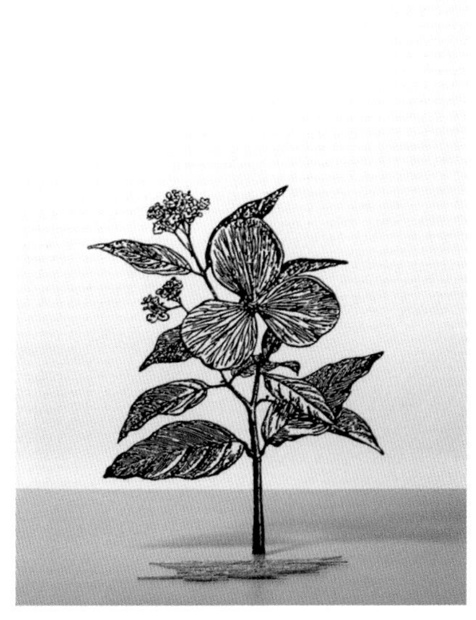

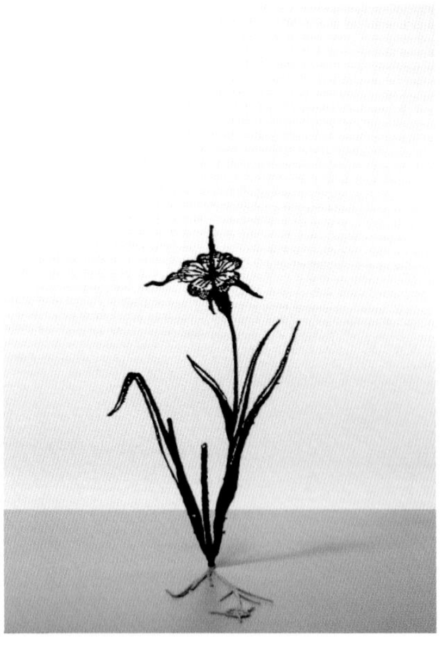 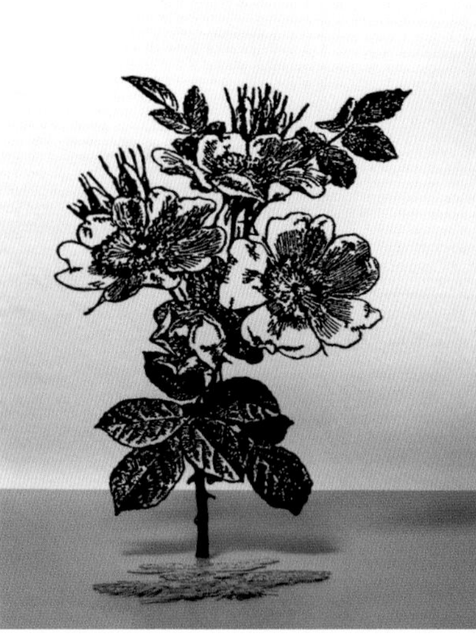 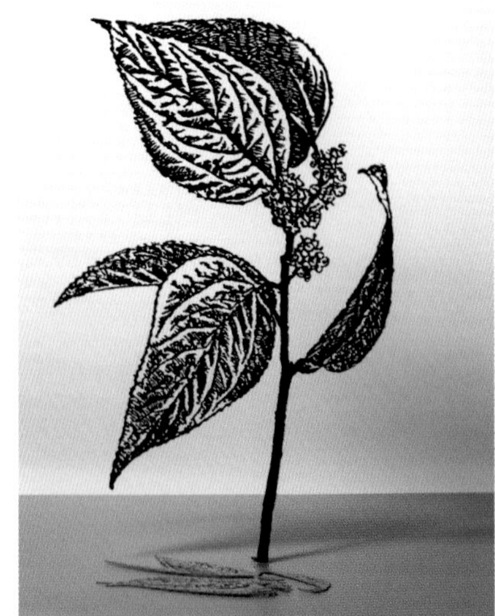

(left)
Midsummer, hand-cut painted aluminium, H91 x W53 cm, 2012.

(centre)
Night Bloom, hand-cut painted aluminium, H165 x W124 cm, 2012.

(right)
North Wind, hand-cut painted aluminium, H151 x W92 cm, 2010.

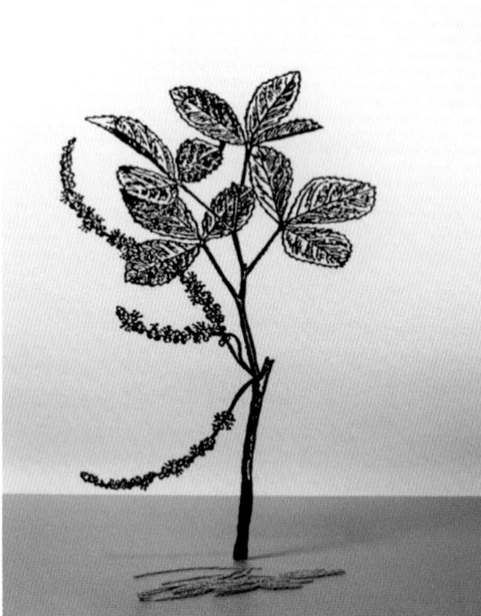 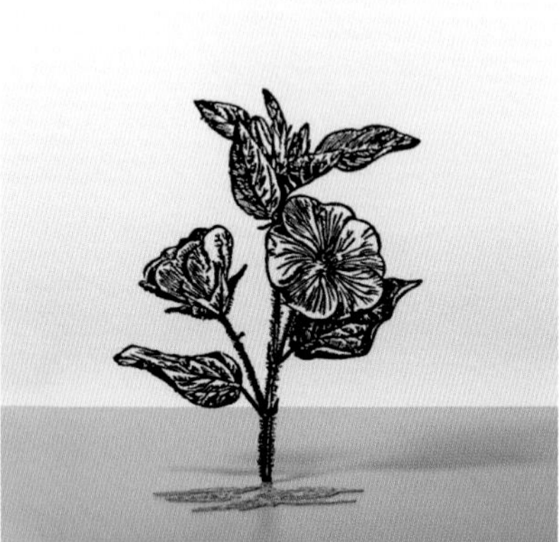 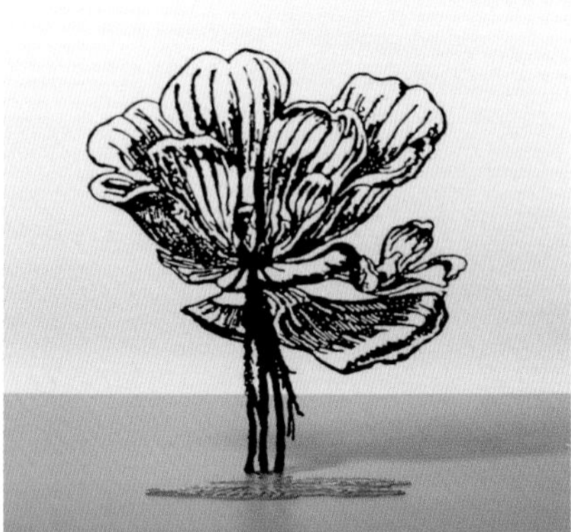

(left)
On the Edge, hand-cut painted aluminium, H146 x W92 cm , 2012.

(centre)
Out of Focus, hand-cut painted aluminium, H84 x W67 cm, 2010.

(right)
Parallel Lines, hand-cut painted aluminium, H90 x W81 cm, 2012.

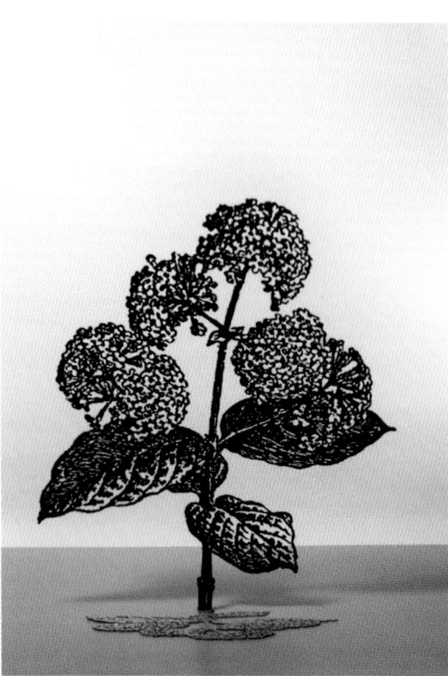 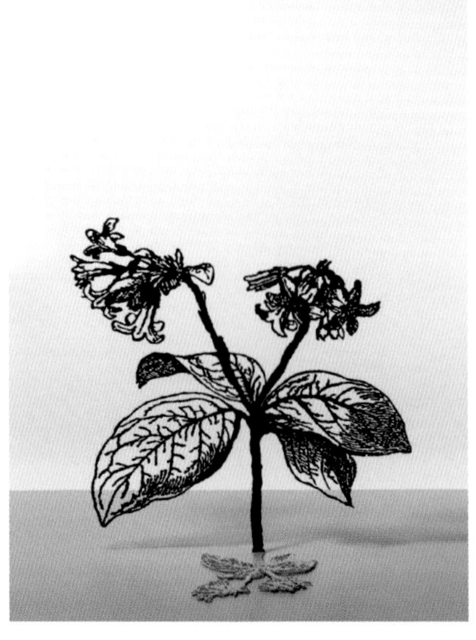 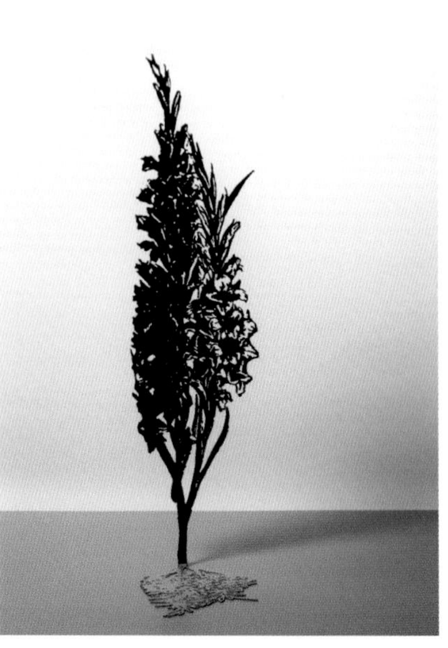

(left)
Perfect Spring, hand-cut painted aluminium, H121 x W106 cm, 2012.

(centre)
Roof Top, hand-cut painted aluminium, H87 x W87 cm, 2012.

(right)
Shadow of the Tail, hand-cut painted aluminium, H180 x W45 cm, 2010.

(left)
Simple Lines, hand-cut painted aluminium, H140 x W113 cm, 2010.

(centre)
Solo Act, hand-cut painted aluminium, H67 x W40 cm, 2010.

(right)
Speaking Loud, hand-cut painted aluminium, H163 x W75, 2012.

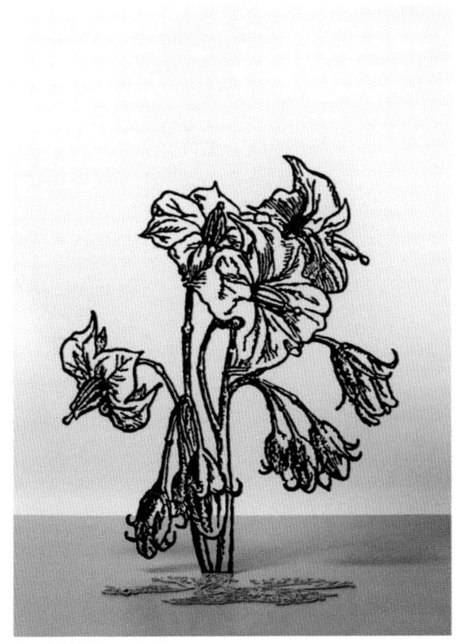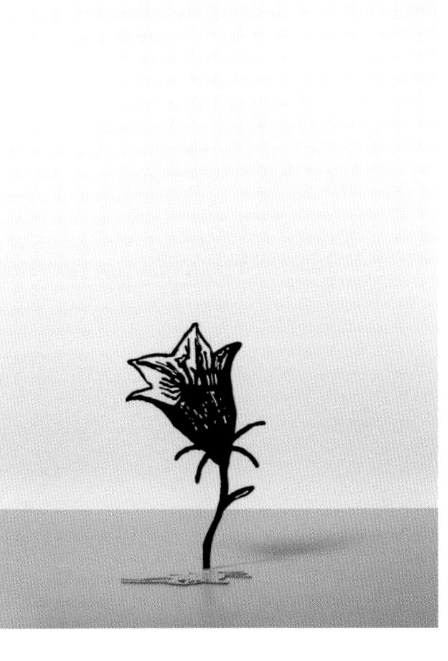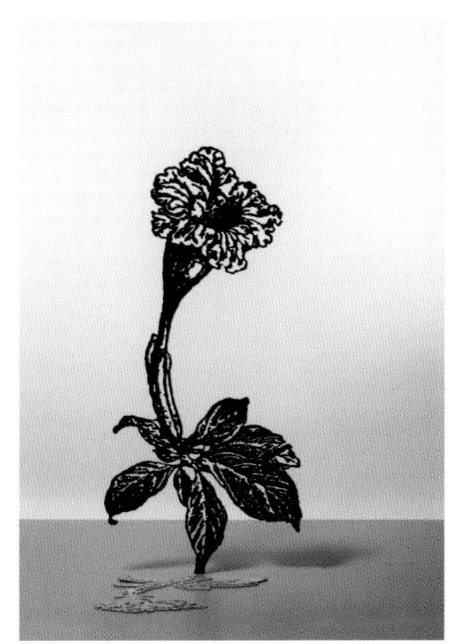

(left)
Spider Dance, hand-cut painted aluminium, H92 x W38, 2012.

(centre)
Spring Time, hand-cut painted aluminium, H180 x W84 cm, 2010.

(right)
Springing Out, hand-cut painted aluminium, H130 x W61 cm, 2012.

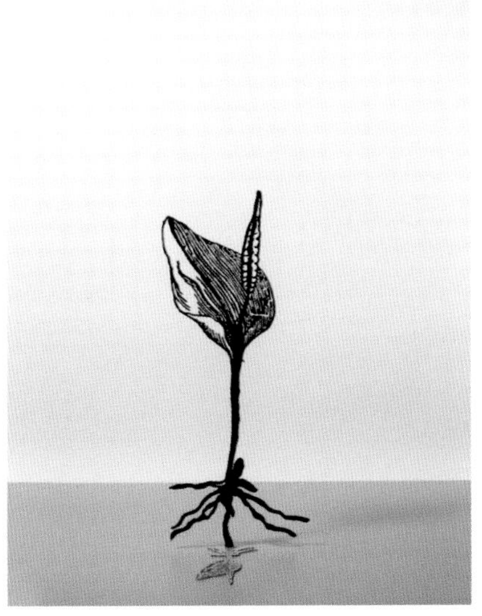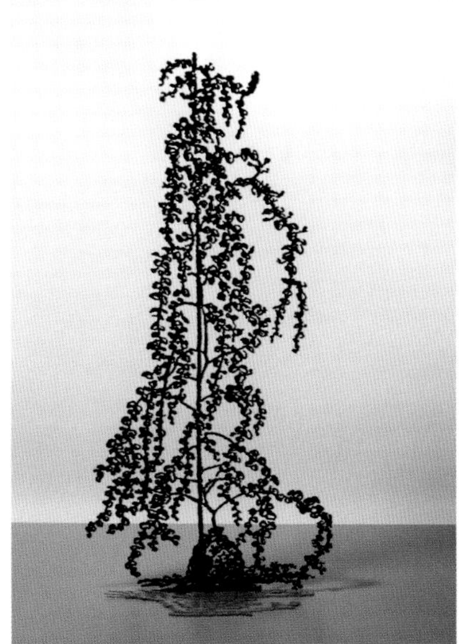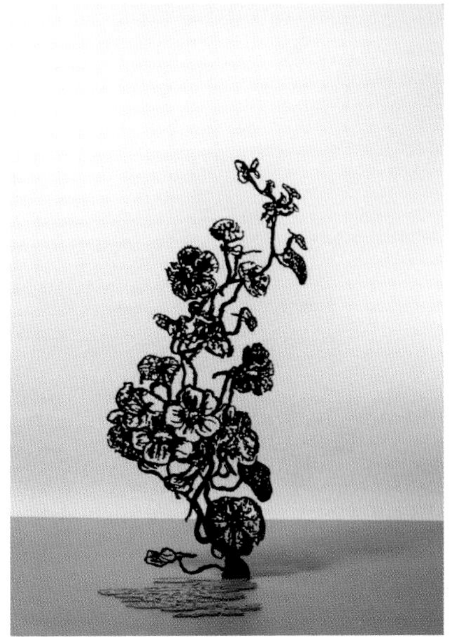

(left)
Stepping Out, hand-cut painted aluminium, H89 x W93 cm, 2012.

(centre)
Stepping Up, hand-cut painted aluminium, H161 x W77 cm, 2010.

(right)
Stretching Out, hand-cut painted aluminium, H163 x W84 cm 2012.

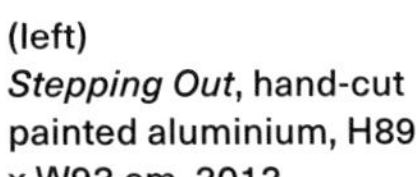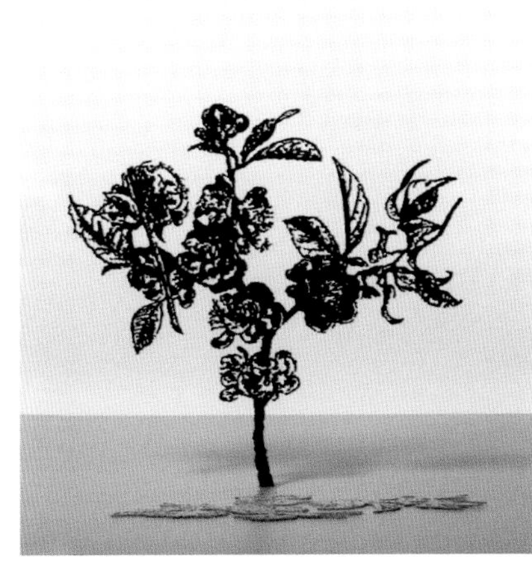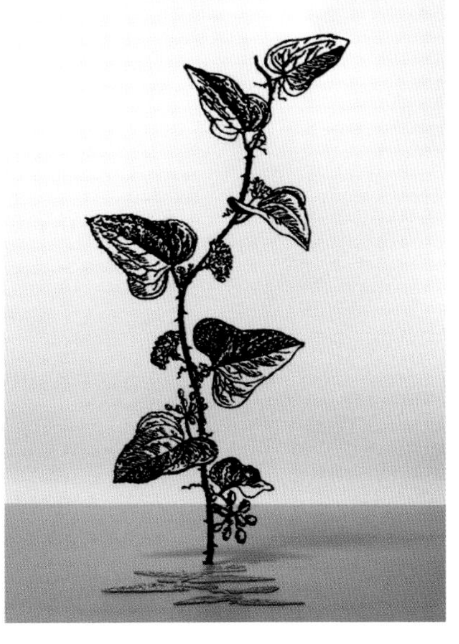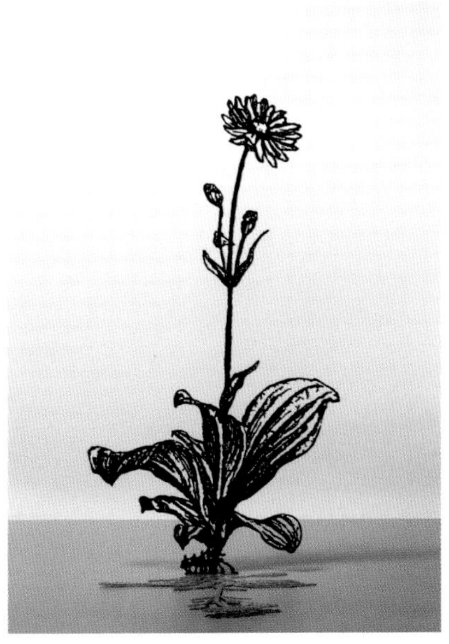

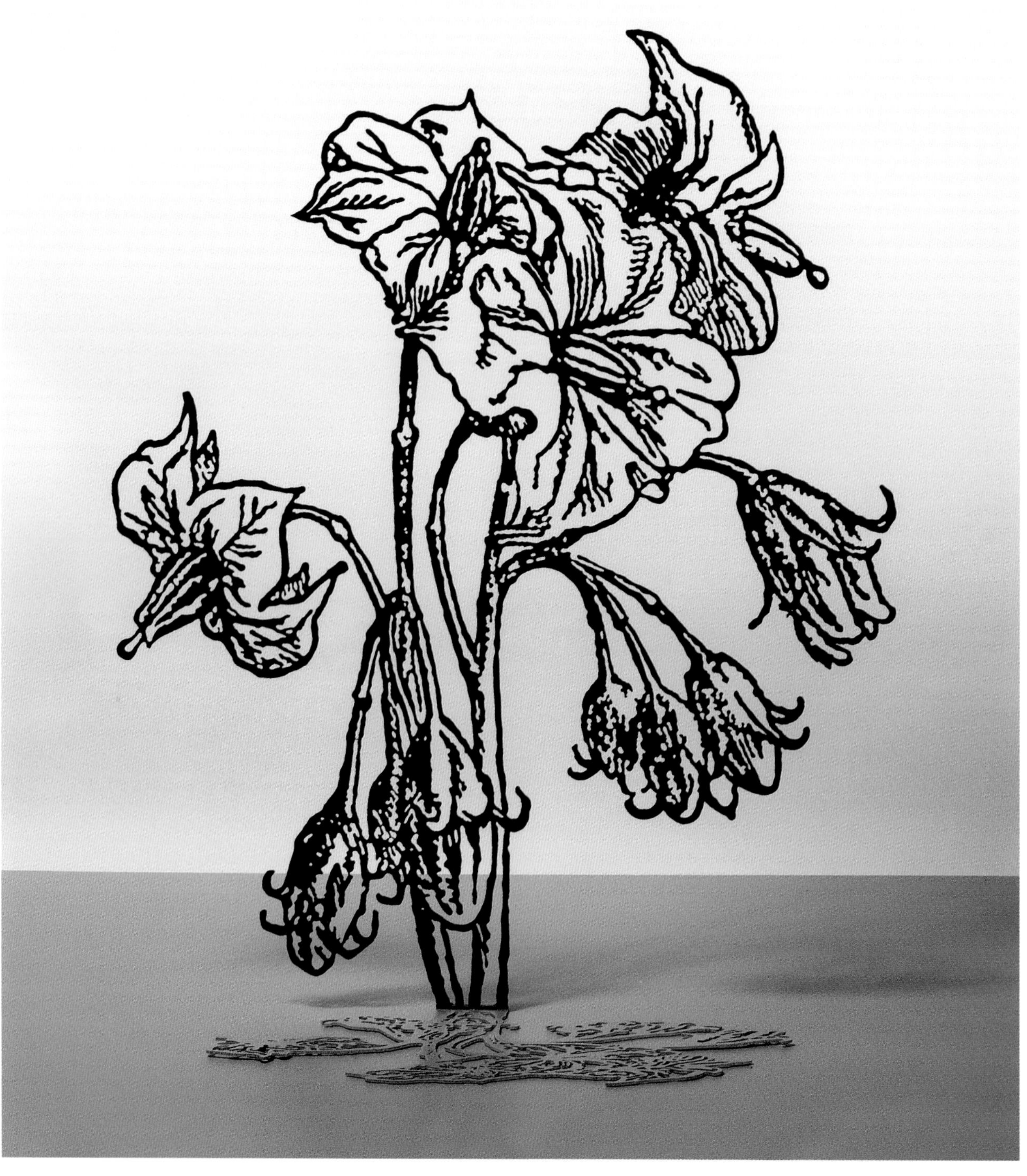

Simple Lines, hand-cut painted aluminium, H140 x W113 cm, 2010.

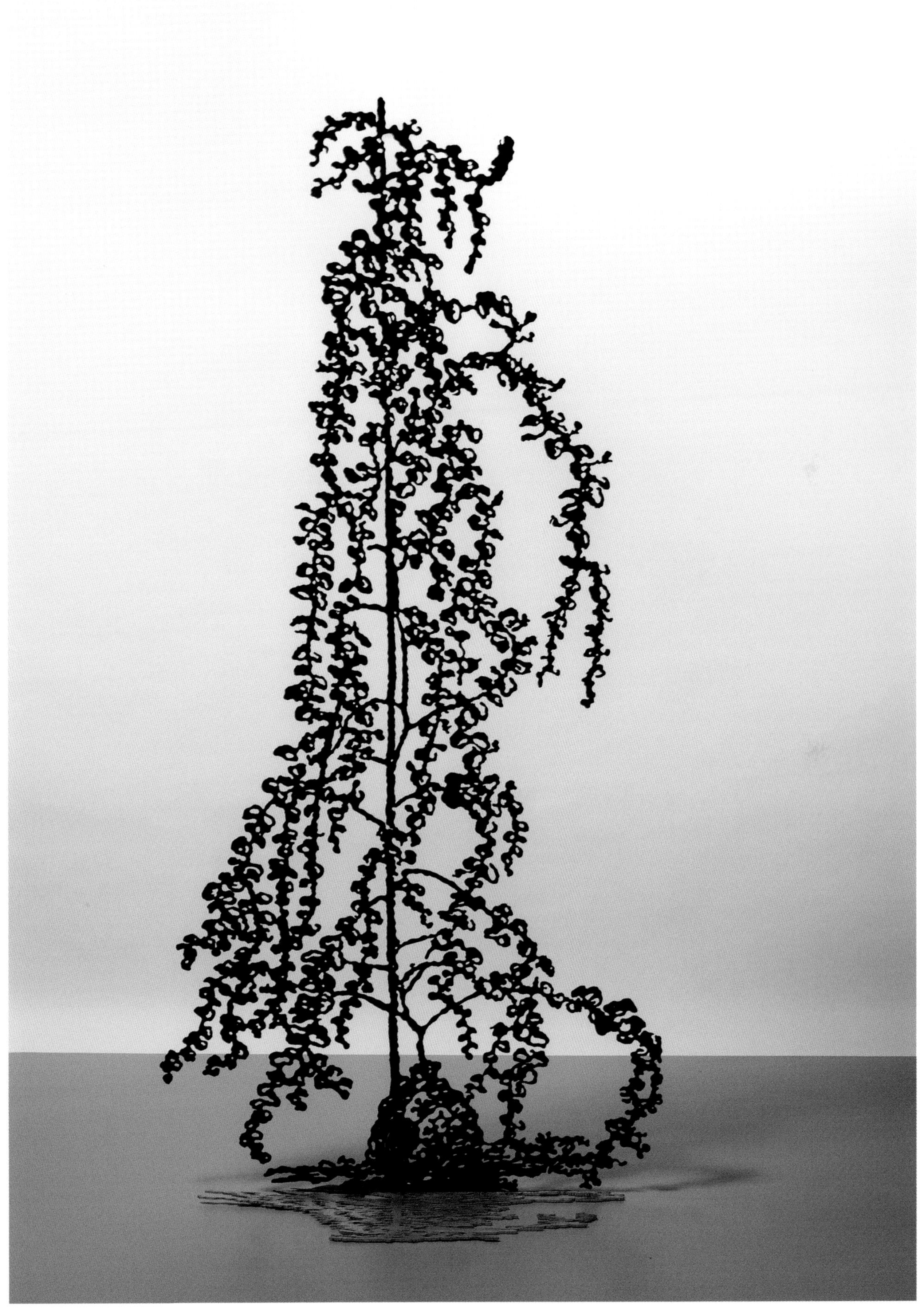

Spring Time, hand-cut
painted aluminium, H180
x W84 cm, 2010.

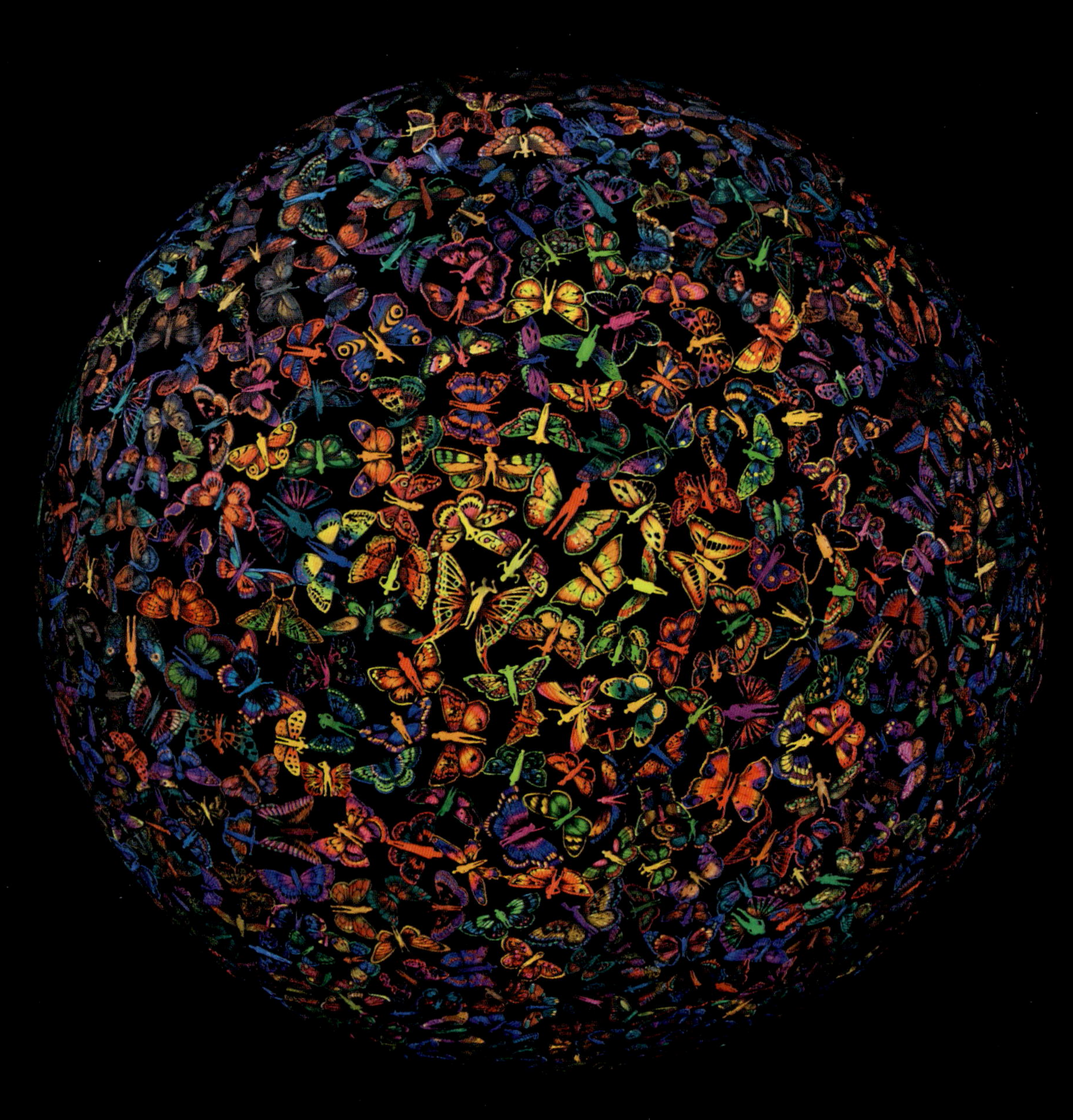

BLACK BOX

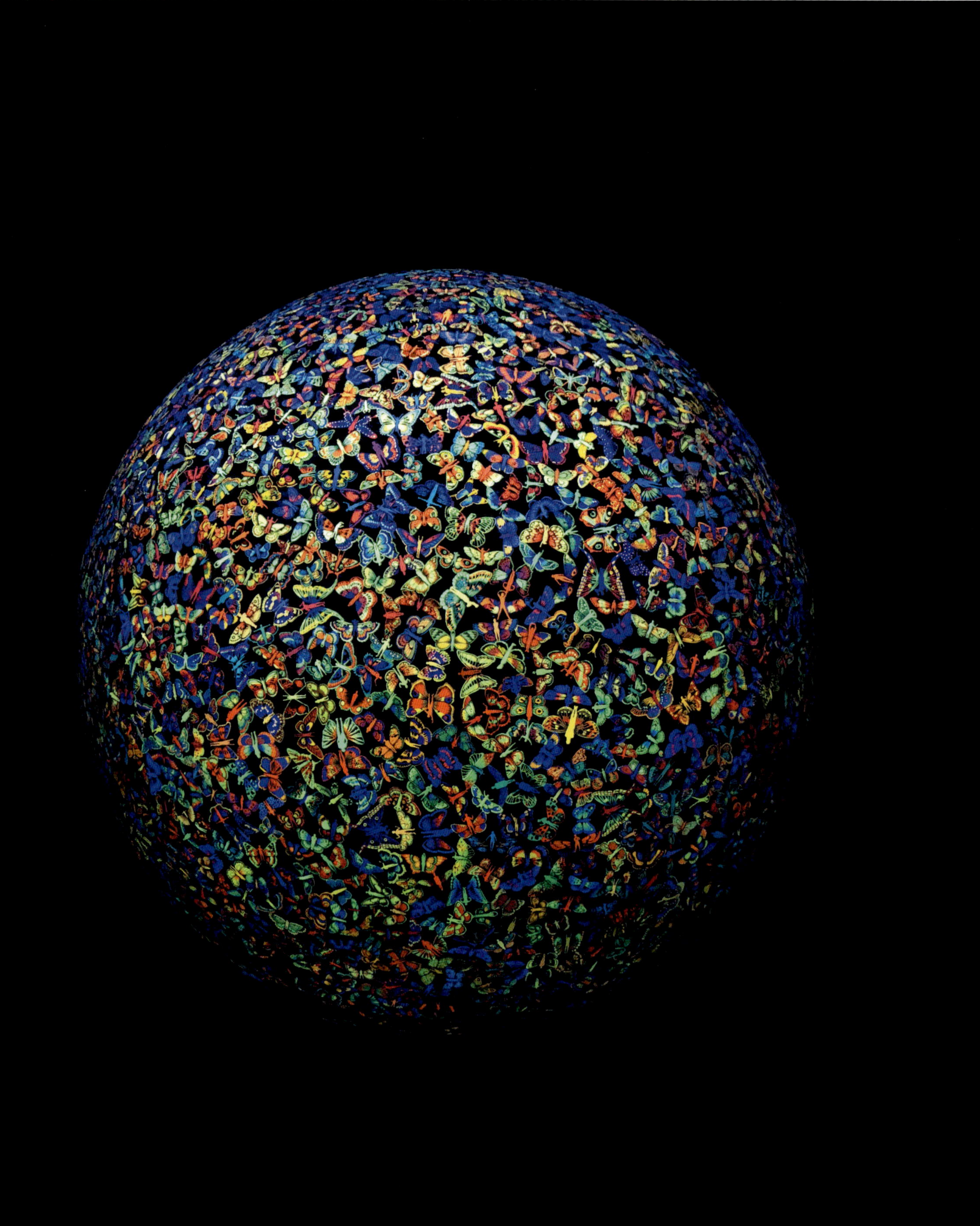

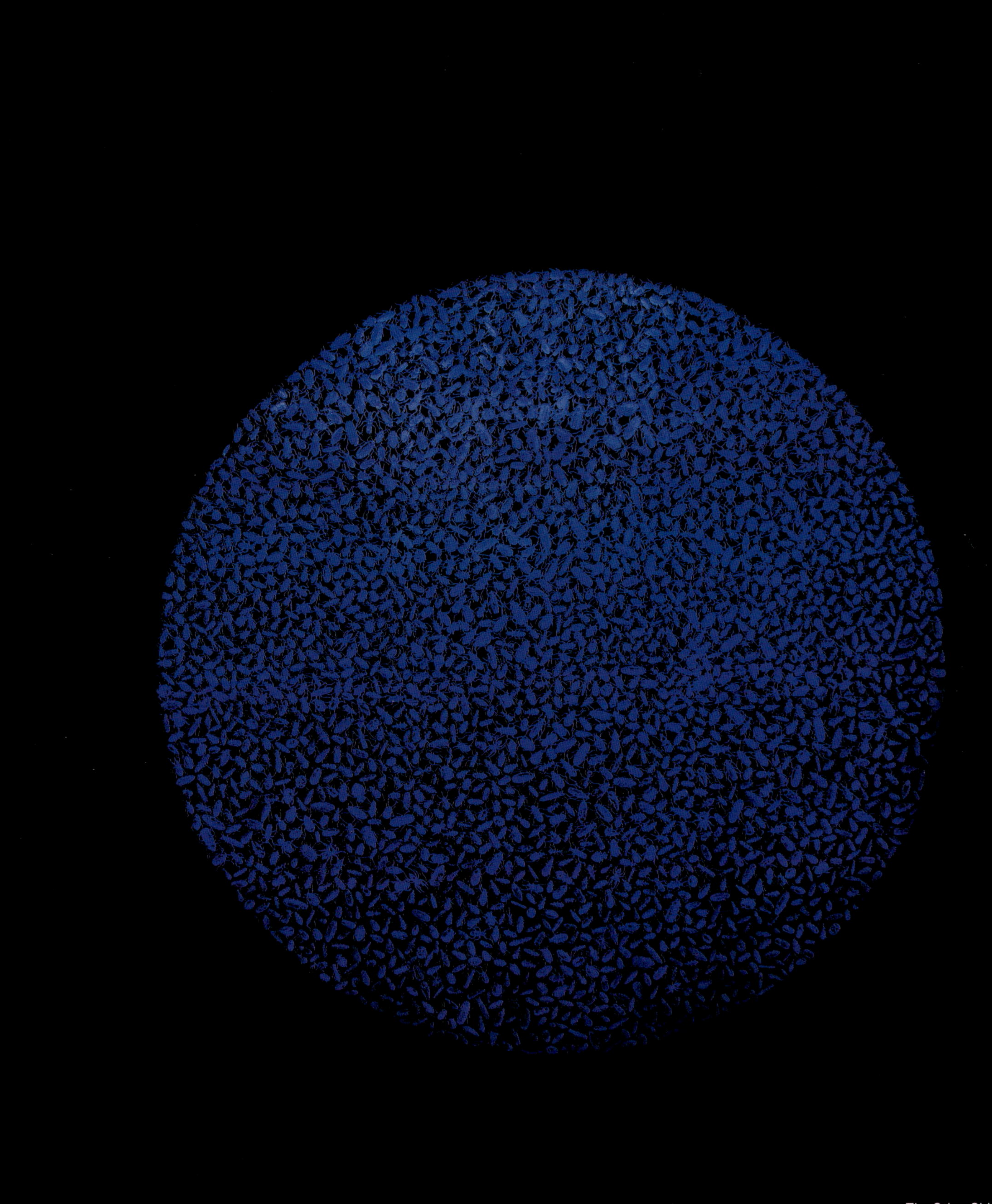

The Other Side Of Midnight, hand painted stainless steel, H300cm x W300 x D0.3cm, Los Angeles, 2012.

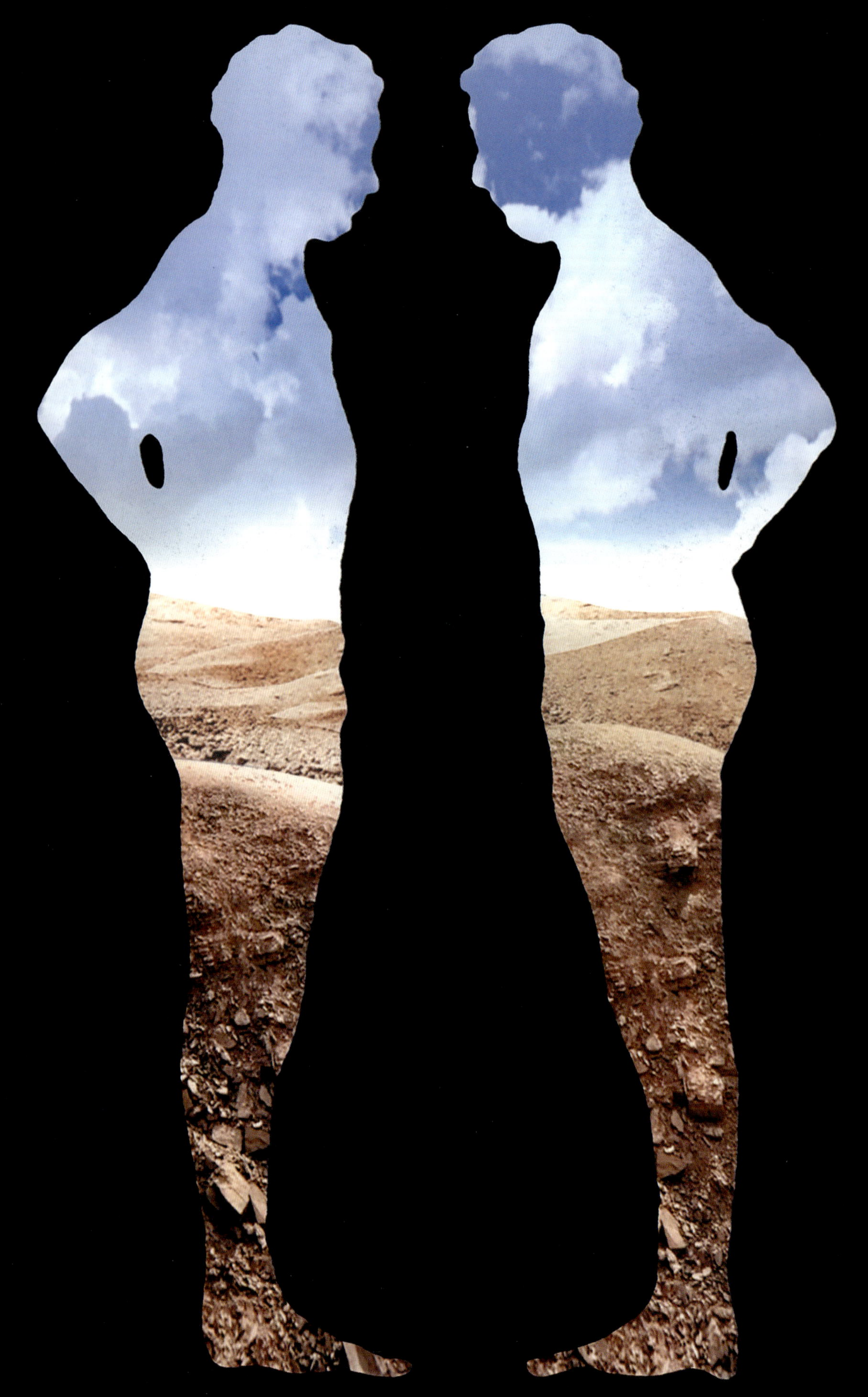

CONVERSATION
PEACE

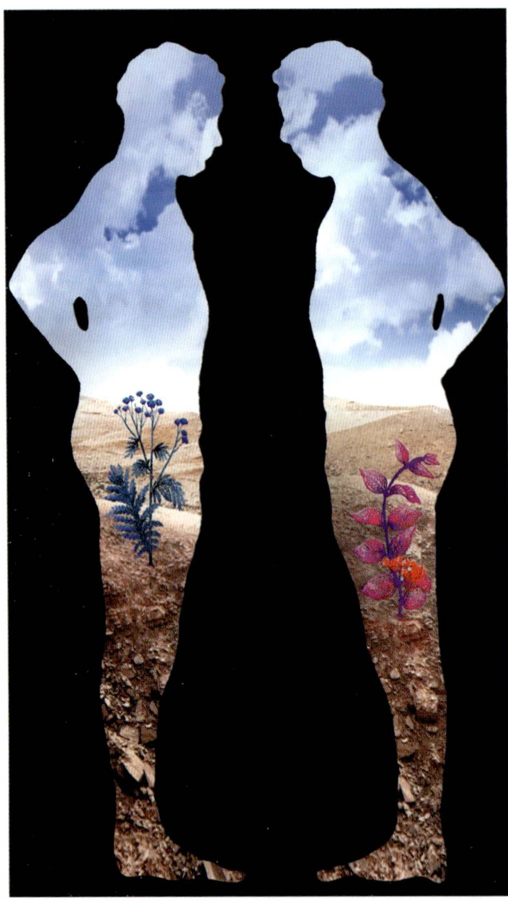
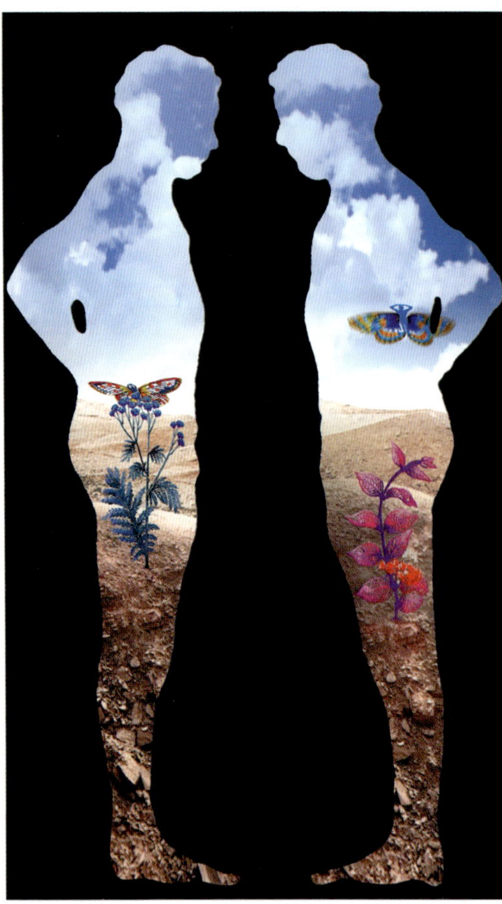
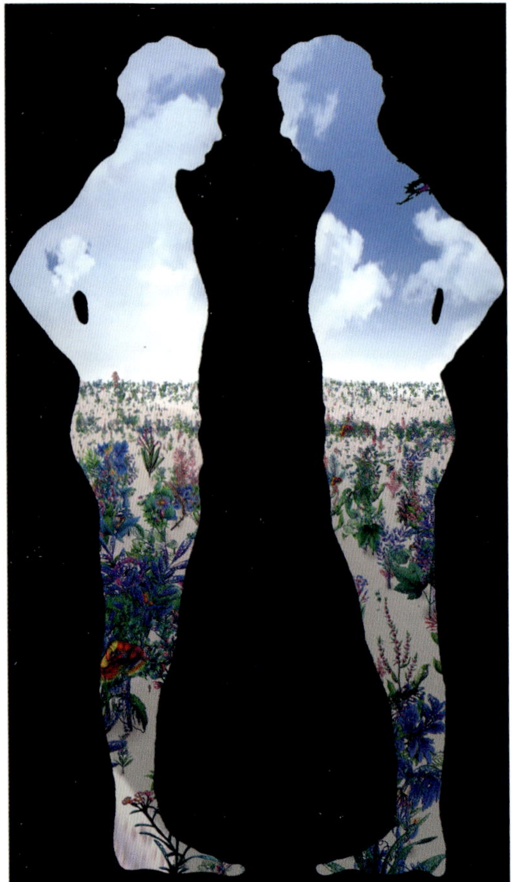
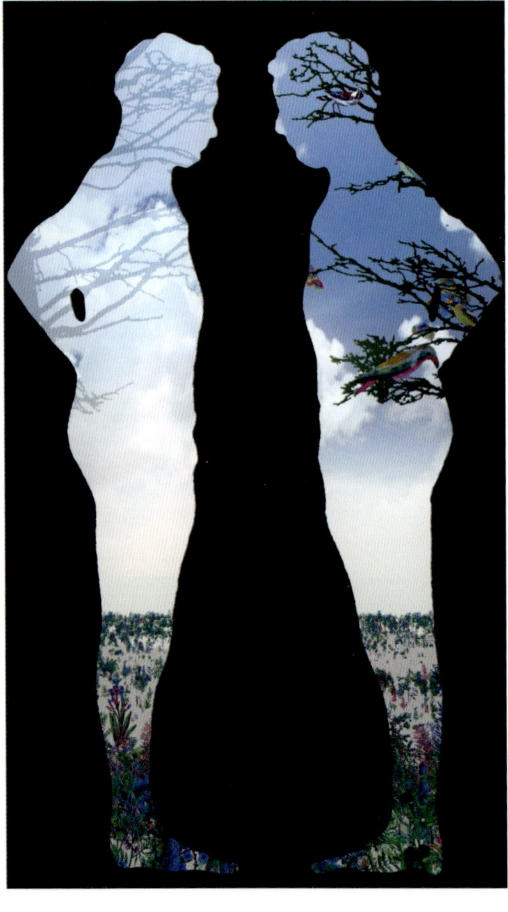

Conversation Peace

Conversation Peace is a 3 minute 52 second video illustrating images of nature taken from Zadok Ben-David's recent installations; trees, butterflies, insects and flowers, telling a story of how peace can easily turn into a futile war.

The video is also about self-destruction and vicious circle…

Stills from *Conversation Peace*, video installation, 2018.

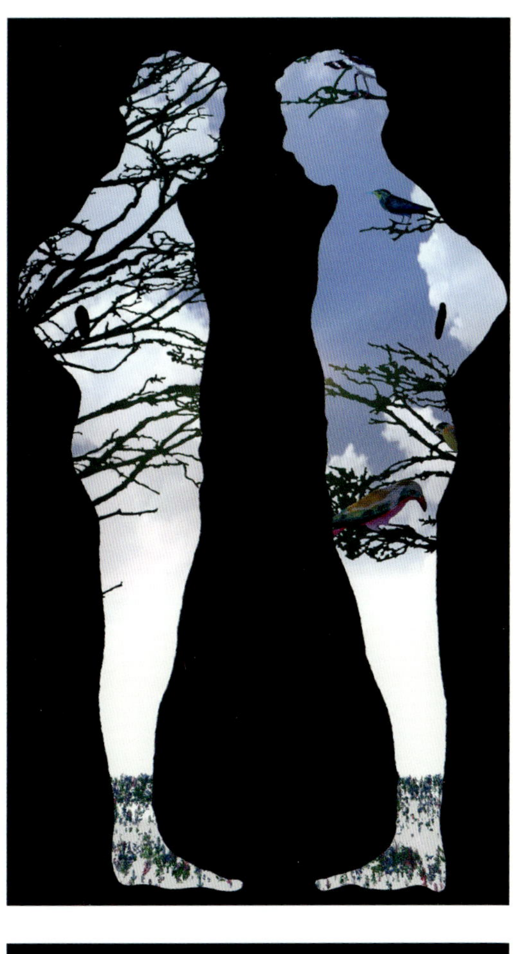
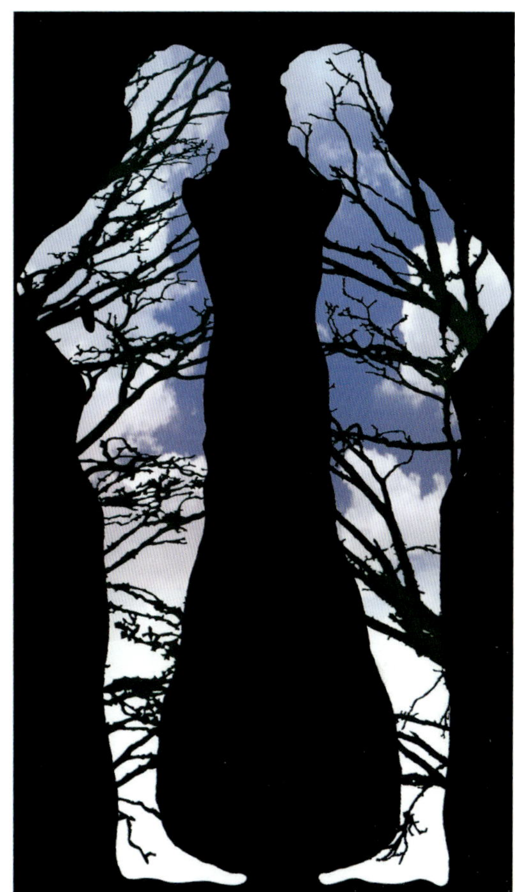
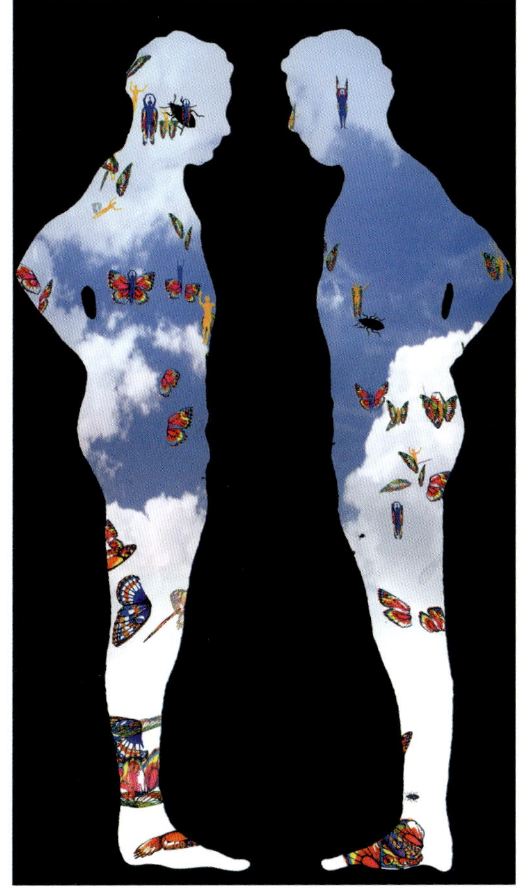
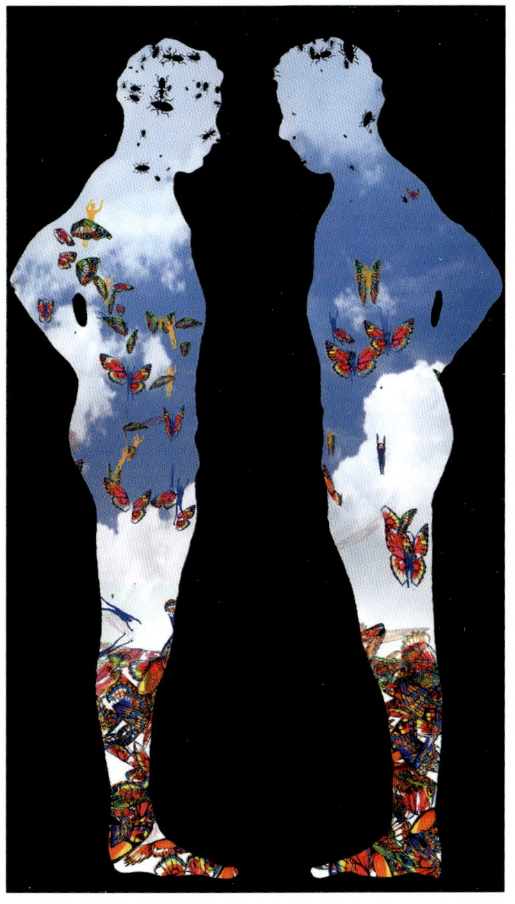

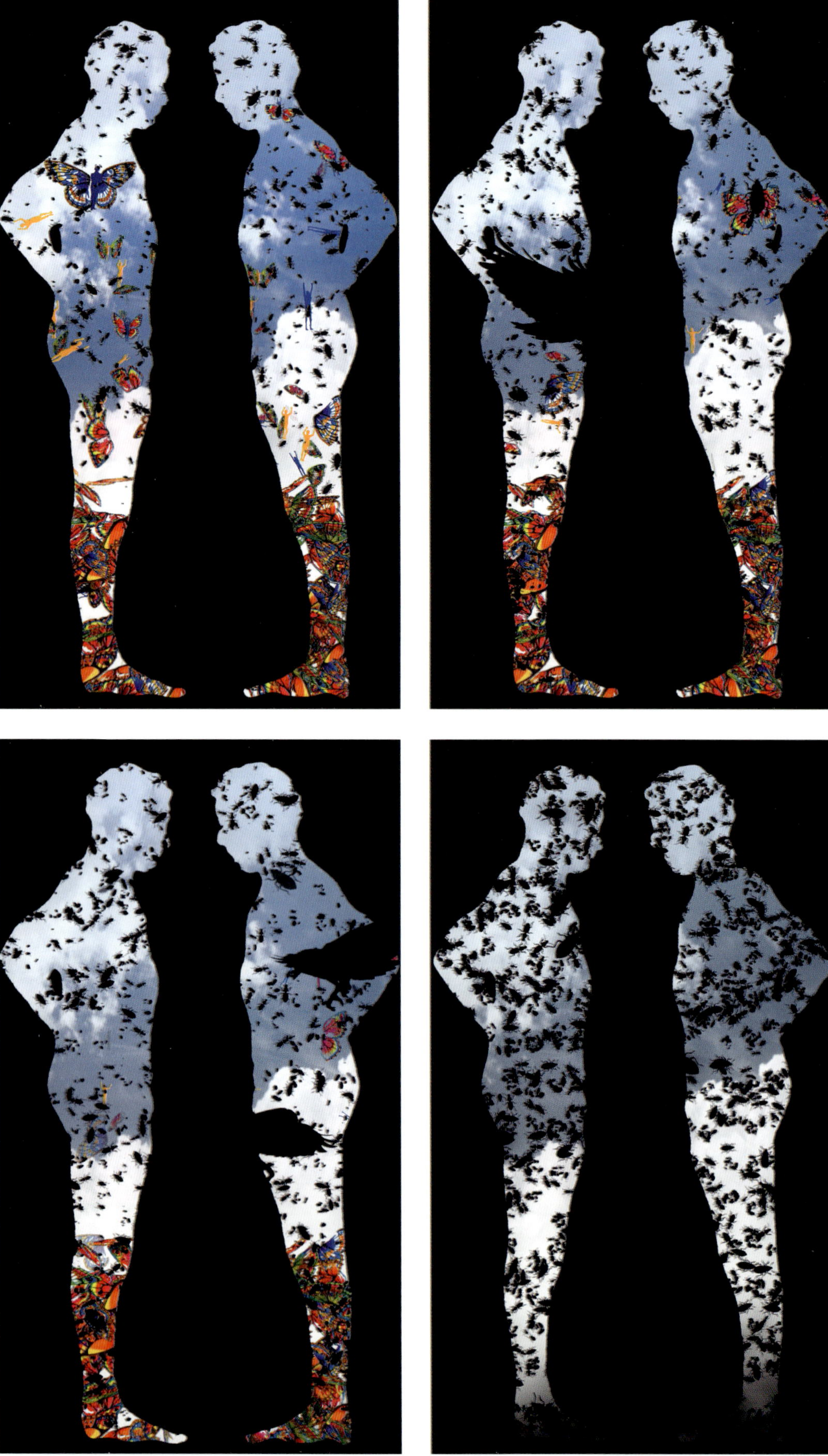

Stills from *Conversation Peace*, video installation, 2018.

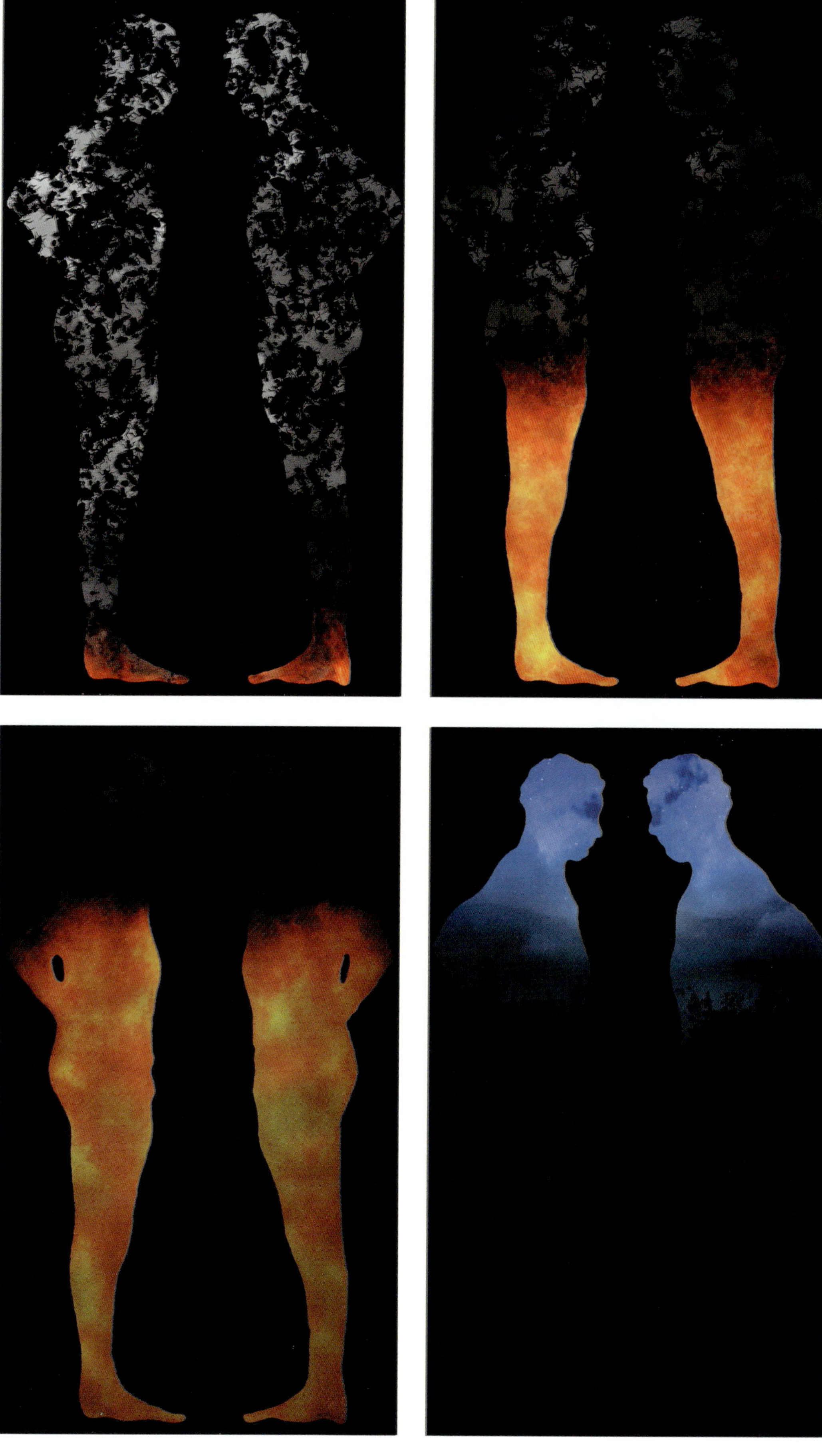

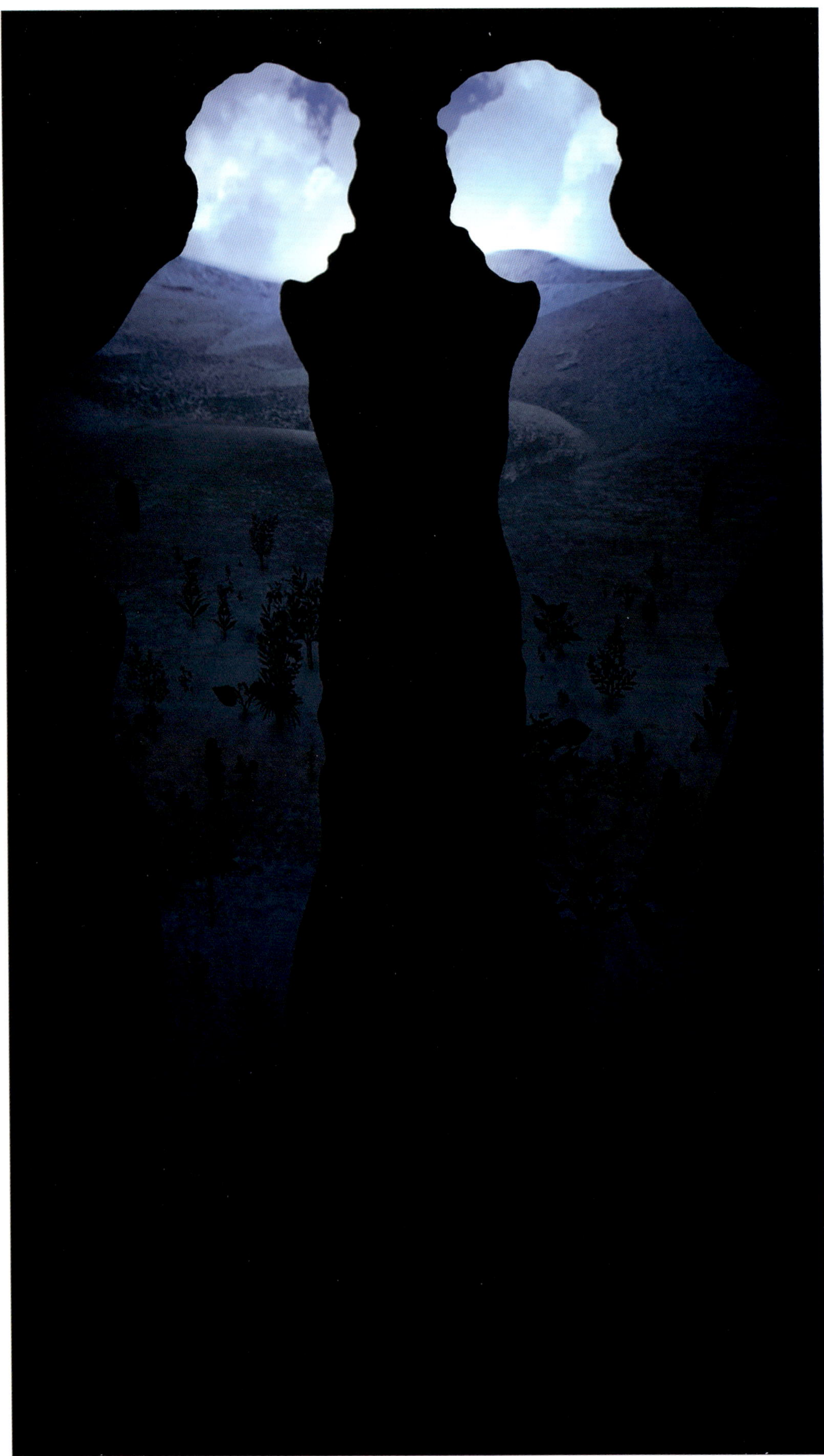

Stills from *Conversation Peace*, video installation, 2018.

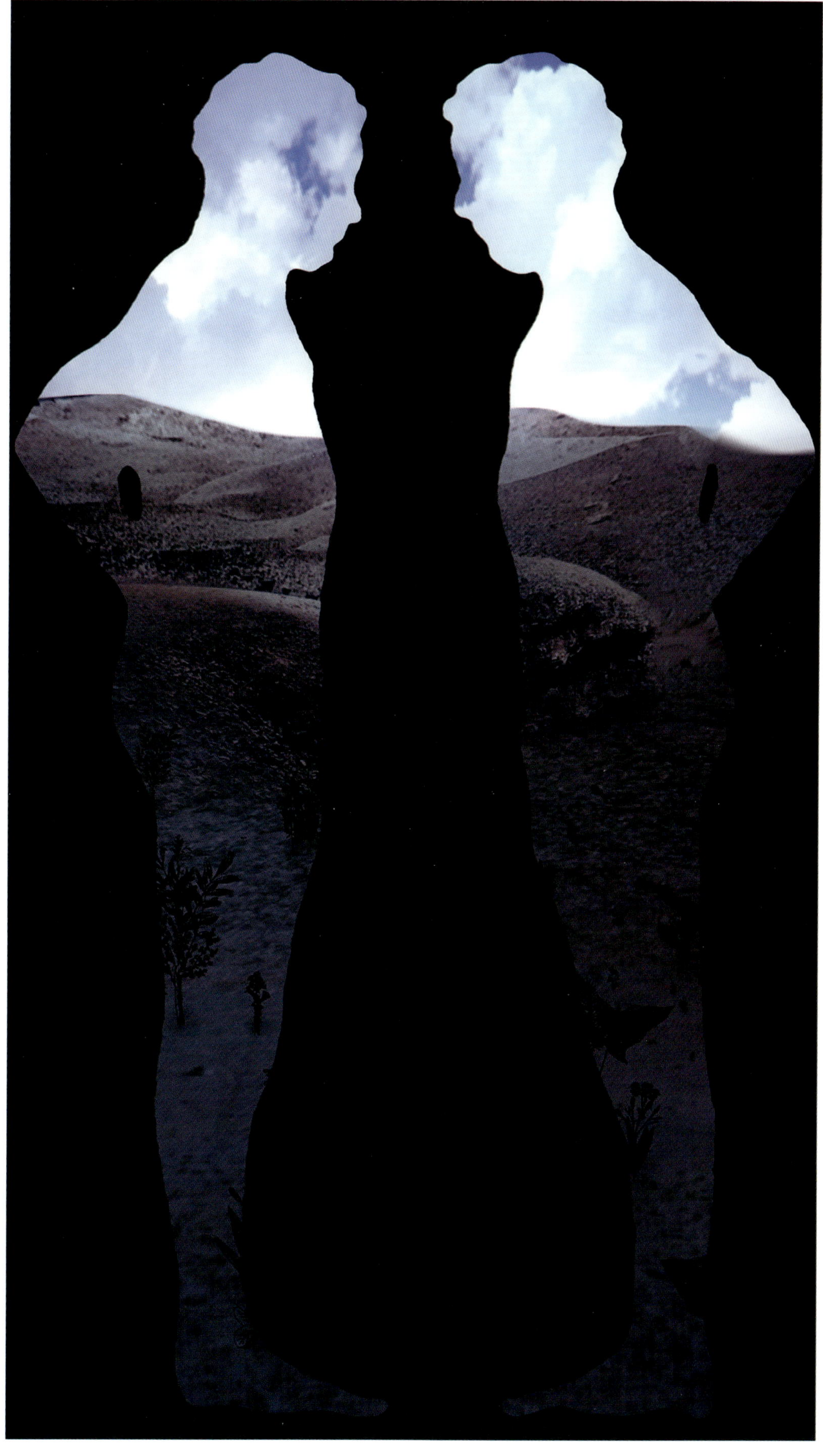

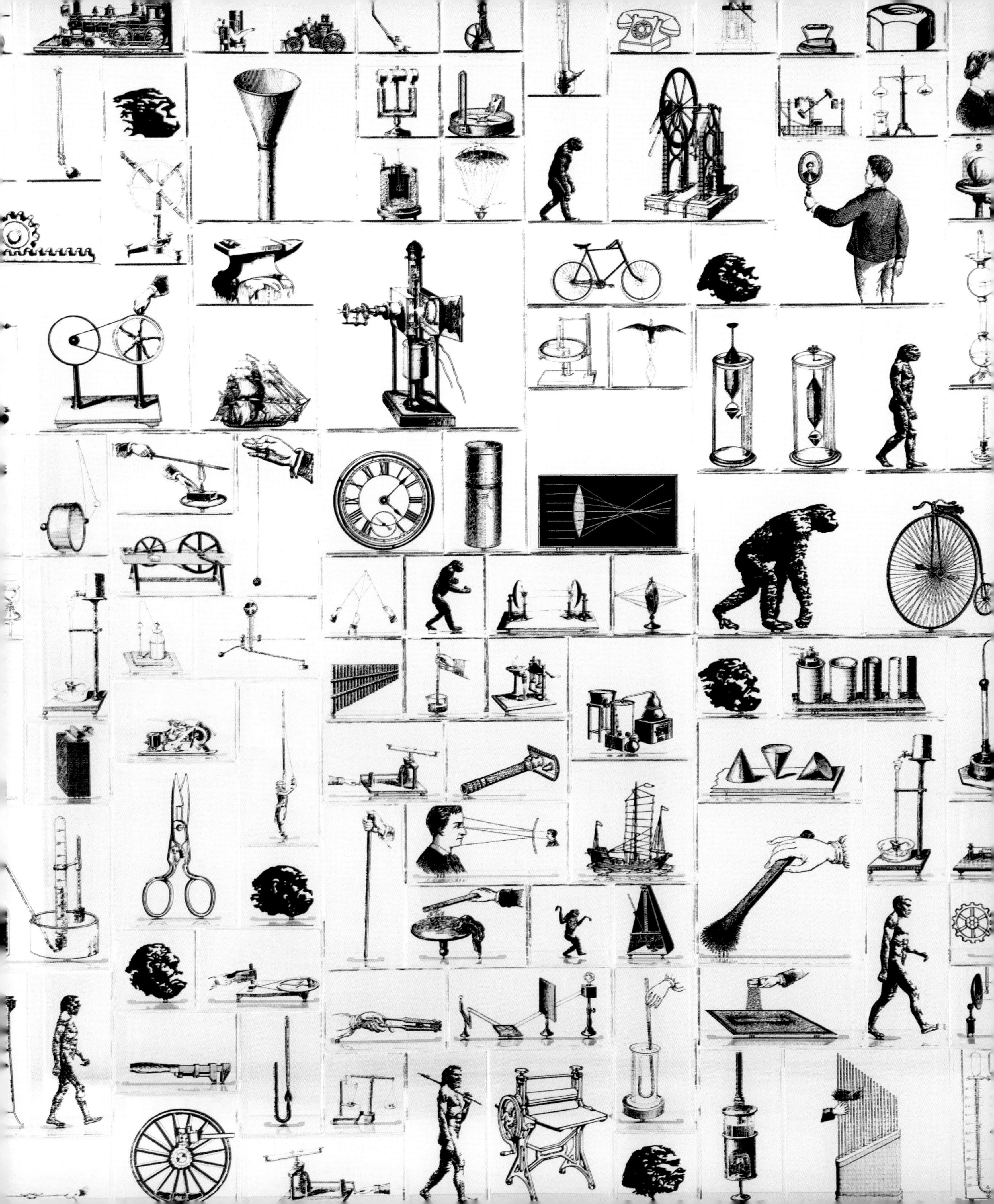

EVOLUTION AND THEORY

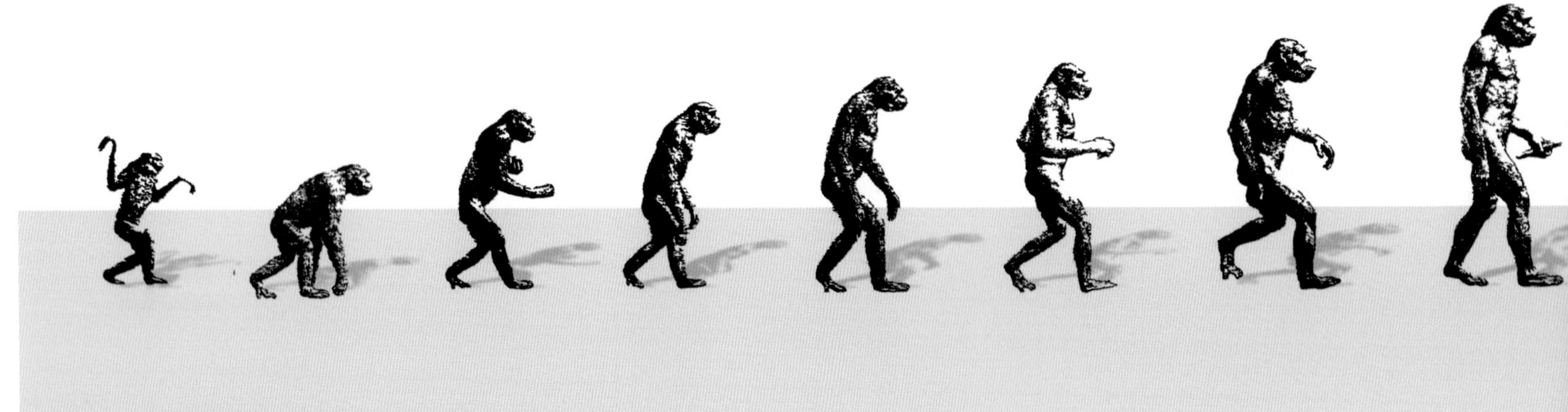

Evolution and Theory

Evolution and Theory is my largest installation so far.
It contains 250 scientific images drawn from Victorian
science education books and encyclopaedias, hand cut
and painted from aluminium.

This new wall version, especially made for the exhibition
at Kew Gardens contains most of the original images plus
a few that are new. They are placed inside transparent
boxes containing scientific instruments and illustrations
of laboratory experiments, all appearing with a strong
optical illusion.

The images cover themes like gravity, magnetism, gases,
optical illusion, machine technology and many more. This
mini-installation contains images from the evolution
of scientific theories of the 19th century, together with
Darwin's theory of evolution. One is dealing with the past,
in search of the origin of man. The other is exploring
science, aiming at the future. There is a nostalgic element
to this installation, a time when one could visualise
experiments with a naked eye. Now everything seems to
be hidden in microchips.

(above)
Detail from *Evolution
and Theory*, based on
the drawings in Charles
Darwin's theory of
evolution as published in
Life magazine, 1977.

(right)
Evolution and Theory,
hand-cut painted
aluminium, Museum
Beelden aan Zee, The
Hague, Netherlands,
1998.

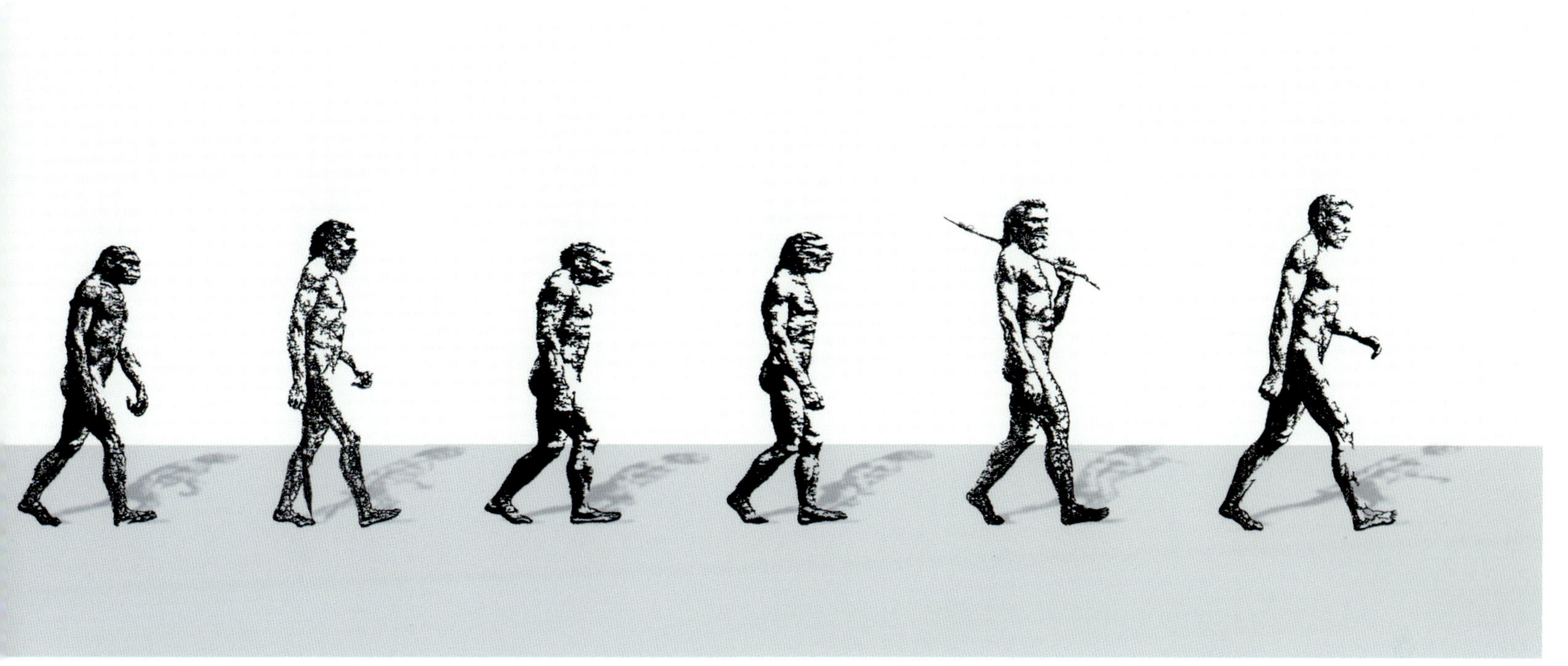

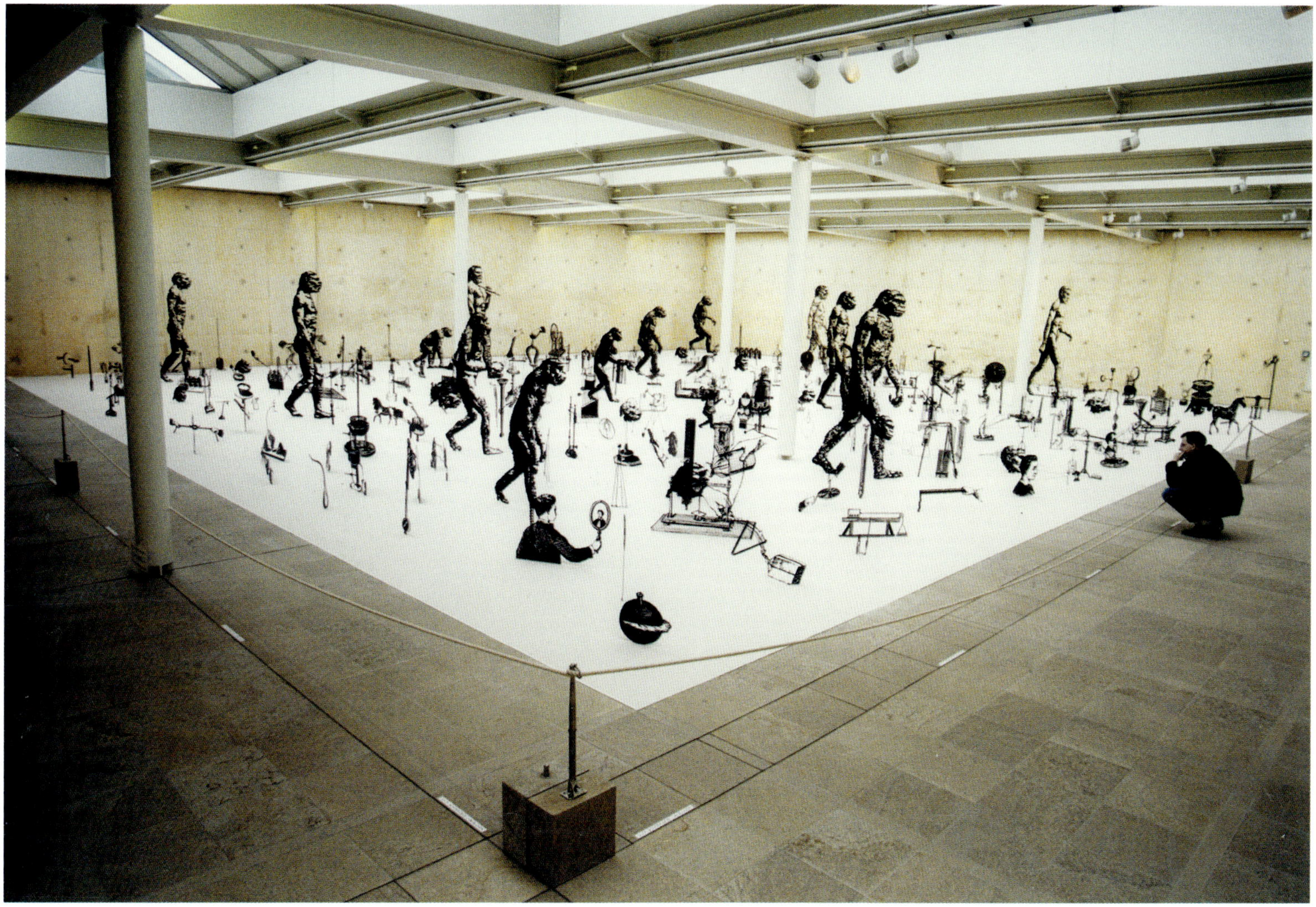

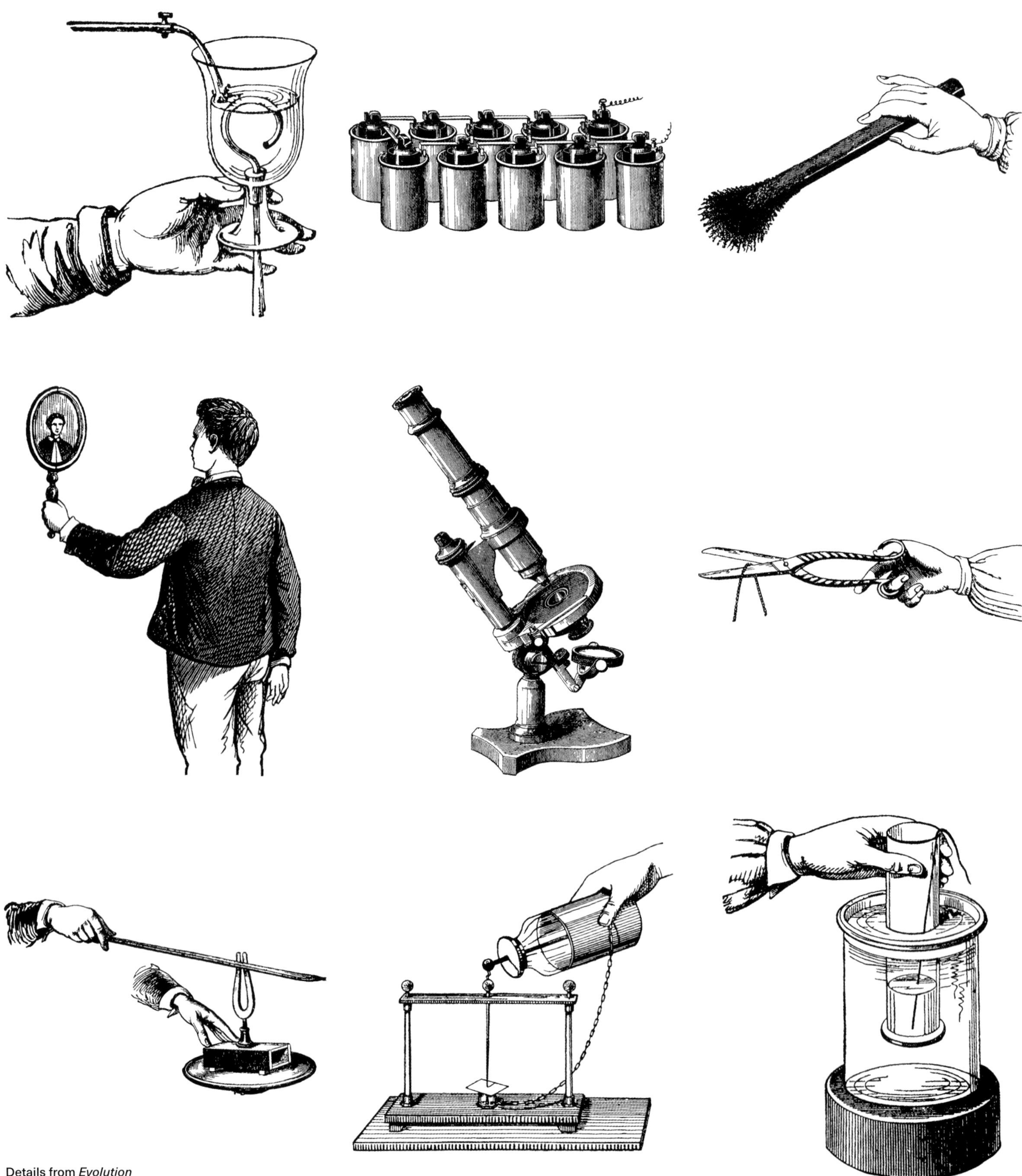

Details from *Evolution and Theory*, 2018.

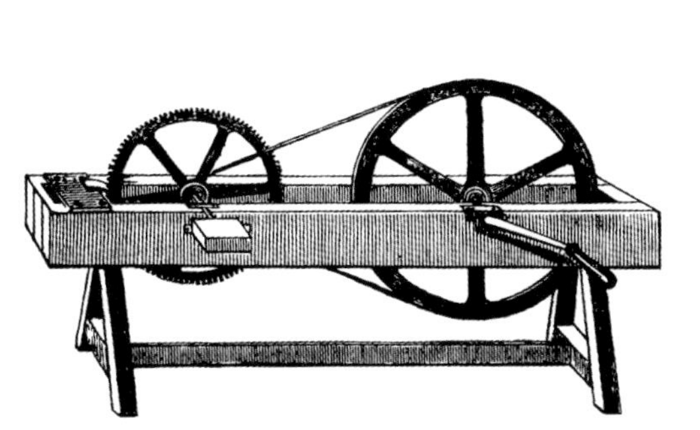
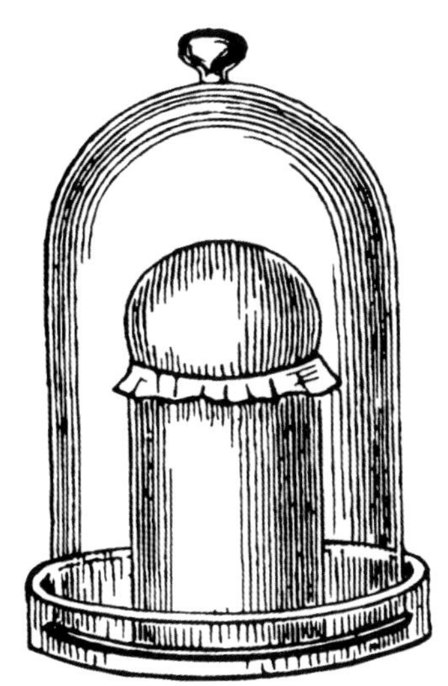
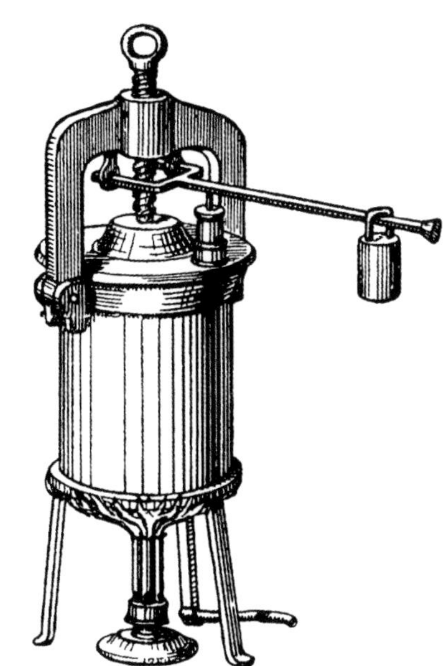
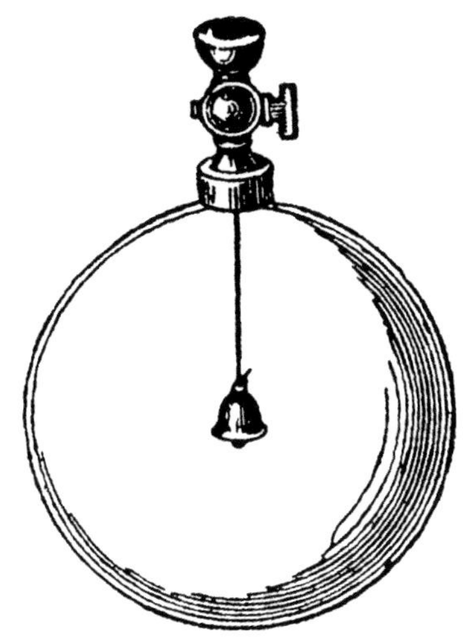
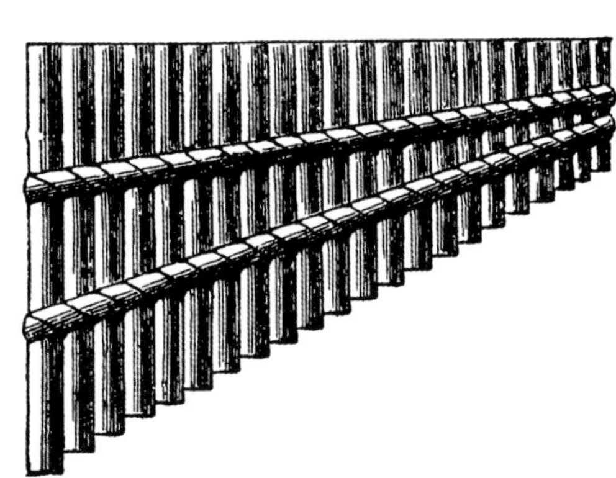
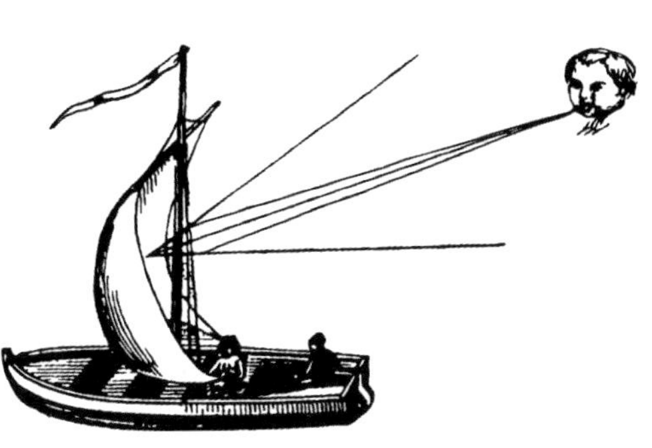
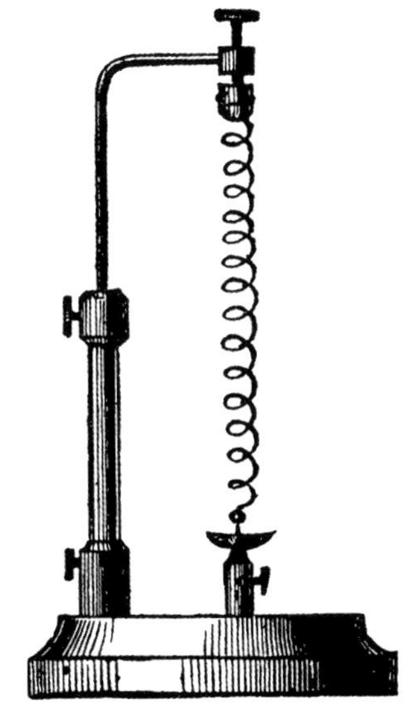
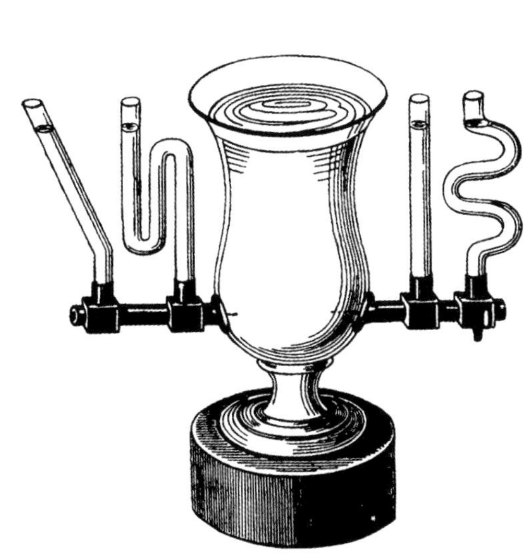
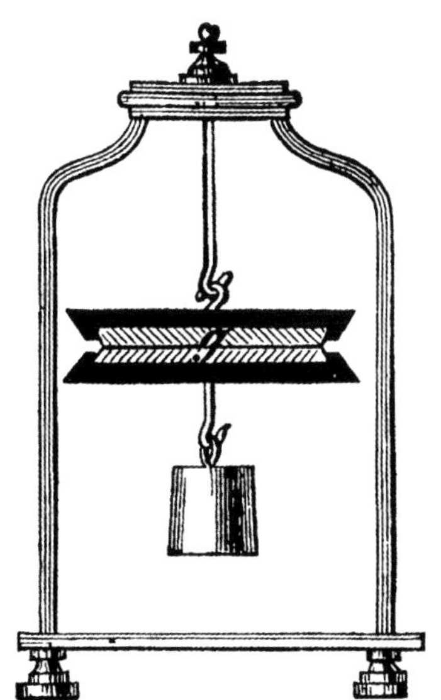

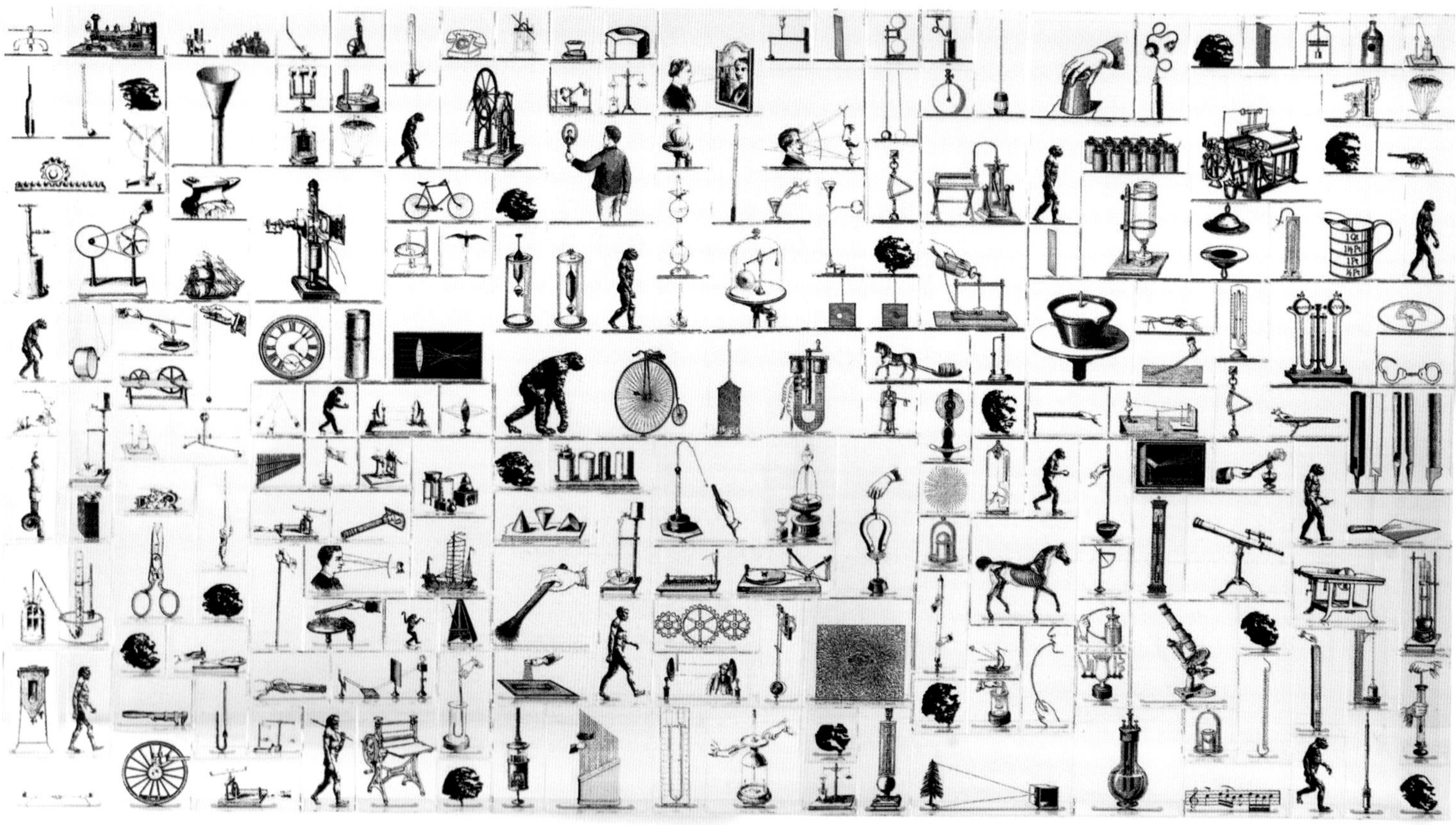

Evolution and Theory,
painted stainless steel,
H246 x W137.5 x D11 cm,
2021.

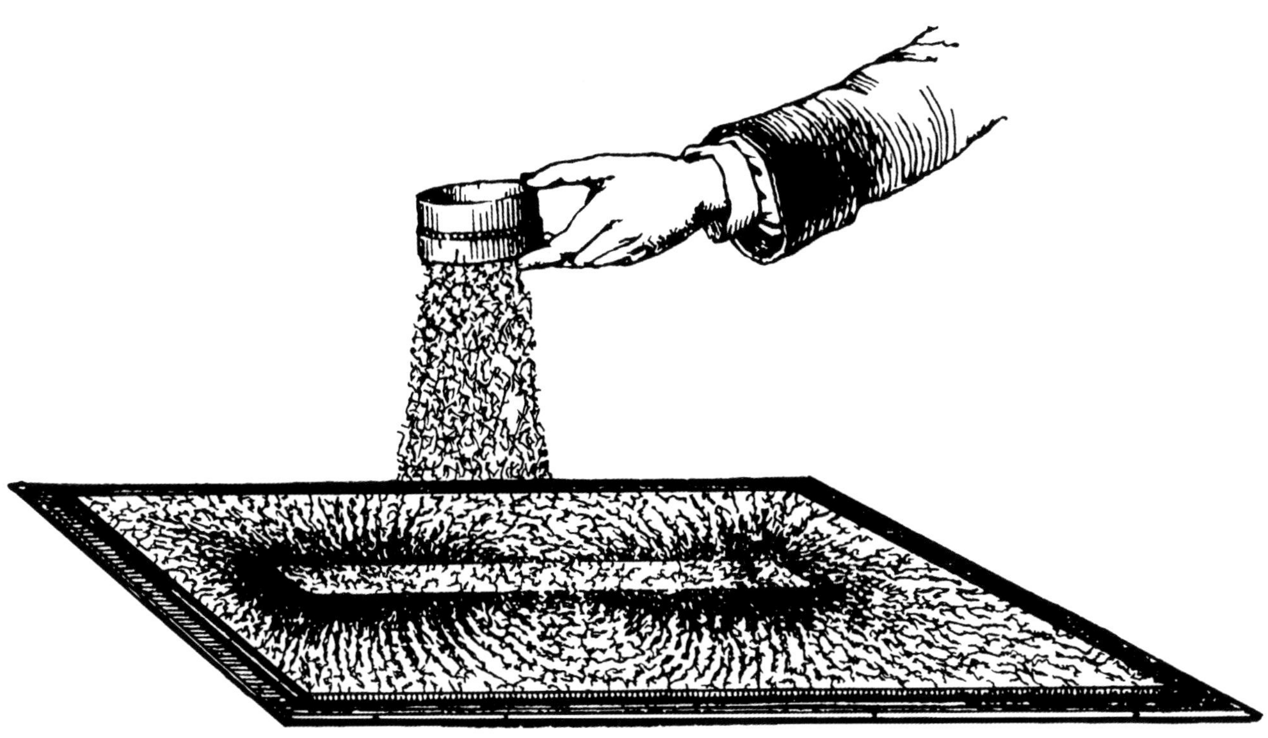

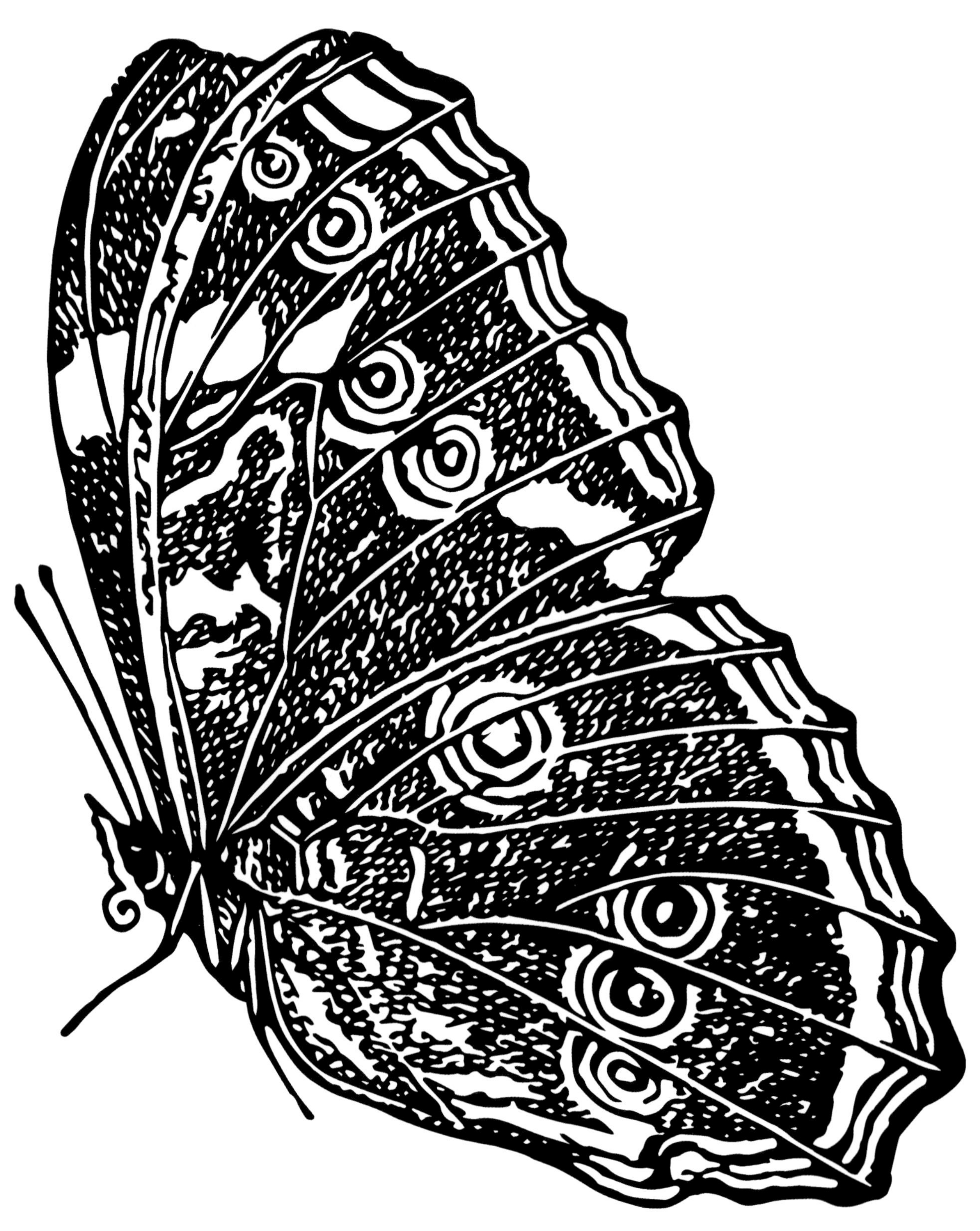

NATURAL RESERVE

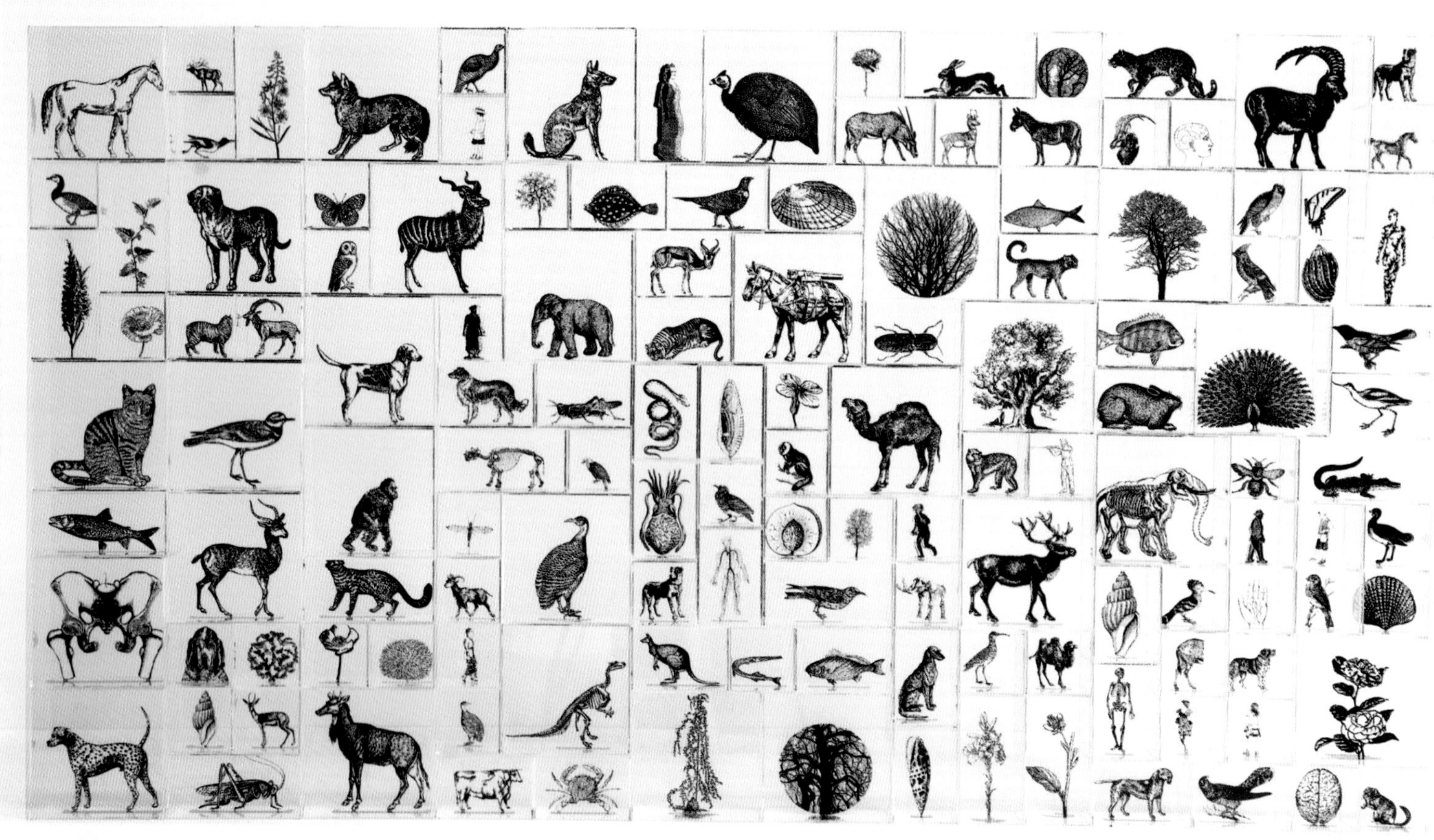

Natural Reserve, painted
stainless steel, H192 x
W108 x D11 cm, 2021.

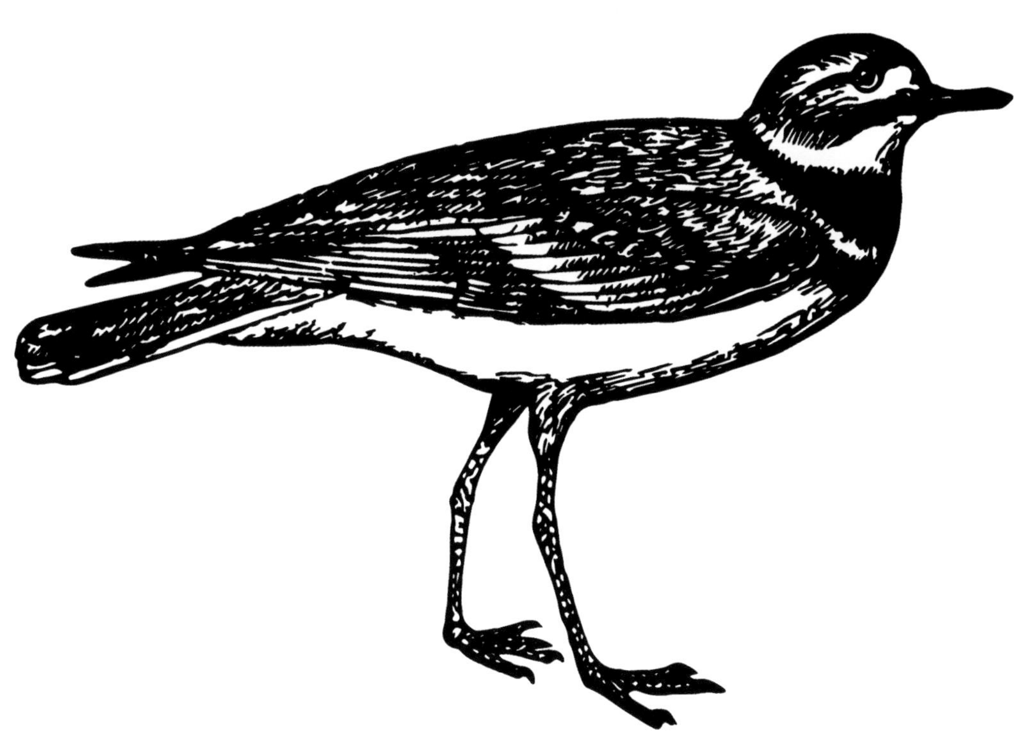

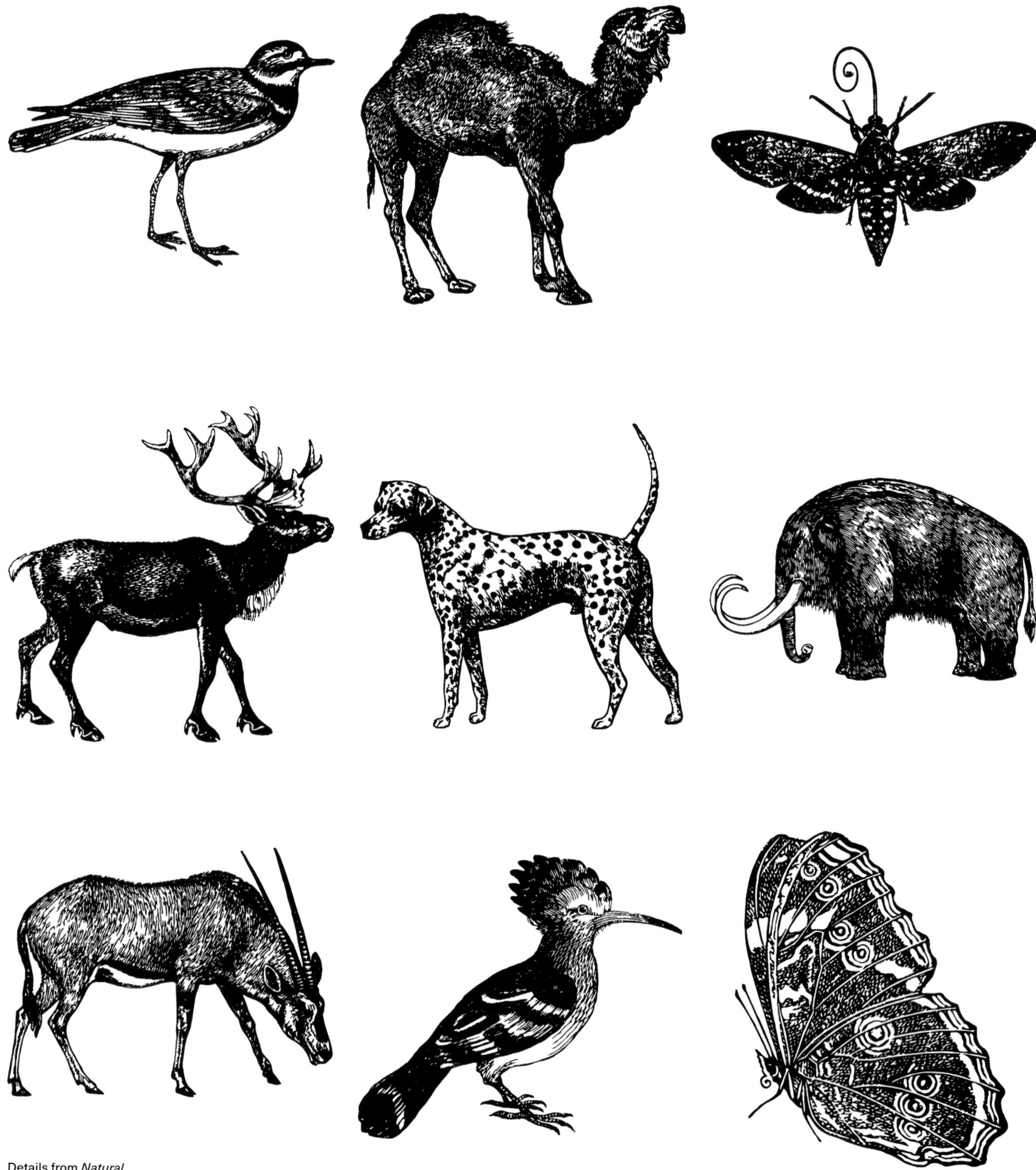

Details from *Natural Reserve*, 2021.

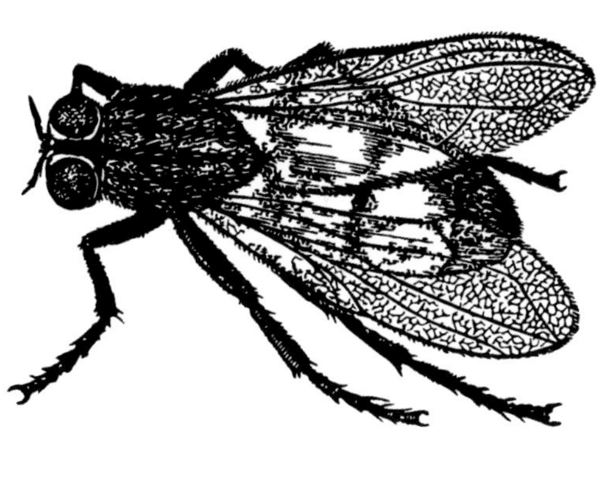

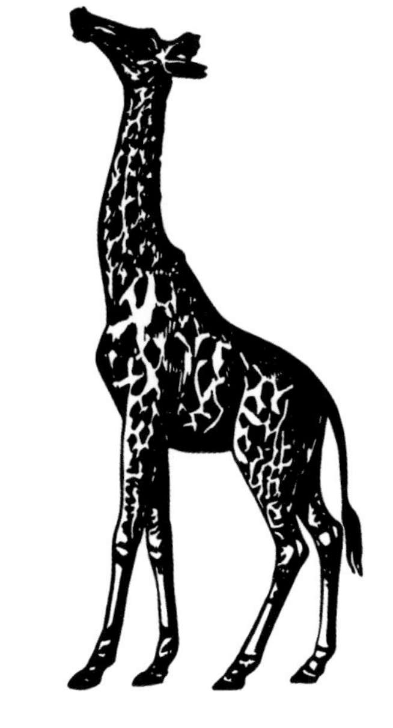

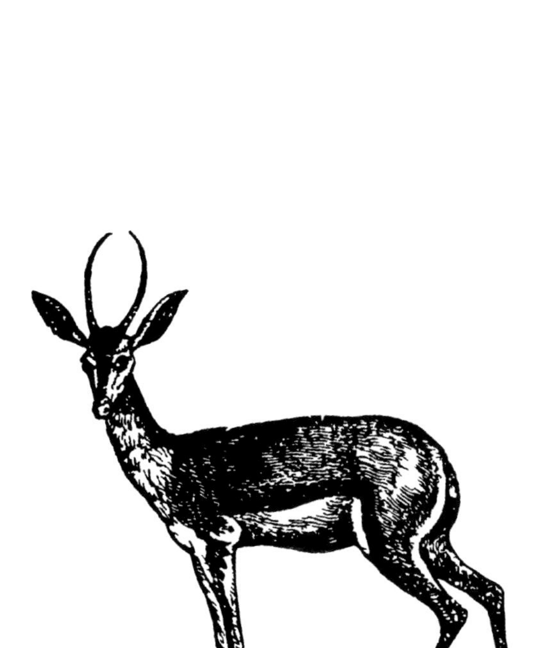

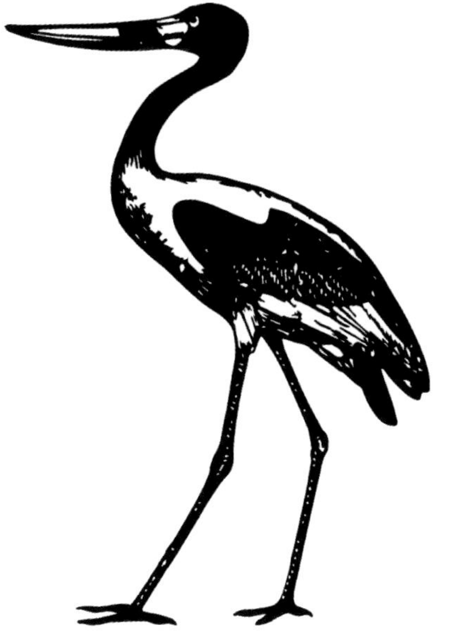

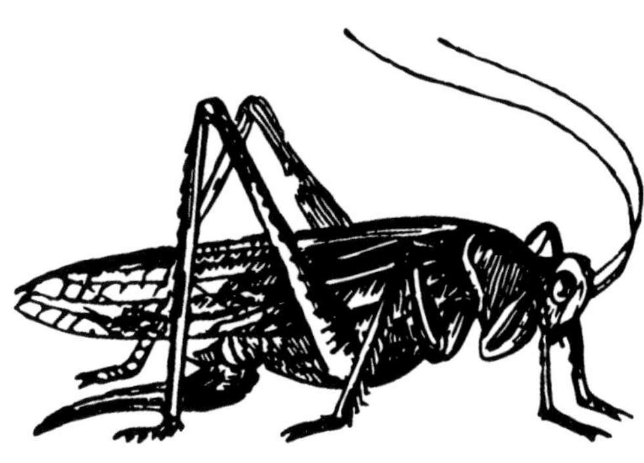

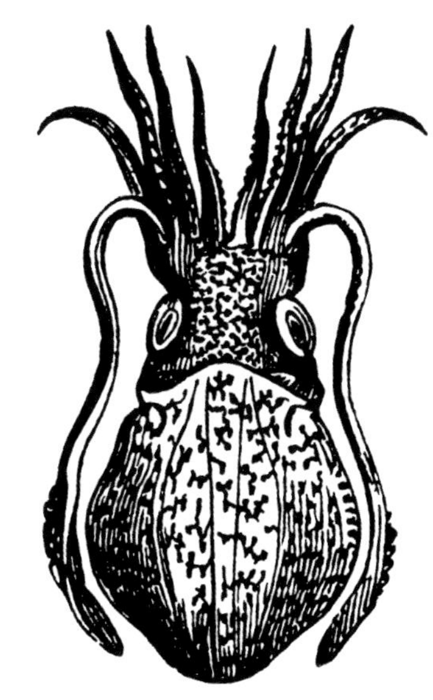

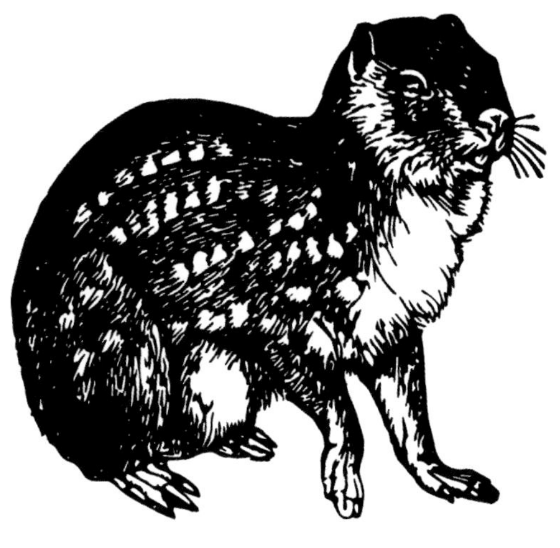

Natural Reserve

Natural Reserve continues my interest and commitment to ongoing universal concerns around humankind and our relationship to the planet.

We tend to forget that we are part of nature. We are all guests on our planet just like other creatures. Every year a great number of creatures become extinct forever due to our actions.

In this wall installation I tried to include various aspects from the nature that surrounds us; animals, plants and human beings. They are randomly mixed, creating a mosaic of nature.

Like *Evolution and Theory* most of the images were drawn from 19th century illustrated books, encyclopaedias and dictionaries.

Zadok Ben-David, October 2021

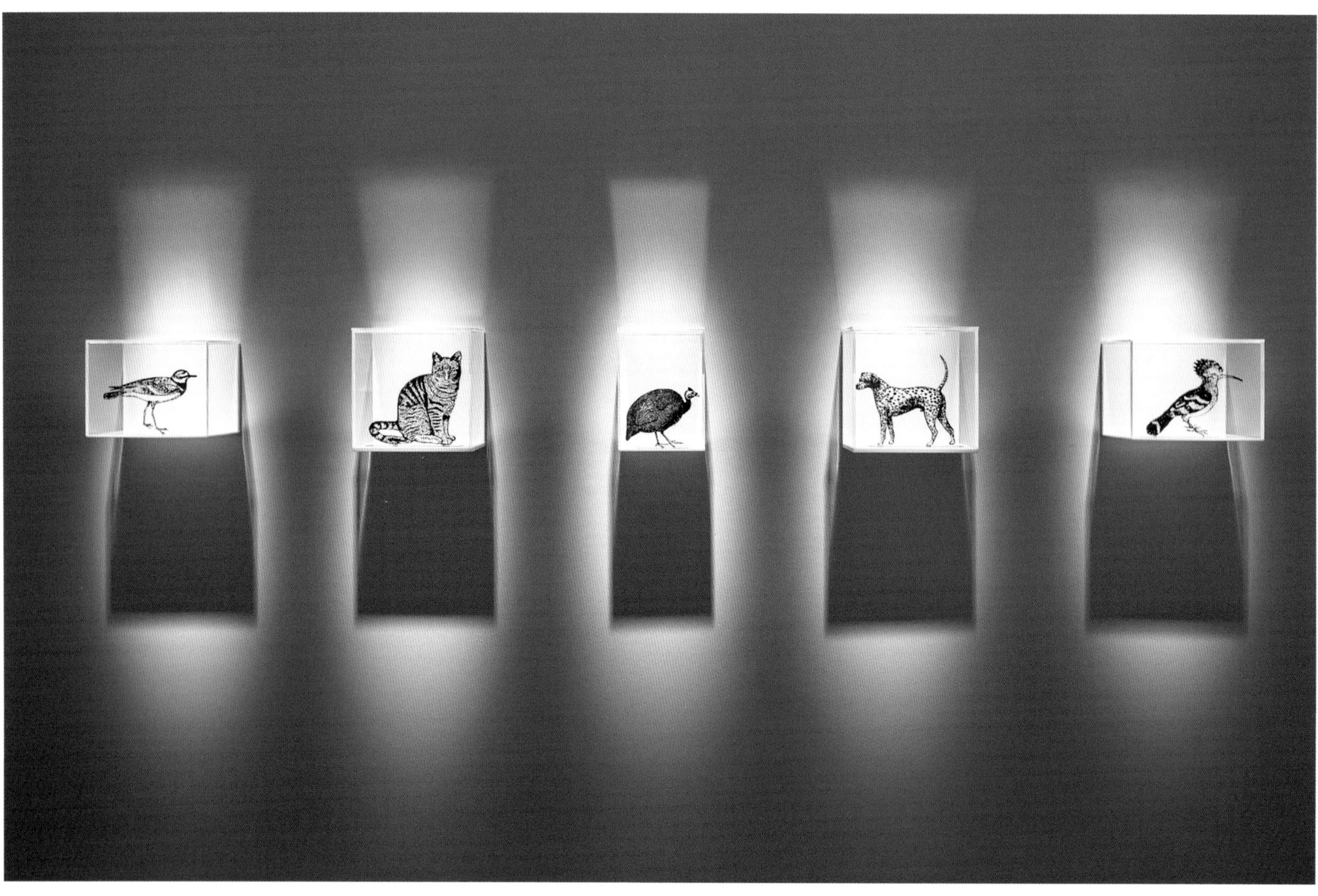

Details from *Natural Reserve*, hand-painted stainless steel and plexiglass, Royal Botanic Gardens, Kew, UK, 2021.

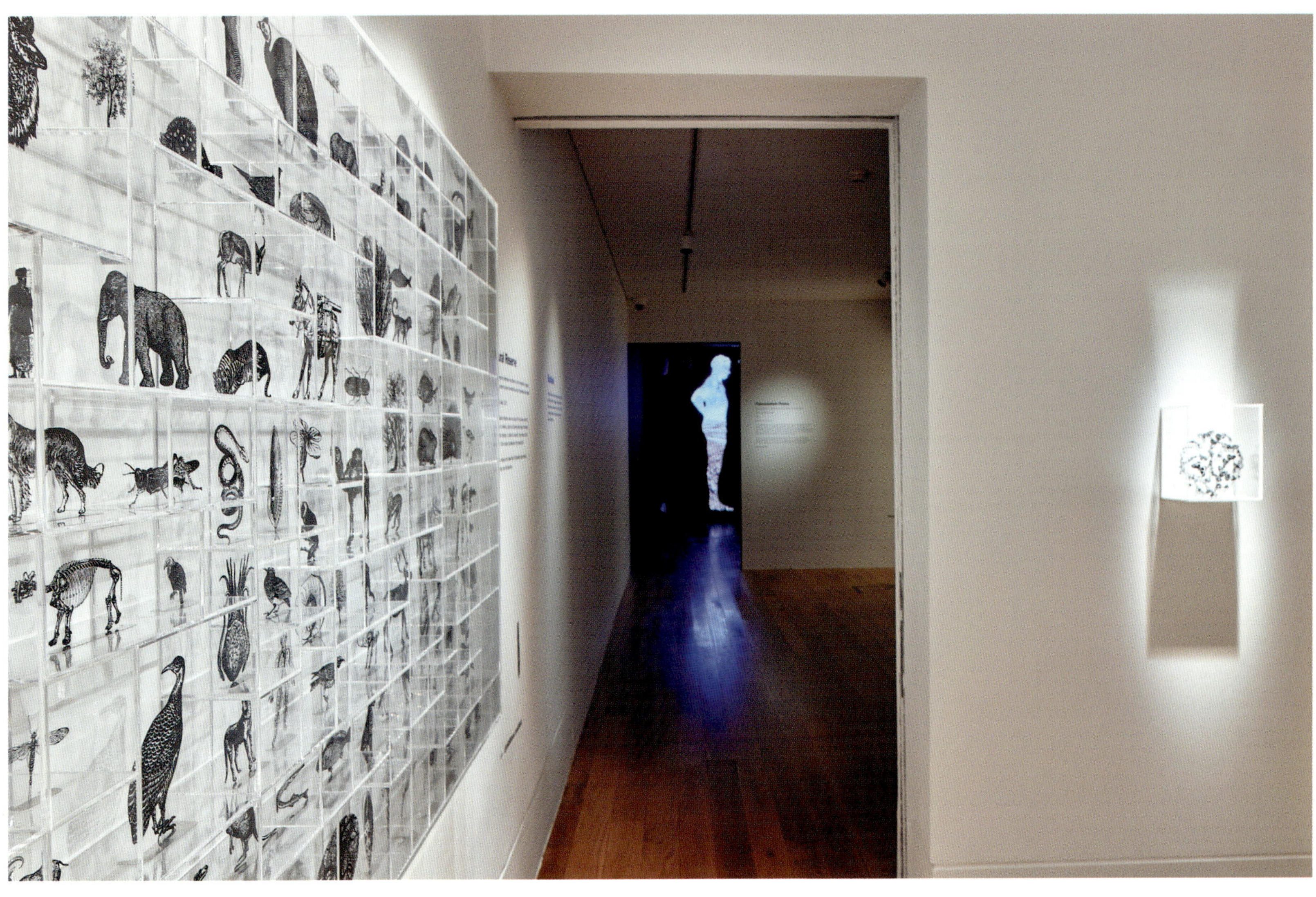

Natural Reserve, Royal
Botanic Gardens, Kew,
UK, 2021.

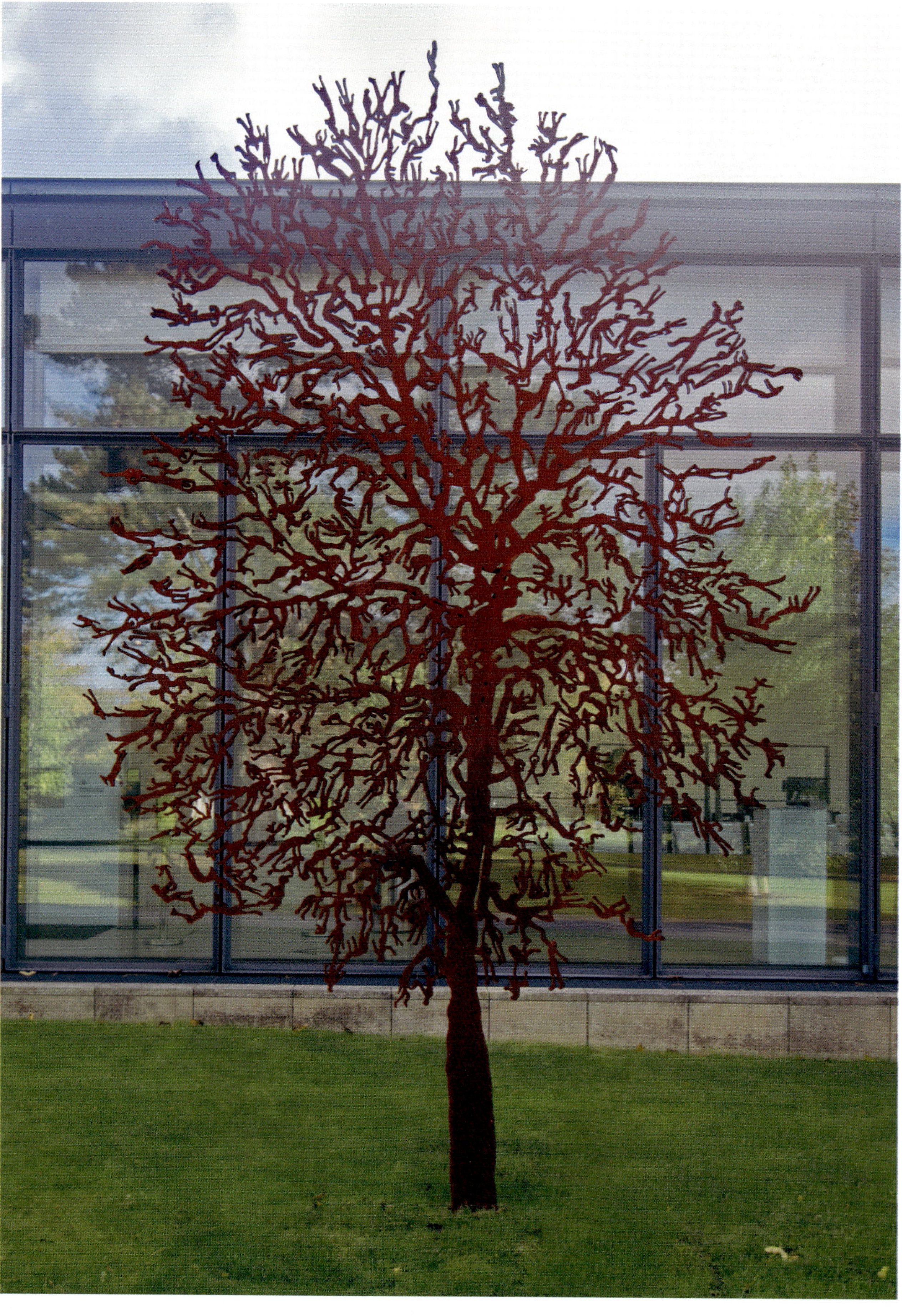

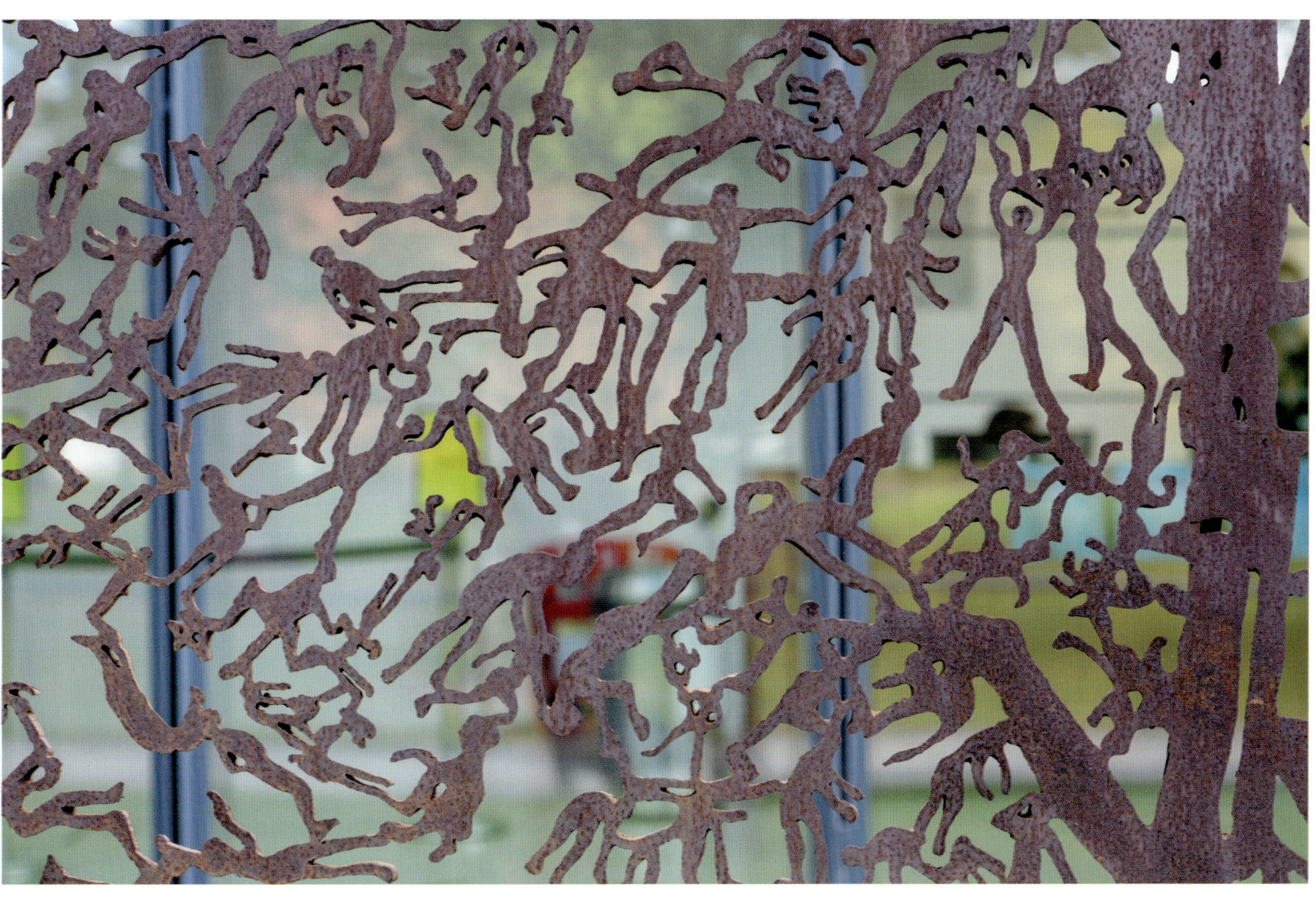

Winter Lights, hand-cut
corten steel, H450 x W257
x D30cm, Royal Botanic
Gardens, Kew, UK, 2021

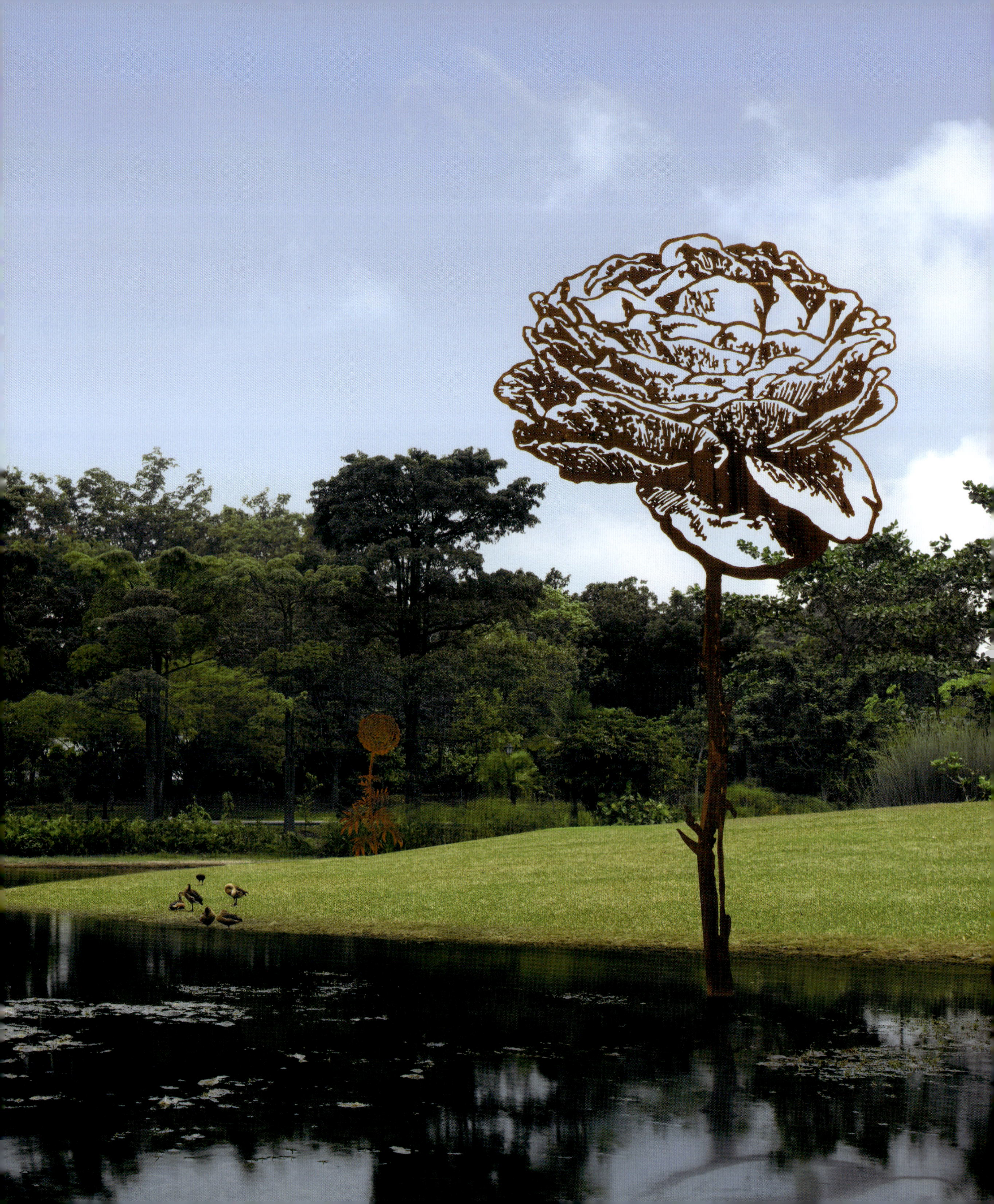

OUTDOOR SCULPTURES

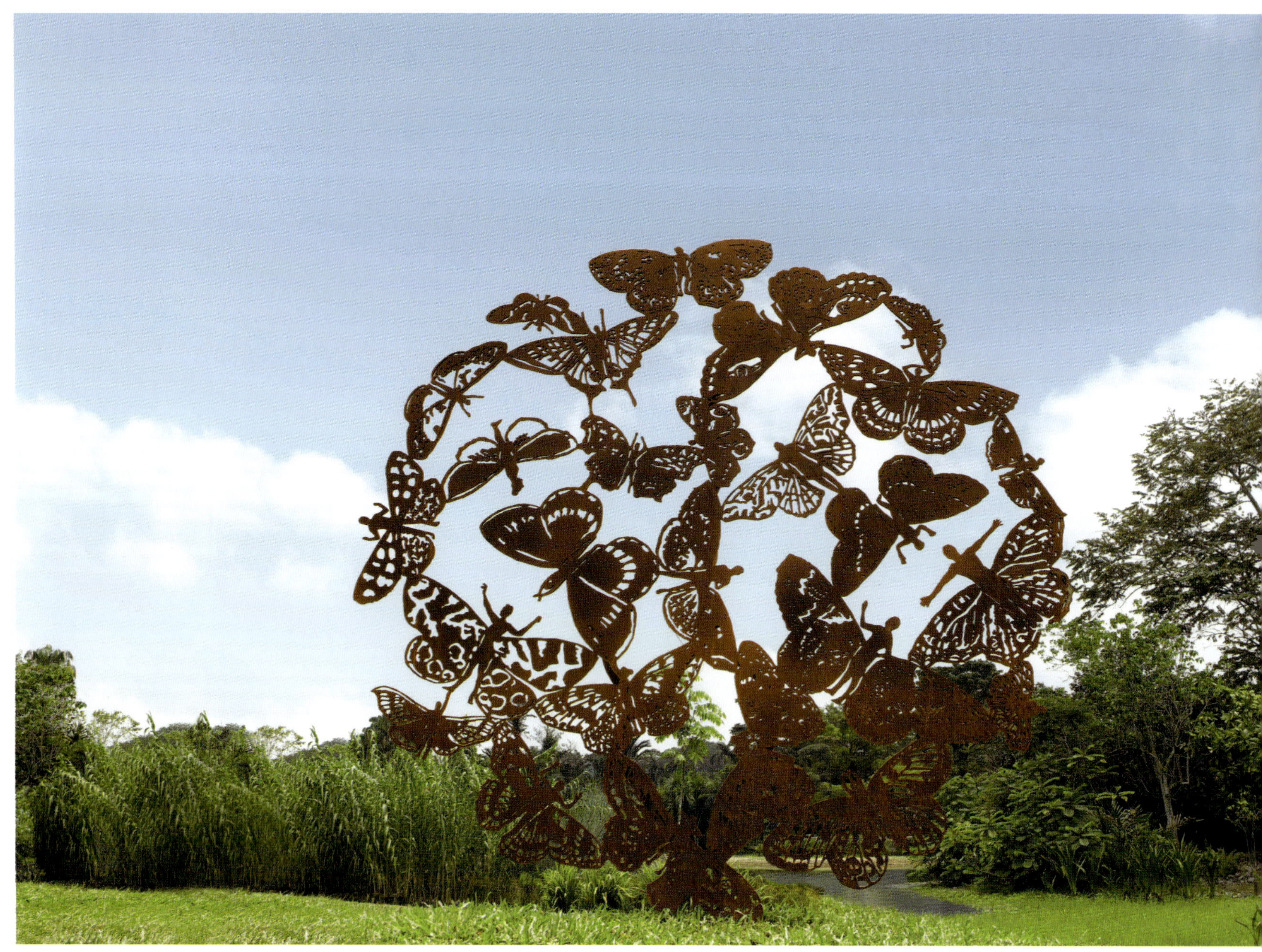

Midnight Dance, hand-
cut corten steel, diameter
300 cm, Singapore
Botanic Gardens, 2012.

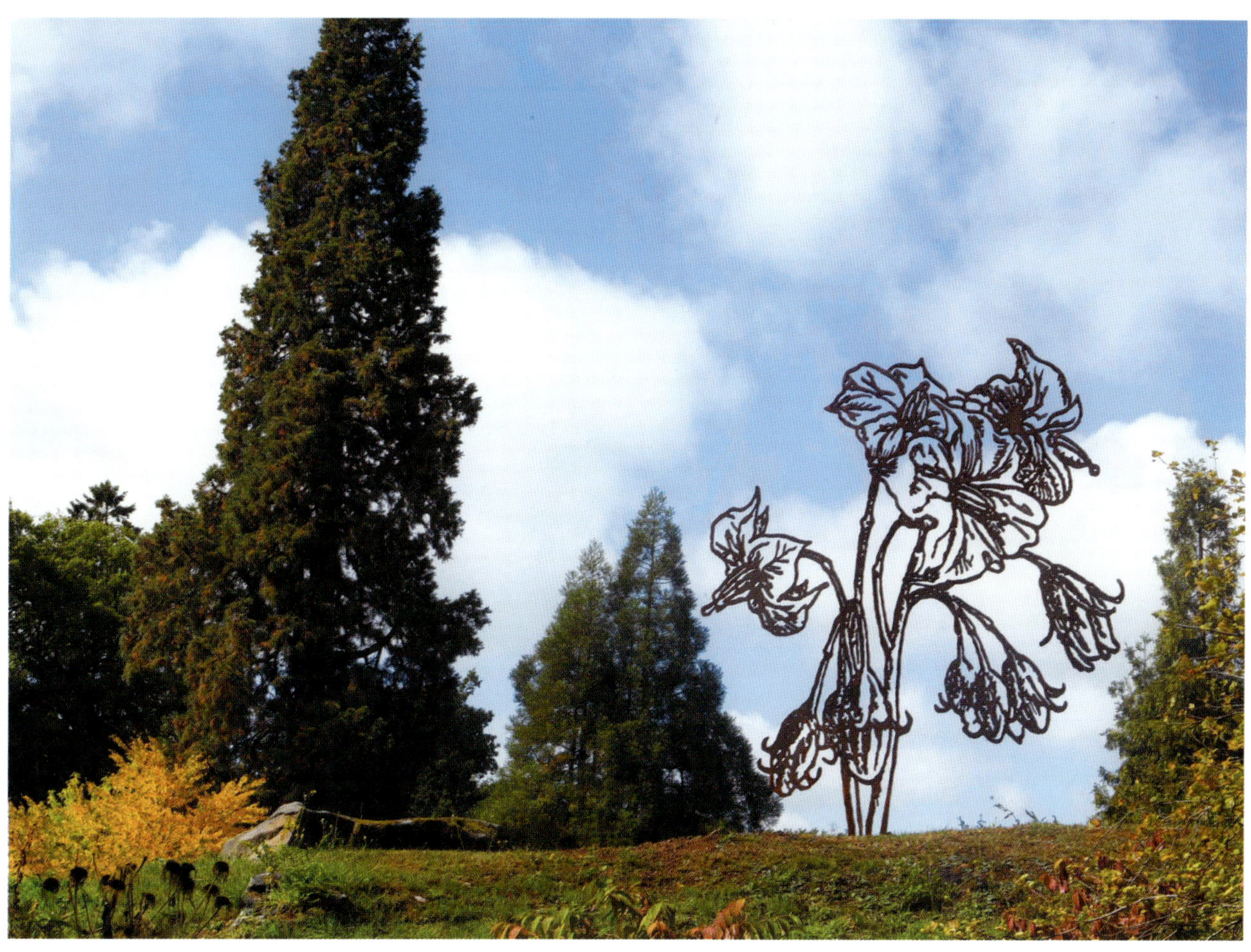

Simple Lines, hand-
cut corten steel, H323
x W248 x D17 cm
Singapore, Botanic
Gardens, 2012.

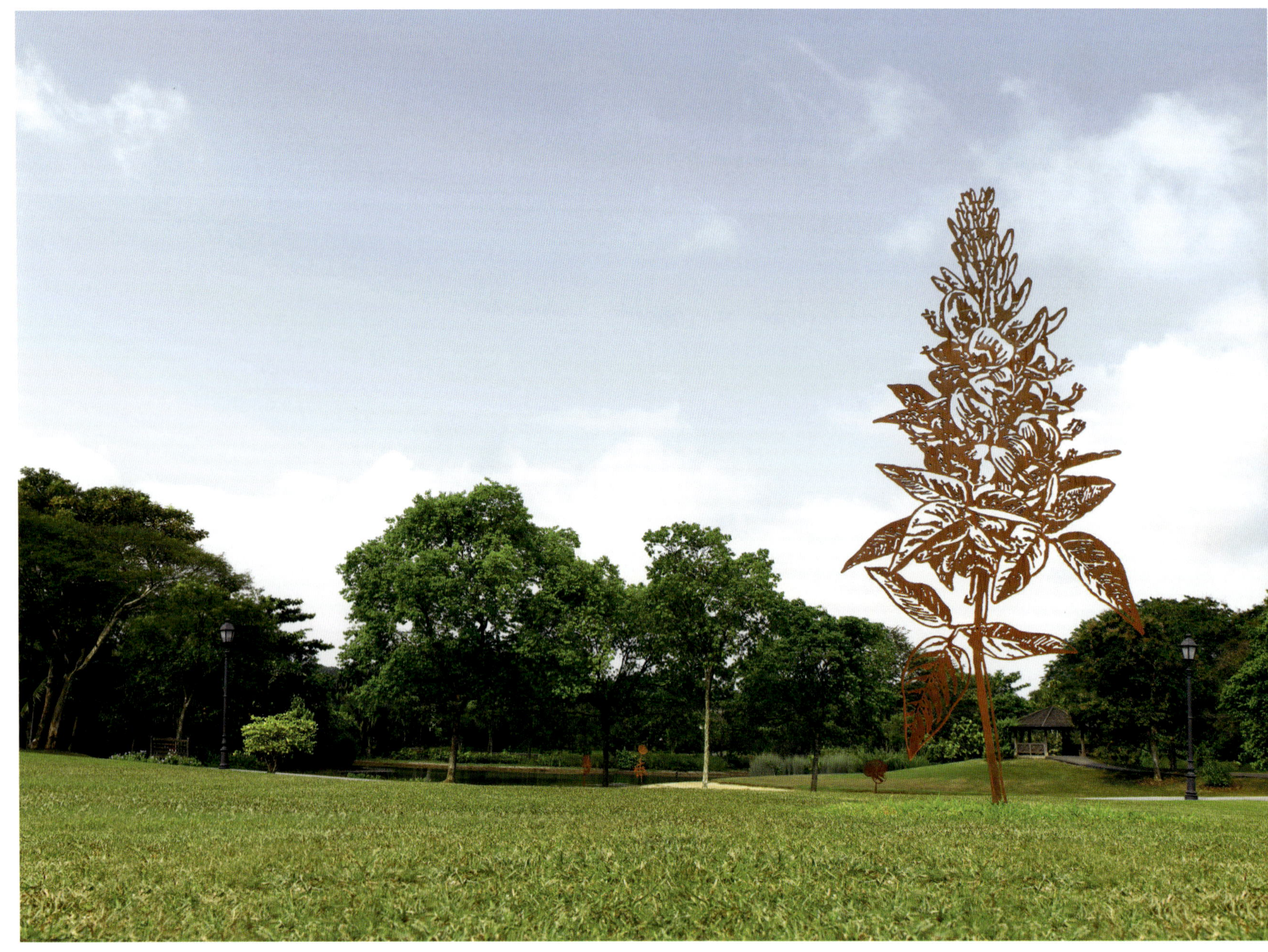

Over the Top, hand-cut corten steel, H347 x W160 x D1.5 cm, Singapore, Botanic Gardens, 2012.

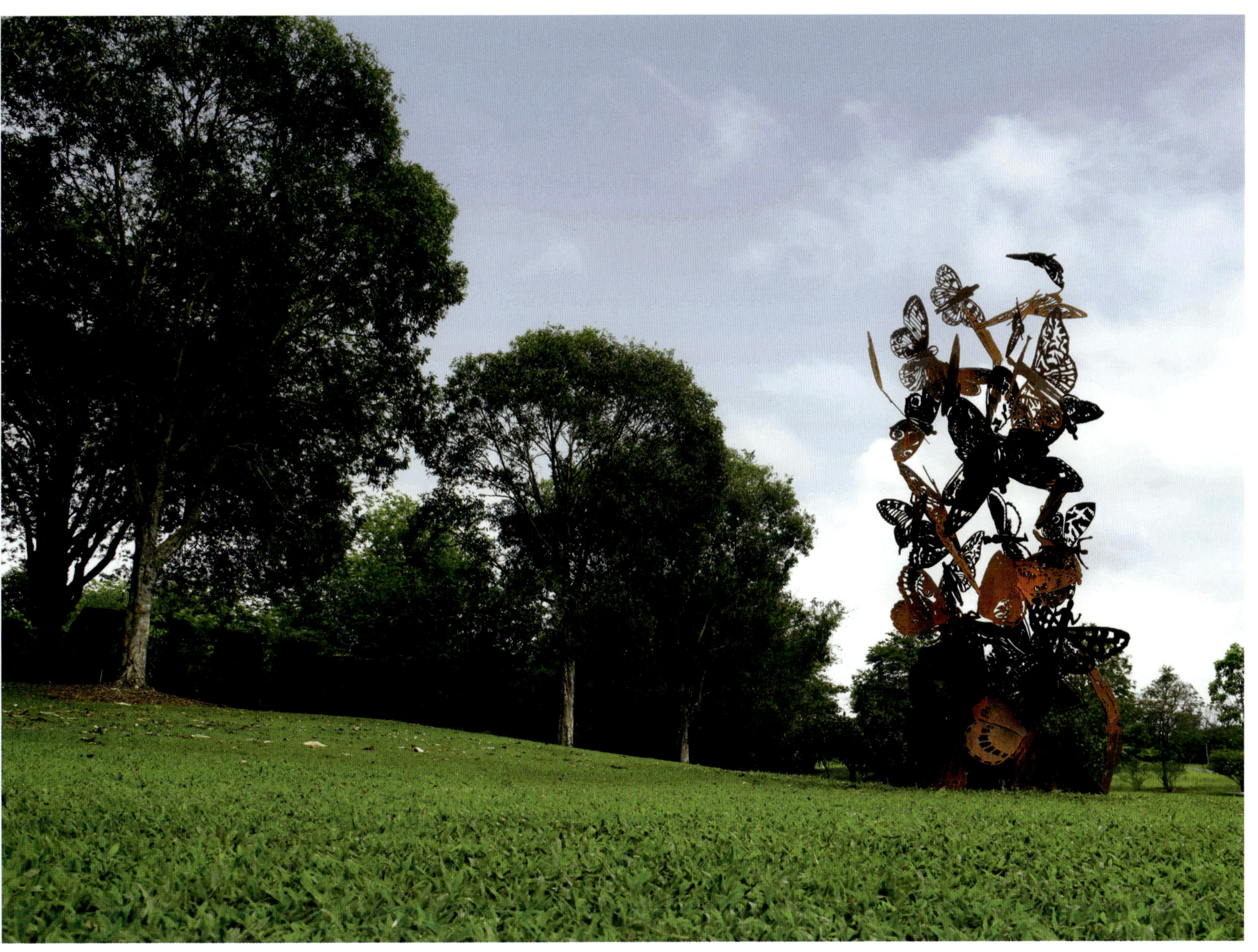

Natural Tower, hand-
cut corten steel, H445
x W212 x D171 cm,
Singapore Botanic
Gardens, 2012.

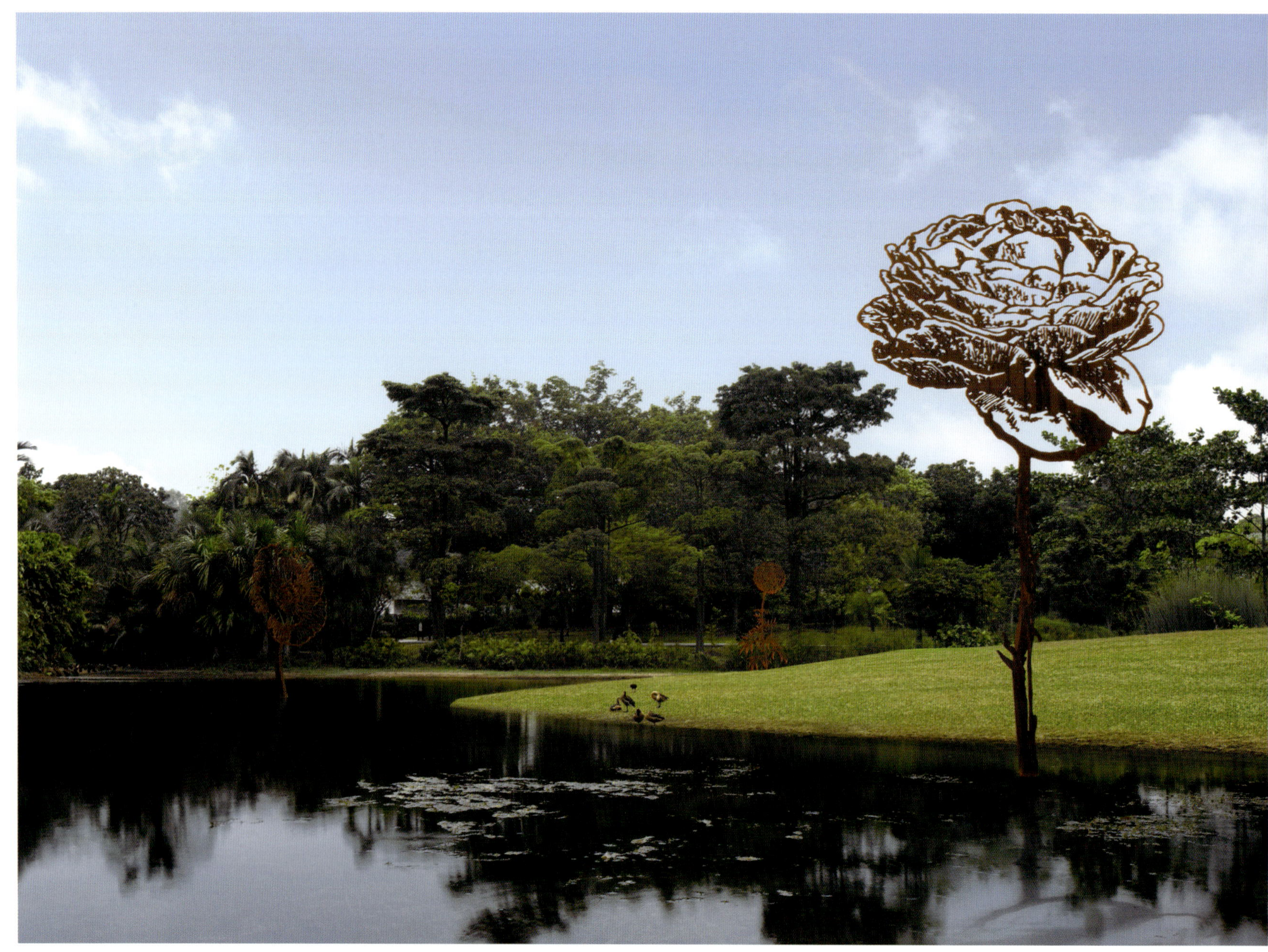

Tongue In Cheek, hand-cut
corten steel, H290 x W157
x D1.5 cm, Singapore
Botanic Gardens, 2012.

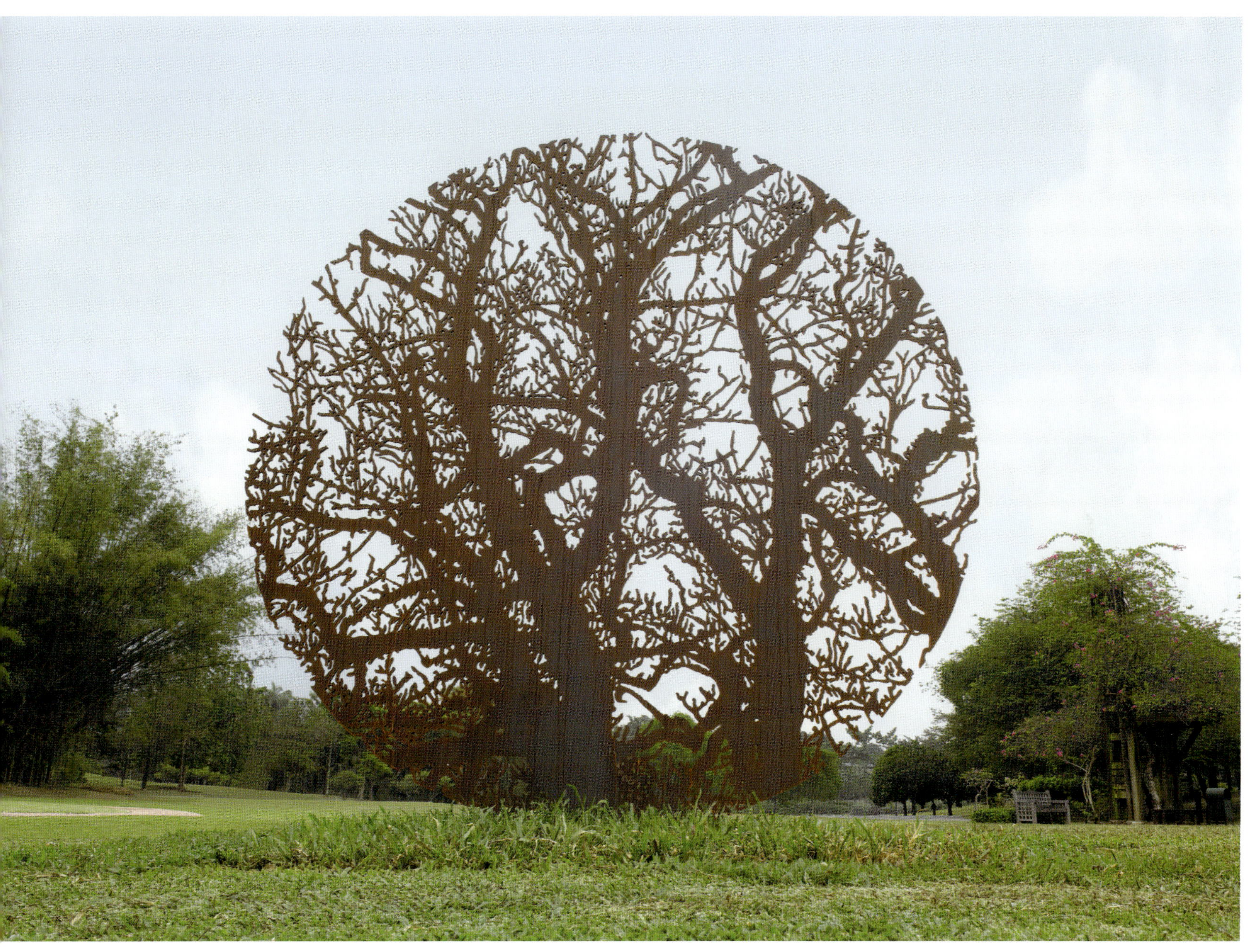

Mid Spring, hand-cut
corten steel, diameter
249 cm x 15 cm,
Singapore Botanic
Gardens, 2012.

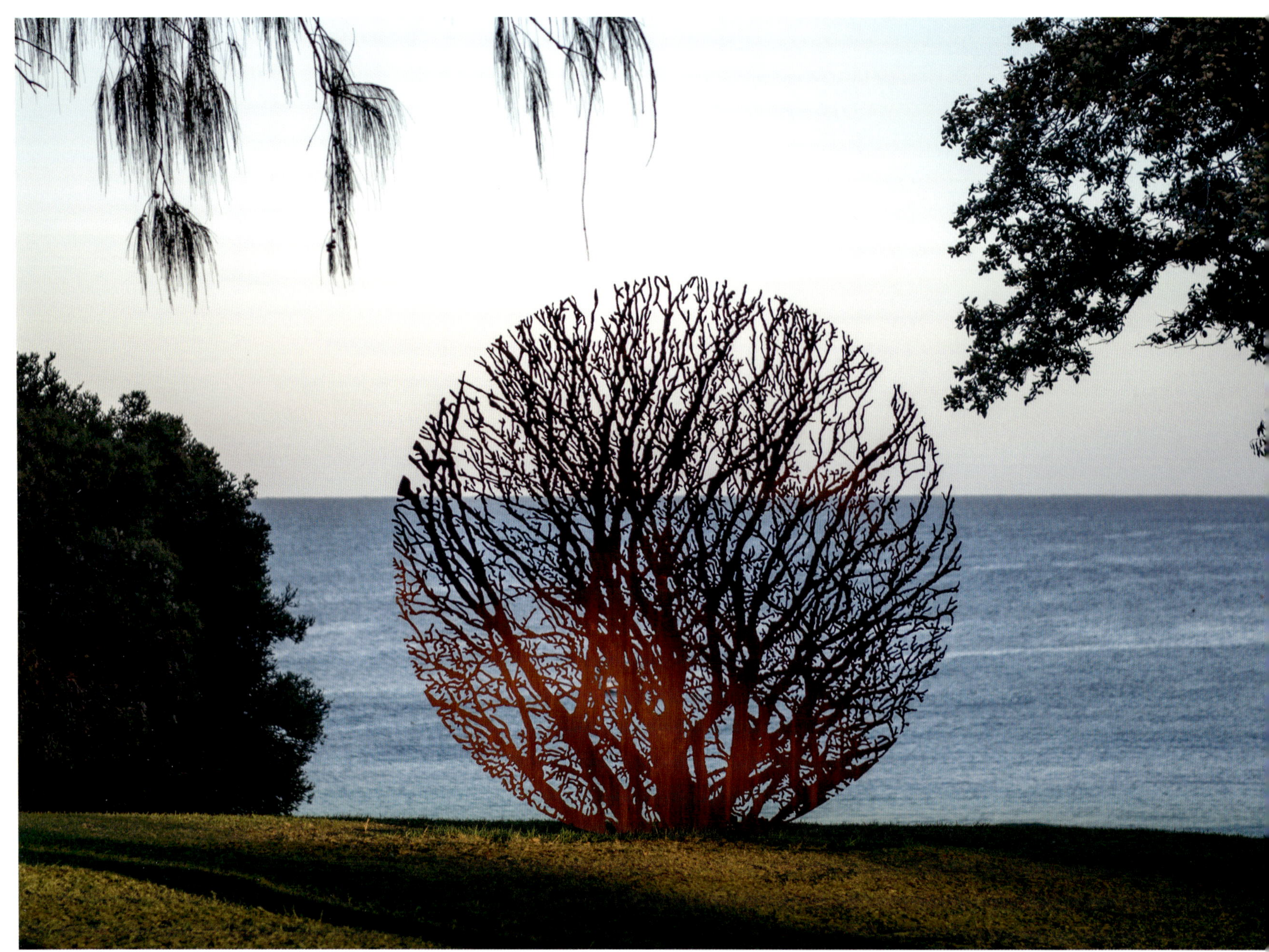

Sunny Moon, hand-cut
corten steel, diameter
271 cm, *Sculpture by
the Sea*, Cottesloe,
Australia, 2008.

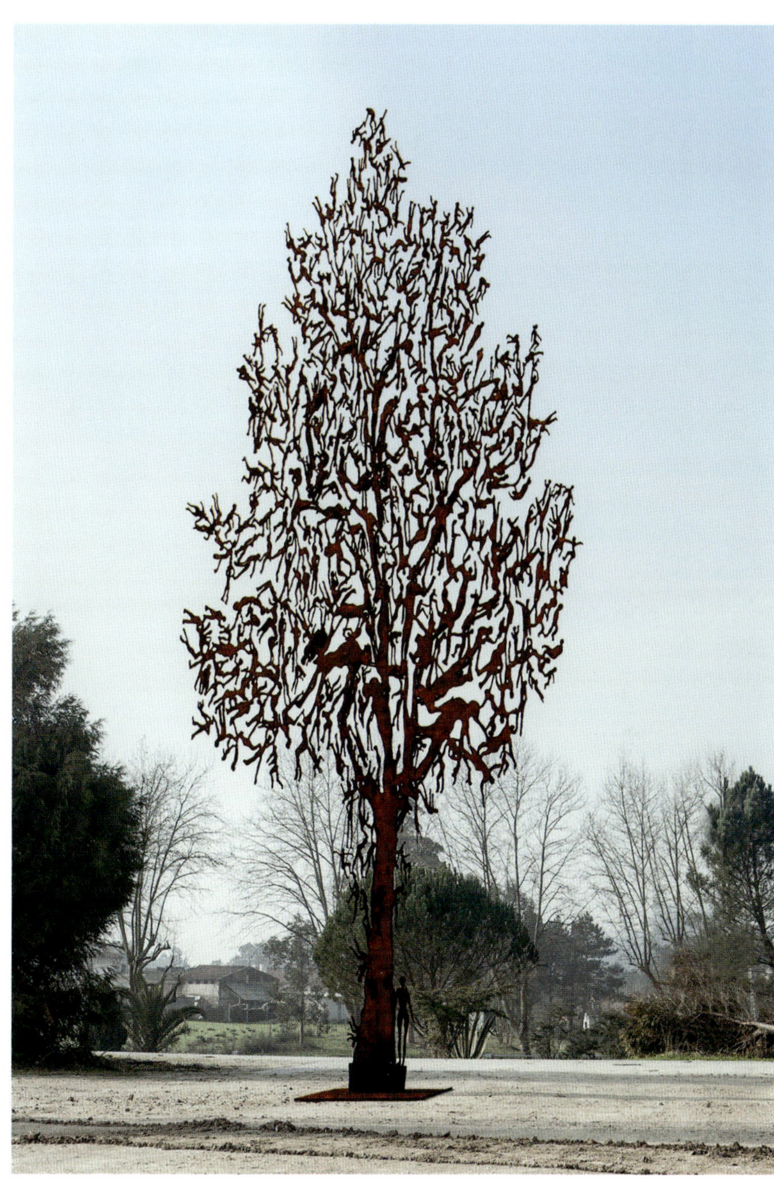

Morning Stretch,
hand-cut corten steel,
H1021.5 x W395 x D2 cm,
Portugal, 2014.

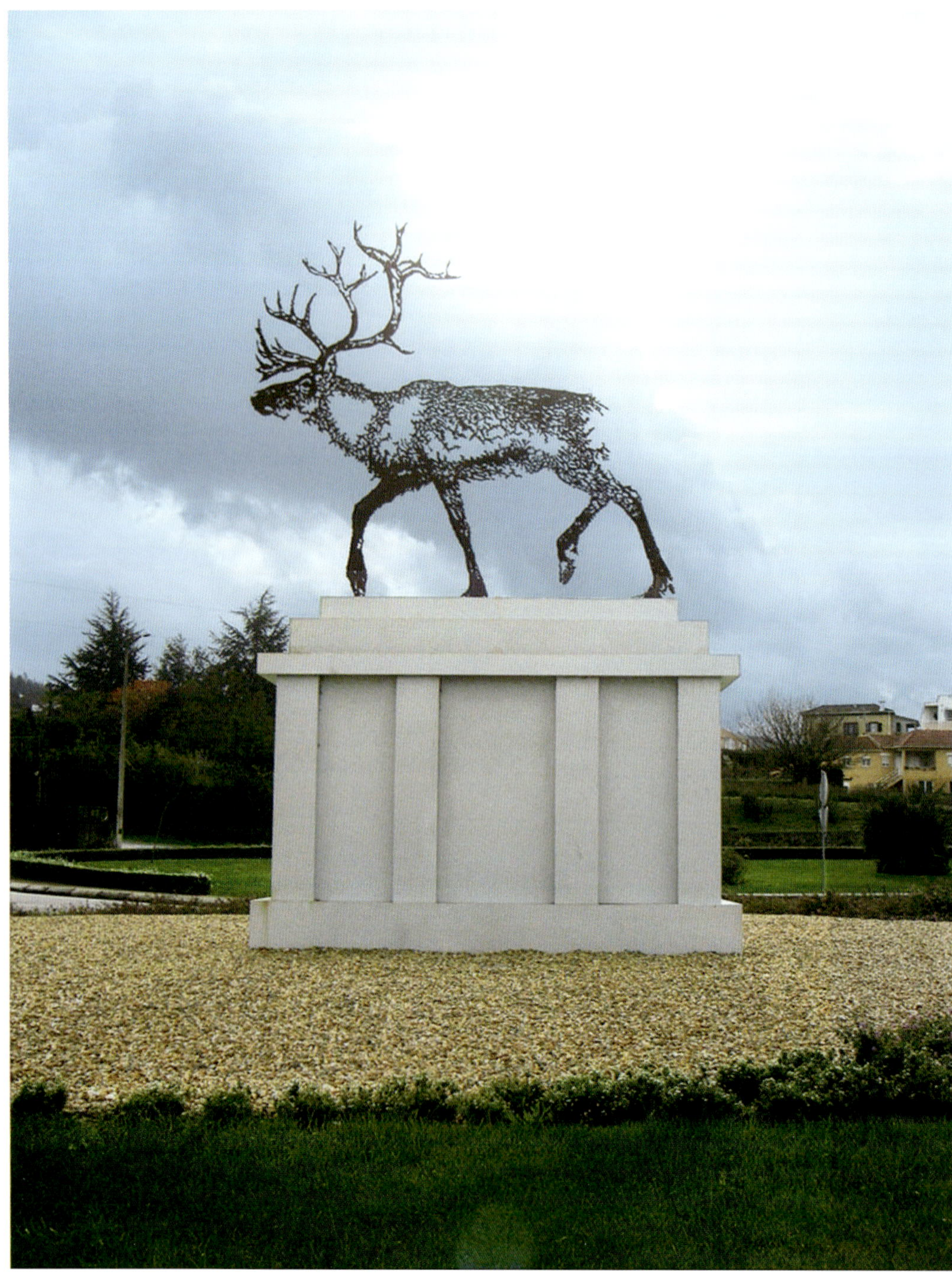

Cervo, hand-cut corten
steel, H400 x W680 x
D134 cm, Vila Nova de
Cerveira, Portugal, 2004.

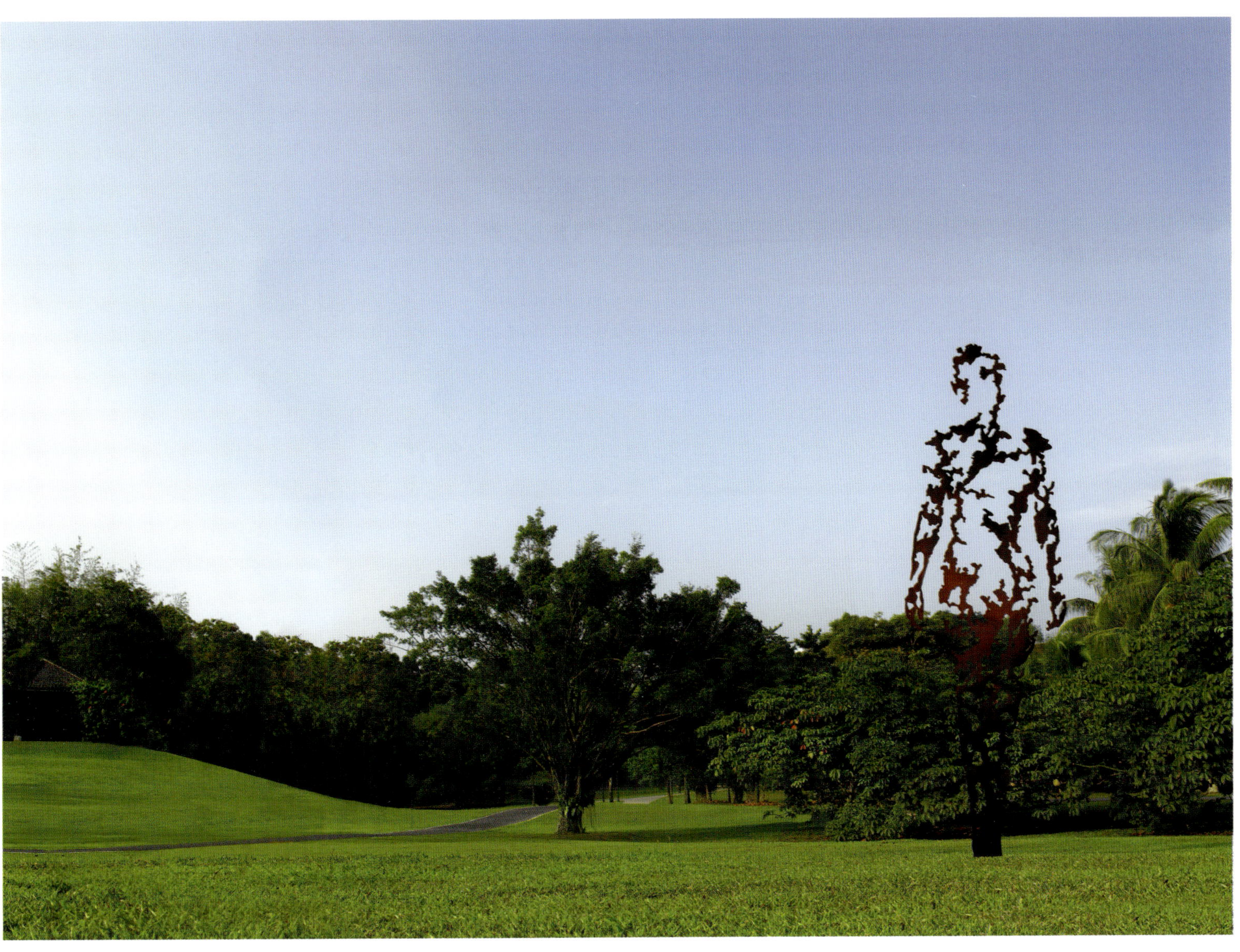

Celine, hand-cut corten
steel, H361 x W112
x D2 cm, Singapore
Botanic Gardens, 2012.

Zadok Ben-David: Life and exhibitions

1949
Born in Bayhan, Yemen, immigrated to Israel

1971-73
Studied at Bezalel Academy of Art & Design, Jerusalem, Israel

1975
Studied at Reading University, Fine Arts, Reading, UK

1976
Studied advanced sculpture course at St Martin's School of Art, London, UK

1977-82
Taught sculpture at St Martin's School of Art, London, UK

Selected Solo Exhibitions

2007
Invisible Reality, Guangdong Art Museum, Guangzhou, China

2008
Blackfield, Annandale Galleries, Sydney, Australia

2009
Human Nature, Tel Aviv Museum of Art, Israel

2010
Blackfield, Verso Arte Contemporanea, Turin, Italy

1918 Art Space, Shanhai, China

Blackfield, Galerie Albrecht, Berlin, Germany

2011
Blackfield, Artclub 1563, Seoul, South Korea

2012
Zadok Ben-David at Singapore Botanic Gardens, presented by Sotheby's, Singapore

Simple Line, Mysteski Arsenal, Kiev, Ukraine

The Story *I Am About to Tell You…, Magic Box*, Vila Nova de Cerveira, Portugal

2013
Bacalhôa Buddha Eden, Bombarral, Portugal

The Other Side of Midnight, Shoshana Wayne Gallery, Los Angeles, USA

2014
National Museum of the Republic of Kazakhstan, Astana, Kazakhstan

2015
The Other Side of Midnight, The Art Gallery of Uzbekistan, Tashkent, Uzbekistan

2016
People I Saw but Never Met, Annandale Galleries, Sydney, Australia

2017
People I Saw but Never Met, collaboration with SUUM Project, Seoul, South Korea

People I Saw but Never Met, Shoshana Wayne Gallery, Los Angeles, USA

2018
Blackfield, Musée de la Chasse et de la Nature, Paris, France

Three installations, Perth Festival 2018, Lawrence Wilson Gallery, Perth, Australia

2019
People I Saw but Never Met, Centro de Arte Contemporânea Graça Morais, Bragança, Portugal

2021
People I Saw but Never Met, Tel Aviv Museum of Art, Israel

Natural Reserve, Royal Botanic Gardens, Kew, UK

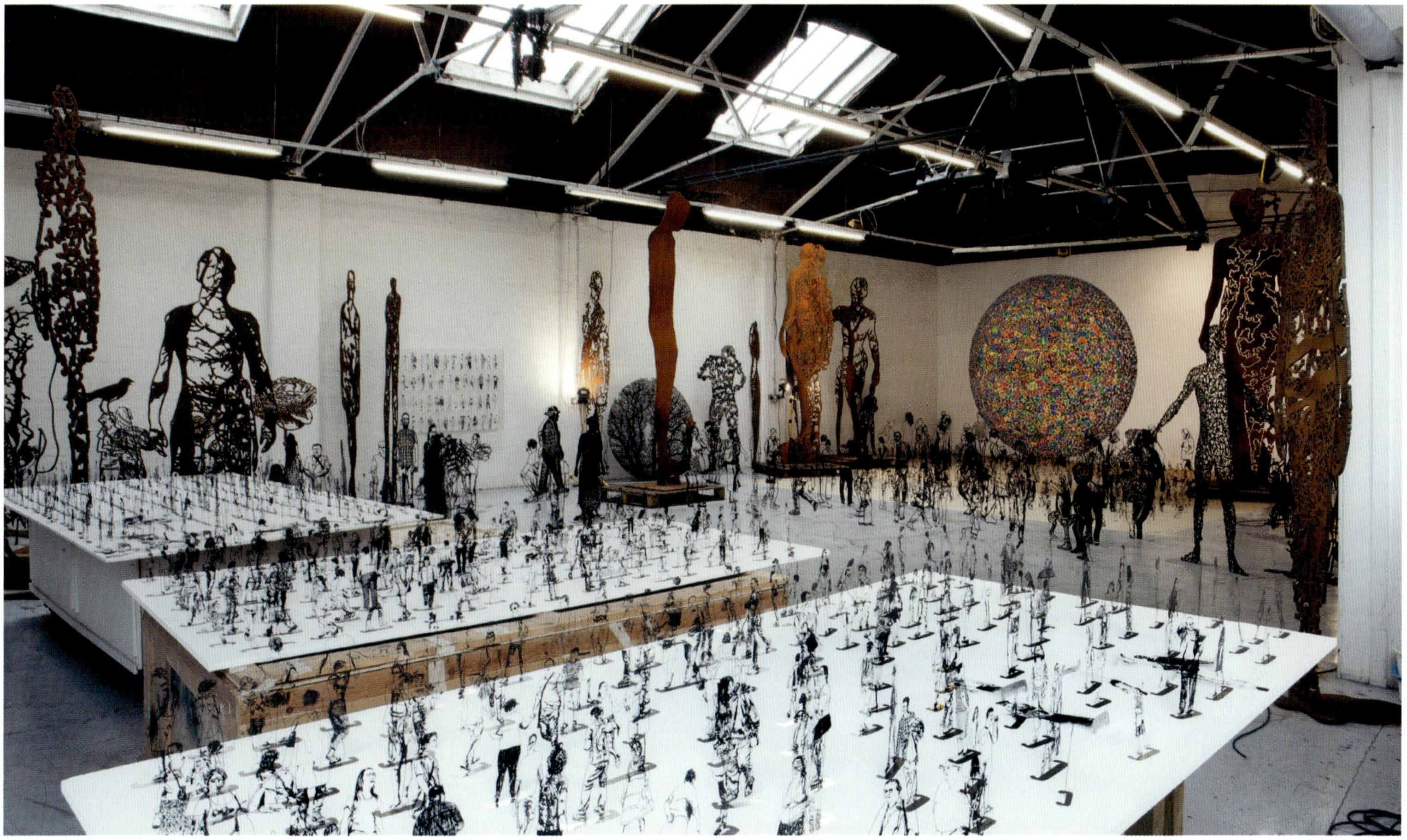

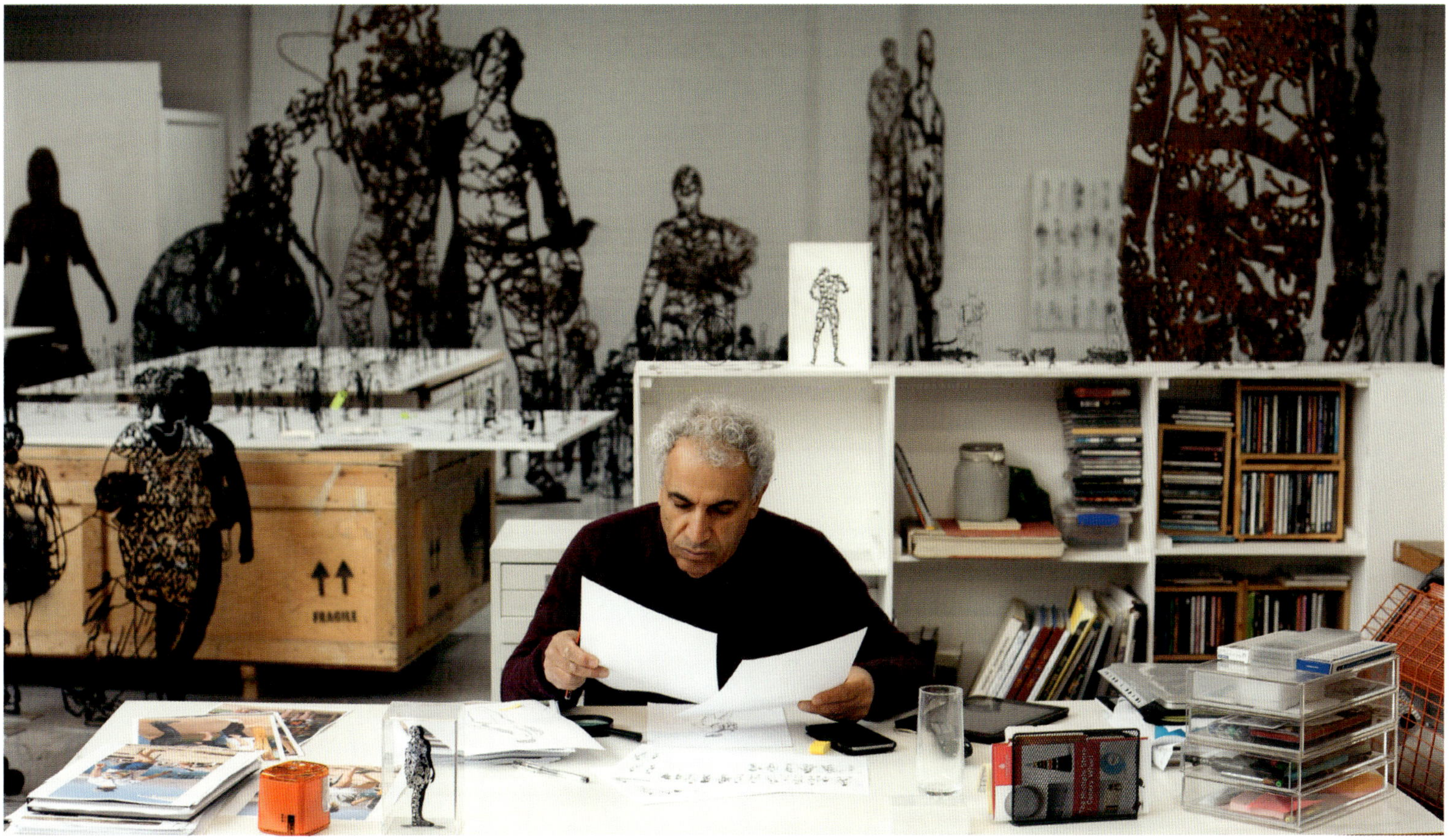

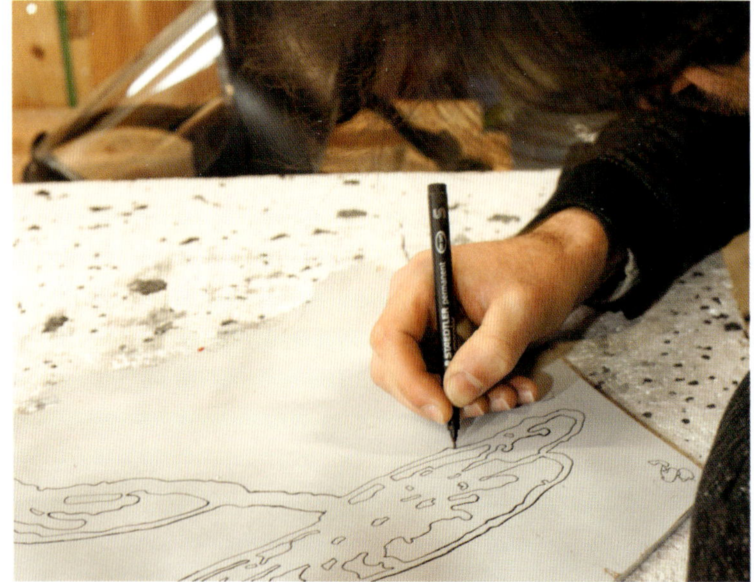
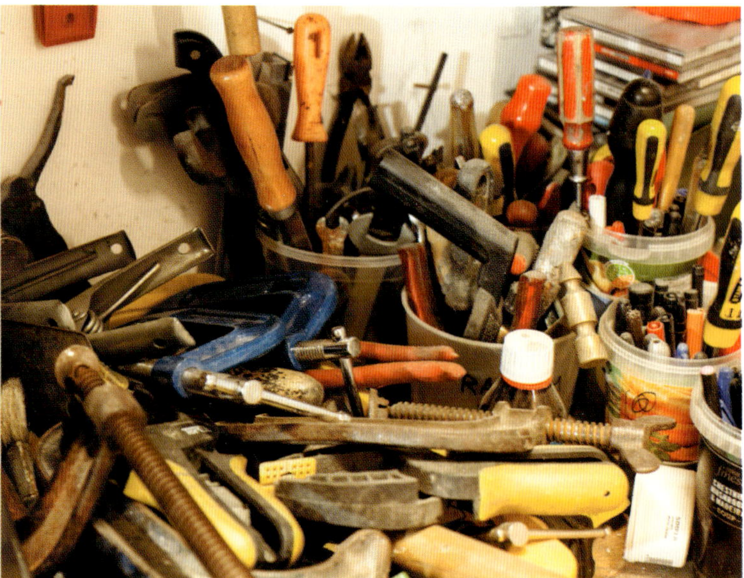
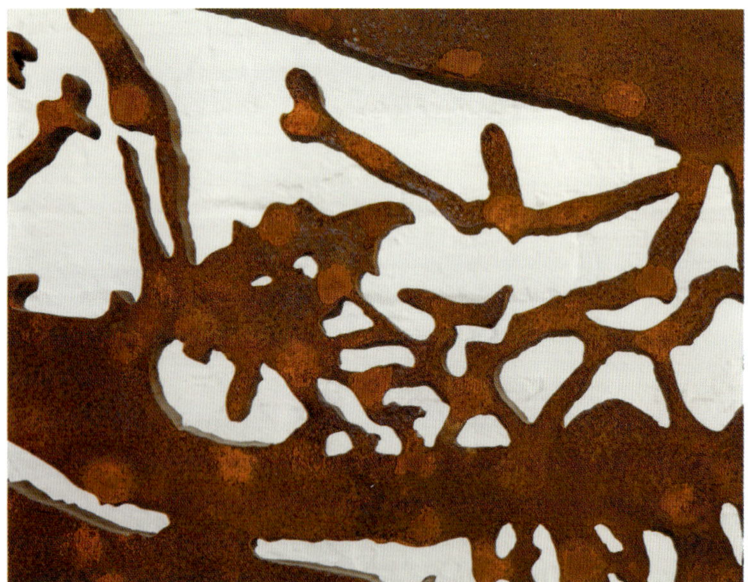
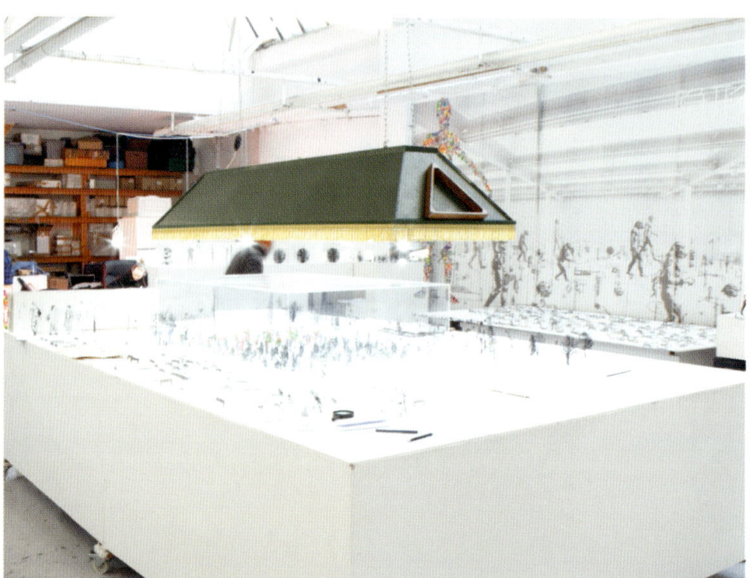
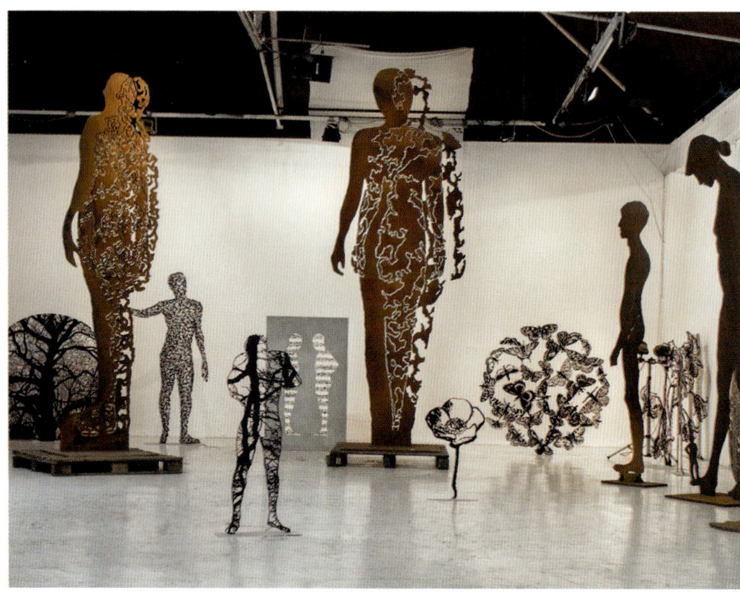
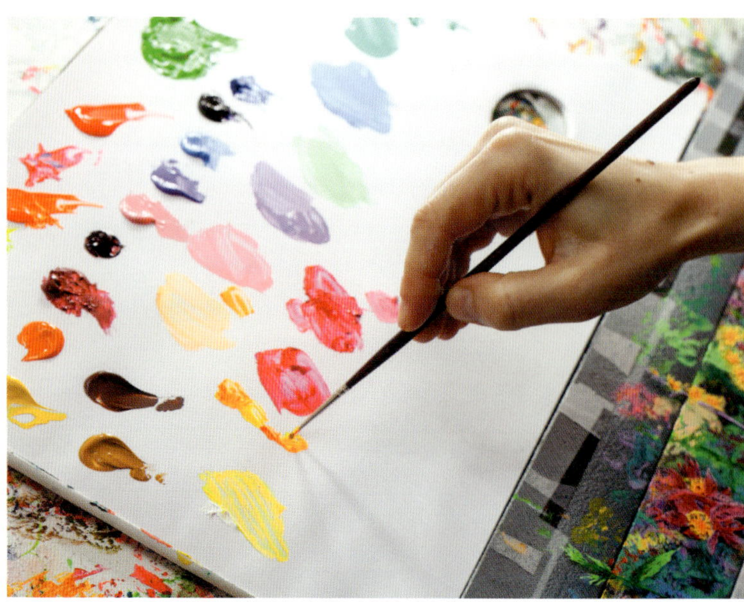

Selected Group Exhibitions

2007
Sculptuur Biennale, Den Haag, Netherlands

2008
Of the Outer World, Duckyong Kim & Zadok Ben-David, I-Myu Projects, London, UK

Dreams, Passage de Retz, Paris, France

Gathering Dreams, Beijing Olympic Games 2008, Beijing, China

Beyond Limits, Sotheby's at Chatsworth, Derbyshire, UK

Animal and Nature, Château des Bousval, Belgium

Wonder, Singapore Biennale 2008, Singapore

2009
OK Biennale Cuvee 2009, Linz, Austria

Vivid Fantasy, KISS (Kunst im Schloss Untergröningen), Untergröningen, Germany

Animals Contemporary Vision, Nave Gallery, Parco Culturale Le Serre, Turin, Italy

2010
City Gallery Wellington, New Zealand

Present and Experience of the Past, International Sculpture in Racconigi, Turin, Italy

Living in Evolution, Busan Biennale, Busan, South Korea

Ten Monumental British Sculptures, Berardo Collection, shown at Cerro da Vila Museum and Archaeological Site in Vilamoura, Portugal

2011
Beyond Limits, Sotheby's at Chatsworth, Derbyshire, UK

2012
Do not Destroy, Contemporary Jewish Museum, San Francisco, USA

2013
Newland, Kontur, Kunstverein Stuttgart, Germany

2016
Blackfield, Kenpoku Art Festival, Ibaraki, Japan

2017
Big Boy, *Sculpture by the Sea*, Cottesloe, Perth, Australia

2018
Through The Looking Glass, Cob Gallery, London, UK

Sculpture by the Sea, Cottesloe, Perth, Australia

2019
Continuos Regeneration, Columbia Circle, Shanghai, China

People I Saw but Never Met, 13 Krasnoyarsk Museum Biennale, Siberia, Russia

Continuos Refle(a)ction, Riverside Art Museum, Beijing, China

2020
Breda Photo, Breda, Netherlands

XXI Cerveira International Art Biennale Cerveira, Vila Nova de Cerveira, Portugal

2021
Les Extatiques, Paris, France

Bibliography

TO 'INTERPRETING ZADOK BEN-DAVID'S *BLACKFIELD*'
(PAGE 13)

Ben-Ari, Elia T. (1999). Better than a thousand words: Botanical artists blend science and aesthetics. *BioScience*, Volume 49, no. 8.

Bishop, Claire. (2005). *Installation Art: A Critical History*. Tate, London.

Brockway, Lucile H. (1979). Science and colonial expansion: The role of the British Royal Botanic Gardens. *American Ethnologist*, no. 6.

Cork, Richard, Guilat, Yael, Fenner, Felicity, McDonald, John and Nabjo, Fumio (2017), *Zadok Ben-David – Human Nature*. Circa, London.

Furst, Benny. (2012). Morphology of a cultural change: The information campaign for the protection of wildflowers as an effective factor on shaping space [in Hebrew]. *Ofakim in Geography*, no. 78.

Gothein, Marie-Luise, Wright, Walter Page, ed., and Archer-Hind, Laura, trans. (2014). *A History of Garden Art: From the Earliest Times to the Present Day*. Cambridge University Press, Cambridge.

Groys, Boris. (2009). Politics of installation. *e-flux* #2, 2009, retrieved from https://www.e-flux.com/journal/02/68504/politics-of-installation

Krauss, Rosalind. (1979). Sculpture in the expanded field. *October*, Volume 8.

Marnin-Distelfeld Shahar. (2019). Images of wildflowers in Israeli visual culture: Representations of a troubled land. *Images*, no. 12 issue 1.

Mitchell, W. J. T. (1994). Imperial landscape, in W. J. T. Mitchell (ed.), *Landscape and Power*. Chicago University Press, Chicago.

Sherwood, Shirley S. (2005). *1000 Years of Botanical Art*. Ashmolean Museum, Oxford.

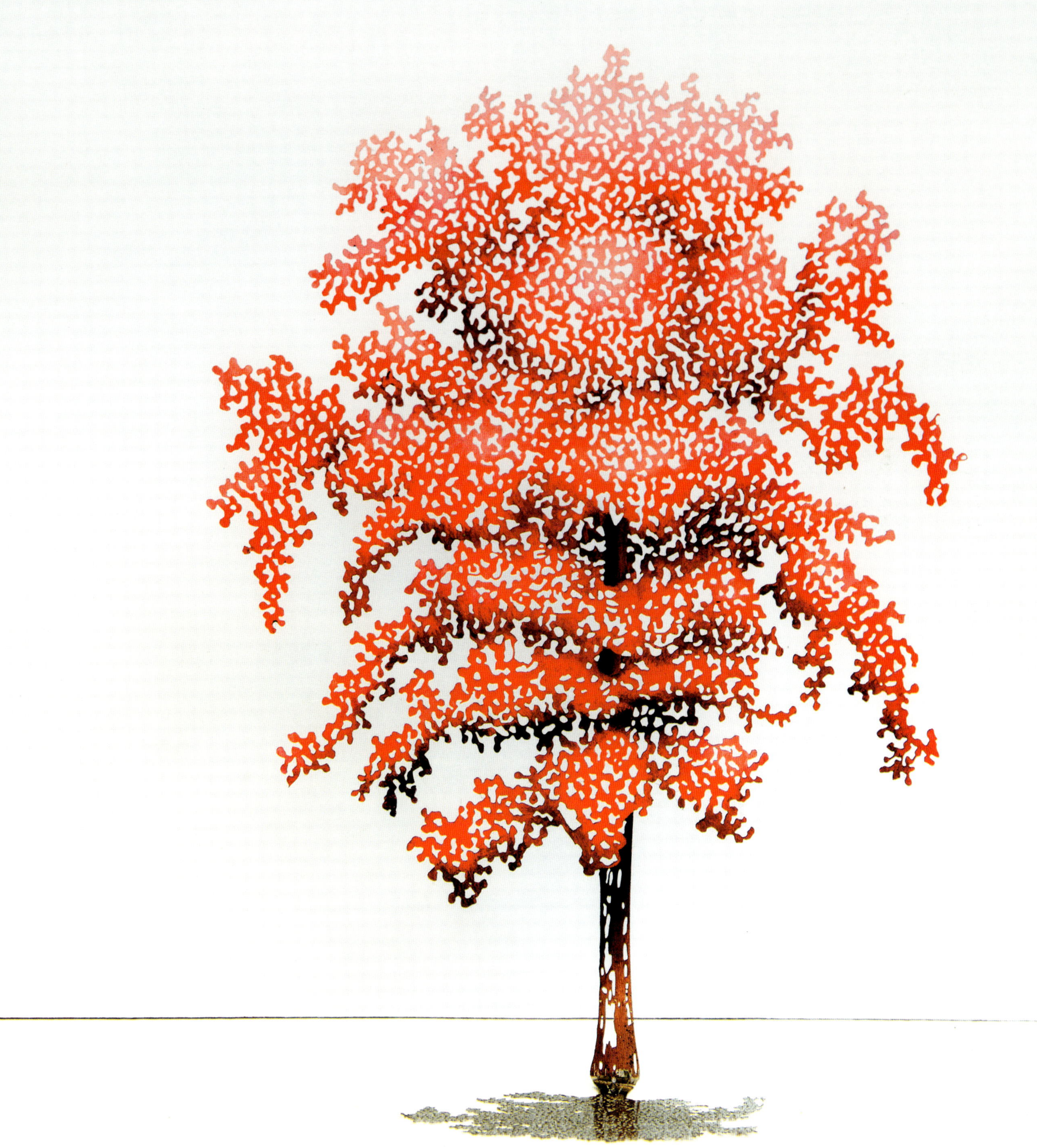

Further reading

Selected Books and Exhibition Catalogues

Cork, Richard, Guilat, Yael, Fenner, Felicity, McDonald, John and Nabjo, Fumio, *Zadok Ben-David: Human Nature*. Circa Press, London. 2017.

De Circasia, V. *Zadok Ben-David: Blackfield*, Verso, Italy. 2010.

De Circasia, V. Agassi, M. *Zadok Ben-David*. Artnews Contemporary Art, Italy. 2007.

De Circasia, V. *Zadok Ben-David: Magica Realta*. International Service Editore, Italy. 2003.

Zadok Ben-David. *Sculpture 1987-1990: Exhibition Tour*. Collins Gallery, Glasgow. 1990.

Zadok Ben-David: The Other Side of Midnight. Annandale Galleries, Sydney. 2013.

Zadok Ben-David: Human Nature. Tel Aviv Museum of Art, Israel. 2009.

Zadok Ben-David: Blackfield. Annandale Galleries, Sydney. 2008.

Zadok Ben-David: The Venice Biennale 1988. The Israeli Pavilion. Venice 1988

Zadok Ben-David. Albert Totah Gallery, New York. 1987.

Online

www.zadokbendavid.com

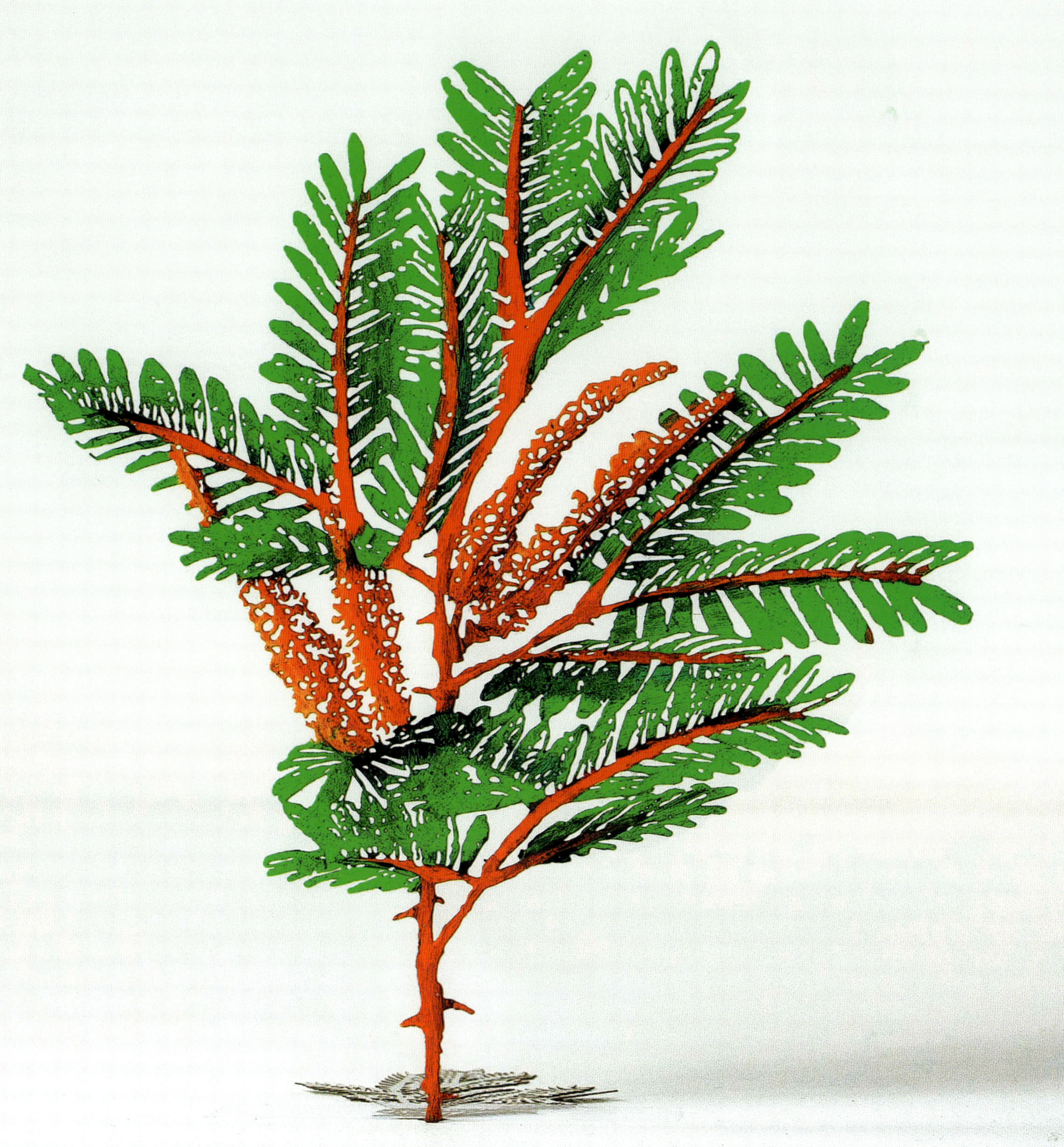

Acknowledgements

Thanks to the team from the Royal Botanic Gardens, Kew. To Maria Devaney the Galleries and Exhibition Leader and curator of the exhibition. To Paul Denton who introduced my work to Maria.

To the rest of the team from Kew.

To the knowledgeable Yael Guilat who never ceases to surprise me with her fresh insight.

To gallery owners Shoshana and Wayne from Los Angeles and to Bill and Anne Gregory from Sydney.

Last but not least, to my wonderful devoted team in London: Inês Magalhães, Adam David, Oona Culley, Lisa Chang Lee and Alexandra Hincapie.

Image credits

Key: numbers are references to pages.
t= top row, m=middle row, b=bottom row,
l=left, c=centre, r=right.

Photography

Maksym Bilousov 60

Carlo Carossio 28

Nerea Castro 62m-l, 62m-c, 63t-r, 63m-l, 63m-r, 64t-l-c,
64m-l, 64b-l, 65t-r, 65m-r, 108

T. Chapotot 30–33

Heath Cooper 109

Jeff Eden / RBG Kew 26, 96–7

Barnaby Hindle 98, 100–6

Keizo Kioku front cover, 44–5

Shira Klasmer 58, 62t-l-c-r, 62b-c, 63t-l, 64tr, 65t-l,
65m-c, 66, 67

Lisa Chang Lee 86–7, 90–3

Virginie Litzler and Duncan Wooldridge 64b-r

David Scheinmann back cover, 2,4, 6, 8, 10, 12, 17, 18, 22,
38–9, 46–57, 80, 115

Ido Sherf and Shahar Brill (*Conversation Peace* stills) 72–9

Meidad Sochowolsky 34

Soupdemots 1, 36, 37, 38–9, 40–43, 61, 62m-r, 62b-l, 62b-r,
63t-c, 63m-c, 63b-l-c-r, 64m-c-r, 64b-c, 65t-c, 65m-l,
65b-l-c-r, 68, 70–1, 82–3t, 84–5, 107, 111–2

John C. Steenwinkel 83

Ines Stuart-Davidson / RBG Kew 27

Suum Project 35

Lawrence Wilson Gallery 29

Roger Wooldridge 24–5, 94–5

Video

Conversation Peace 2018

Ido Sherf (light director) and Shahar Brill,
music by Avshalom Caspi

Other images

Front cover: Detail from *Blackfield*, Kenpoku Art Festival,
Japan, 2016

Back cover: *Happy Days*, see p.49

Frontispiece: *Sour Sweet*, 2021

p.1: Detail from *The Other Side of Midnight*

p.10, 12, 17, 18, 22: Details from *East and West*, 2021

p.58: *Dry Leaves*, see p.63

p.68: *Blackbox*, London, 2017

p.72: Still from *Conversation Peace*, see p.74

p.80: Detail from *Evolution and Theory,* see p.86

p.98: *Tongue in Cheek*, see p.104

p.111–2: Zadok Ben-David studio

p.115: Detail from *East and West*, 2021

p.117: Detail from *Blackfield*

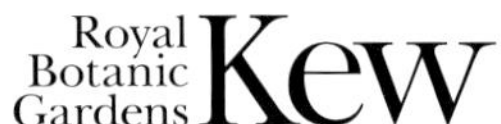

First published in 2021 by
Royal Botanic Gardens, Kew,
Richmond, Surrey, TW9 3AB, UK
www.kew.org

ISBN 978 1 84246 754 1

Distributed on behalf of the Royal Botanic Gardens, Kew in North America by the University of Chicago Press, 1427 East 60th St, Chicago, IL 60637, USA.

British Library Cataloguing in Publication Data
A catalogue record for this book is available from the British Library

Design and page layout: Ocky Murray
Production management: Georgie Hills, Jo Pillai
Copy-editing: Michelle Payne
Proofreading: Gina Fullerlove

For information or to purchase all Kew titles please visit shop.kew.org/kewbooksonline or email publishing@kew.org

Zadok Ben-David: Natural Reserve
at the Shirley Sherwood Gallery of Botanical Art, Kew Gardens
16 October 2021–27 March 2022

Kew's mission is to be the global resource in plant and fungal knowledge and the world's leading botanic garden.

Kew receives approximately one third of its funding from Government through the Department for Environment, Food and Rural Affairs (Defra). All other funding needed to support Kew's vital work comes from members, foundations, donors and commercial activities, including book sales.

Printed and bound in Italy by Printer Trento srl.

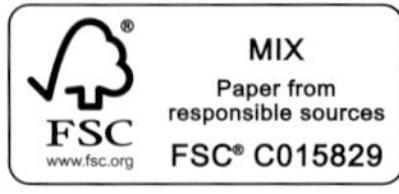